CONSTRUCTING COLONIAL DISCOURSE

Constructing Colonial Discourse

Captain Cook at Nootka Sound

NOEL ELIZABETH CURRIE

McGill-Queen's University Press

Montreal & Kingston • London • Ithaca

© McGill-Queen's University Press 2005
ISBN 0-7735-2915-2

Legal deposit third quarter 2005
Bibliothèque nationale du Québec

Printed in Canada on acid-free paper that is 100% ancient forest
free (100% post-consumer recycled), processed chlorine free

This book has been published with the help of a grant from the
Canadian Federation for the Humanities and Social Sciences,
through the Aid to Scholarly Publications Programme, using funds
provided by the Social Sciences and Humanities Research Council
of Canada.

McGill-Queen's University Press acknowledges the support of the
Canada Council for the Arts for our publishing program. We also
acknowledge the financial support of the Government of Canada
through the Book Publishing Industry Development Program
(BPIDP) for our publishing activities.

Library and Archives Canada Cataloguing in Publication

Currie, Noel Elizabeth
    Constructing colonial discourse : Captain Cook at
Nootka Sound / Noel Elizabeth Currie.
(McGill-Queen's native and northern series: 48)

Includes bibliographical references and index.
ISBN 0-7735-2915-2

    1. Cook, James, 1728–1779. 2. Ethnology – Philosophy.
3. Ethnocentrism – Europe. 4. Discourse analysis. 5. Travelers'
writings, English–18th century – History and criticism.
6. Nootka Indians – British Columbia – Vancouver Island –
Social life and customs. 7. Nootka Sound (B.C.) – Discovery and
exploration. I. Title.

FC3821.2.C87 2005   305.8'001   C2005-901286-2

Typeset by Jay Tee Graphics Ltd. in Sabon 10/13

Contents

Acknowledgments

I first started the project that became this book in early 1990, and although it has sometimes felt like a solitary process, I have found help in many places. A friend's chance remark at a party led me to Nootka Sound, via Coast Guard helicopter, in August of 1994. For their help in arranging my trip, I am grateful to Operations Officer Michael Gardiner (as he was then), Captain F.I. Sacré of the Coast Guard Fleet Systems in Vancouver, and to Vivian Skinner in Victoria. Although my trip lasted only a day, it was a spectacular day, thanks to the help and friendliness of Supervisory Helicopter Pilot Glenn Diachuk and Kipling Hedley, formerly of Nootka Light Station, who shared his materials on (and enthusiasm for) Nootka Sound with me. After scrambling among the rocks at Nootka Sound in the rain, I was grateful for the hospitality offered by Ed and Pat Kidder of Nootka Light Station. Approaching Nootka Sound from the air, I found Beaglehole's description of the coast, which was running through my mind, to be more apt than I could have imagined.

And of course I have found a great deal of help in more familiar places. Several people have read parts or all of the manuscript, and I wish to thank Ian Dennis, Wilson Durward, Margery Fee, Carole Gerson, Derek Gregory, Karen Harlos, Cole Harris, Joanne Horwood, I.S. MacLaren, Maria Ng, M.J. Powell, Anne Rayner, Cy-Thea Sand, Dorothy Seaton, and Betty Schellenberg for their comments. Like those of the anonymous readers for the Humanities and Social Sciences Federation, their responses sharpened my analysis. Special thanks must go to Janice Fiamengo, the late Gabriele Helms, and Joel Martineau, who patiently read and commented on more stages of this manuscript than I like to remember.

In the early 1990s a study of an explorer's journals was a more unconventional topic for a PhD dissertation than it is now, but the University of British Columbia's Department of English offered a supportive environment. Eva-Marie Kröller, Laurie Ricou, and, especially, W.H. New nurtured and challenged me over the long haul of the PhD; I would wish every doctoral candidate the kind of support they gave me. I should also mention my thanks to members of the Special Collections division of the University of British Columbia Library for their help with source materials. Financial support for the research of this book came from the Social Sciences and Humanities Research Council of Canada, and for its publication from the Humanities and Social Sciences Federation's Aid to Scholarly Publishing Program.

Thanks are due to the people and institutions that allowed me to use the images discussed in the book. For permission to reproduce *A View of Christmas Harbour*; *The* Resolution *and* Discovery *in Nootka Sound*; *An Inside View of the Natives' Habitations*; and *A Man of Nootka Sound* and *A Woman of Nootka Sound*, all by John Webber, I am grateful to the British Library, the National Maritime Museum in Greenwich, Harvard University's Peabody Museum, and the Dixson Library, State Library of New South Wales, respectively. Thanks to the National Gallery of Canada for permission to reproduce Benjamin West's *Death of General Wolfe* and to Stephen Nothling, Phyllis Paterson, Robyn McDonald, and the Queensland Art Gallery for permission to reproduce the book's one contemporary image, *Lets Have a Drink and Celebrate*. Thanks are also due to the Hakluyt Society for allowing me to quote so extensively from J.C. Beaglehole's editions of Cook's *Voyages*. Very early drafts of chapters two and four came into being as conference papers, "Approaching the Northwest Coast: Art, Exploration, and Cook's Third Voyage" at the 1992 meeting of the Northwest Society for Eighteenth-Century Studies, February 1993 in Portland, Oregon, and "Cook and the Cannibals: Nootka Sound, 1778" at the Canadian Society for Eighteenth-Century Studies Conference, in St. John's, Newfoundland, October 1992. The latter paper was published under the same title in *Lumen: Selected Proceedings from the Canadian Society for Eighteenth-Century Studies* 13 (1994): 71–78, and I am grateful to the Society for permission to reprint this greatly-expanded argument.

I am grateful to my parents, Dan Currie and Dorothy Wright, for their lifelong encouragement of this and other projects. I owe a debt of gratitude to Deanne Achong and John Egan for technical and moral support in forms too various to list. Finally, my thanks and love go to Jocelyne Valcourt, who patiently lived with this "Cook book" for many years and whose support makes everything possible.

Figure 1   John Webber, *A View of Christmas Harbour,* 1776. Reproduced by permission of the British Library, London.

Figure 2   John Webber, *The Resolution and Discovery in Nootka Sound*, 1778. Reproduced by permission of the National Maritime Museum Picture Library, Greenwich, London.

Figure 3   Benjamin West, *The Death of General Wolfe*, 1770. Reproduced by permission of the National Gallery of Canada, Ottawa, Canada K1N 9N4. Transfer from the Canadian War Memorials, 1921 (Gift of the 2nd Duke of Westminster, Eaton Hall, Cheshire, 1918).

Figure 4   John Webber, *An Inside View of the Natives' Habitations*, 1778. Photo #N36062. Reproduced by permission of the Peabody Museum, Harvard University, Cambridge, Mass.

Figure 5   John Webber, *A Man of Nootka Sound*, c. 1781–83.
Reproduced by permission of the Dixson Library, State Library
of New South Wales, Sydney.

Figure 6   John Webber, *A Woman of Nootka Sound*,
c. 1781–83. Reproduced by permission of the Dixson Library,
State Library of New South Wales, Sydney.

Figure 7 Stephen Nothling, Phyllis Paterson, and Robyn McDonald, *Lets Have a Drink and Celebrate* (from "Right here right now – Australia 1988" portfolio) 1987. Screenprint on paper ed. 3/30, 72 x 56.5 cm. Purchased 1989. Andrew and Lilian Pedersen Trust Collection: Queensland Art Gallery, Brisbane, Australia. Reproduced by permission of the artists.

CONSTRUCTING COLONIAL DISCOURSE

Life in the Contact Zone

We no sooner drew near the inlet than we found the coast to be inhabited; and at the place where we were first becalmed, three canoes came off to the ship. In one of these were two men, in another six, and in the third ten. Having come pretty near us, a person in one of the two last stood up, and made a long harangue, inviting us to land, as we guessed, by his gestures. At the same time, he kept strewing handfuls of feathers toward us; and some of his companions threw handfuls of a red dust or powder in the same manner. The person who played the orator, wore the skin of some animal, and held, in each hand, something which rattled as he kept shaking it. After tiring himself with his repeated exhortations, of which we did not understand a word, he was quiet; and then others took it, by turns, to say something, though they acted their part neither so long, nor with such vehemence as the other. (James Cook, *A Voyage to the Pacific Ocean* [London, 1784], 265–6)[1]

So begins the first published account of Captain James Cook's encounter with the people of the place now known, as a result of that encounter, as Nootka Sound. The *Resolution* and the *Discovery* stayed there from Sunday 29 March to Sunday 26 April 1778 on Cook's third and last Pacific voyage, this one in search of the Northwest Passage. To British and European readers encountering Nootka Sound in the official edition of 1784, the events of this month were largely overshadowed by the foreknowledge of Cook's death at Hawaii less than a year later. Although the Northwest Coast of North America was exotically different from the South Pacific, it could not hope to compete with the high drama to come at Hawaii in February 1779. Standard landfall activities at Nootka Sound – where the crew replenished the ships' water supplies, made necessary repairs, relieved their sexual frustrations, and traded with the Natives – seemed mundane by comparison.

Cook's words describing his arrival at Nootka Sound belong to a narrative tradition beginning with Columbus: the "discovery" of the New World, a series of first encounters reinscribed across time and space. Cook's place in that tradition bridges his time and ours. No single explorer is more associated with scientific exploration on a global scale than Cook: he and his voyages seem to illustrate for his contemporaries and later generations alike the spirit of the time. Cook was chosen as the commander of the *Endeavour* voyage (1768–71), the purpose of which was to observe the transit of Venus at Tahiti in 1769, because of the skills he demonstrated as a surveyor and astronomer during the Seven Years War. Although the resultant readings were inconclusive, the voyage charted New Zealand and the east coast of Australia, producing impressive enough results that the Admiralty sent Cook to the South Pacific again, this time in search of the Great Southern Continent. On this second voyage (1772–75), accompanied by the *Adventure* under Tobias Furneaux, Cook and the *Resolution* charted Australia and ventured further south than any European had before, well below the latitudes where Alexander Dalrymple had so confidently asserted the Southern Continent must lie. When the Admiralty decided to send a voyage in search of the Northwest Passage shortly after Cook returned to England, who better to lead it than the man whose name was synonymous with Pacific exploration? On this third circumnavigation (1776–80), Cook and the *Resolution*, this time accompanied by Charles Clerke and the *Discovery*, pushed far into the North Pacific, past Bering Strait into the Arctic Ocean. Cook's failure to discover the Northwest Passage – or disprove its existence – was less widely circulated than was the manner of his death in Hawaii on 14 February 1779.

The voyages disproved as much as they "discovered," and it is perhaps for this reason that Cook's name stands for the shift from the romantic, fantastic exploration of centuries past to exploration governed by the norms of empirical science. The endorsement of the Royal Society and the involvement of its members (Joseph Banks, one of the leading scientific figures of the day on the first voyage, Johann Reinhold Forster and his son Georg on the second) supported that image. At a time when the Royal Navy doubly overstaffed long ocean voyages on the assumption that half the crew would die at sea, not one man died of a nutritional-deficiency disease on any of Cook's three circumnavigations.[2] He earned the Royal Copley Gold Medal in 1776 for a paper presented to the Royal Society on his innovations in maintaining the health of the men who served with him; these included frequent fumigations of the ships and the use of "anti-scorbutics" such as sauerkraut, carrot marmalade, citrus fruits, and fresh greens whenever possible. Recognized for his contributions to European knowledge about the world, Cook was posthumously constructed as a founding figure for both colonial settler societies in Australia and New Zealand (and, to a lesser degree, Canada) and British imperial culture. As James A. Williamson writes, "Cook was the representative not only of England but of civilization, and civilization acknowledged it."[3]

But what of those New World others against whom "civilization" was defined? The resistance of indigenous peoples to the process of colonization that followed in Cook's wake is carried out in the twentieth and twenty-first centuries by reclaiming their hereditary lands, a legal process that casts explorers such as Cook not as givers but as takers of gifts (food, health, culture, land). The land-claims debate has qualified the discussion of "discovery" so that the very word calls to mind two discourses: the old colonial one that validated the dispossession of Aboriginal peoples and the appropriation of their territories, and a postcolonial critique of both dispossession and appropriation.

Even before Darwin and nineteenth-century evolutionary theory, Europeans defined the moment of contact as though it occurred between themselves in the present tense and some version of their own past. Of course, Europeans were not encountering the human past but another human present, one radically different from their own, a distinction that is sometimes difficult to grasp in the overdetermined vocabulary of European contact with the non-European world. By definition, the very existence of such peoples is simultaneously confirmed and denied through the paradox of absence and presence. That is to say, the old colonial notion of "discovery" identifies New World territory as uninhabited "virgin land," there to be claimed by the representative of the European Crown, even though encounters with the inhabitants give psychological and physical impetus to the narrative. Such encounters, ranging from sightings to bloody conflicts, propel the narrative by means of the fear and excitement they generate in Europeans: fear of attack (often of cannibalism) and excitement about moving towards the goal of exploration. When the explorer's journal is edited for publication, the expansionist imperative of exploration often leads to revising the moment of encounter to assert, retroactively, that the land was empty.[4] This assertion may also be a function of perception in the moment of European encounter with the New World, either on its shores or between the pages of a book, a European way of seeing that consists precisely of *not* seeing that which is alien to it.[5]

Notwithstanding the voracious appetite for depictions of the New World in eighteenth-century Britain, its inhabitants had a certain political invisibility for readers who saw non-agricultural societies as inherently inferior to their own, according to the four-stages theory, which ranked societies hierarchically from nomadic (the lowest) to mercantile (the highest).[6] The sexualized context created by the notion of virgin land may also have contributed to this invisibility: the metaphor identifying the European explorer as husband to the territory personified by the Native woman assumed his lawful possession of her body. The rhetoric of natural science also supported the appropriative project by identifying the original inhabitants primarily as natural products of the land rather than as human producers of culture. Such discursive strategies rhetorically emptied out the New World territory, making it available for legitimate European possession.

For most of the two centuries since Cook's Pacific voyages, a generalized notion about the European discovery of the New World was a kind of shorthand for a whole set of assumptions about Europe's relation with the non-European world. The last half of the twentieth century saw challenges to the long-unquestioned assumptions of imperial rhetoric. Postcolonial independence movements underscored the political motivations hidden behind (or justified by) such rhetoric: that the description of Native peoples is virtually a set-piece of any exploration text reveals the logical absurdity of the claim of virgin land. The advent of postcolonial literary theories – of what has come to be known as colonial discourse – and cultural studies as critical projects further repositioned the field. Accompanying these changes in the critical climate, new editions – in Cook's case, the publication of scholarly editions of his journals – revealed the often complex relationship between exploration journal and published text. And sensitive bibliographic work has traced the general process by which an explorer's journal account of the New World is shaped by the demands and concerns of the Old World. As recently as 1978, the bicentenary of Cook's arrival on Canada's west coast, the old understanding of "discovery" still applied; by the time of the Vancouver bicentenary in 1992, however, the term no longer seemed adequate and was replaced with a celebration of a series of "Arrivals and Encounters." In little more than a decade, public perceptions had changed considerably. A relatively unqualified acceptance of the assumptions of imperial rhetoric – that converting Natives to Christianity and making unused land productive were valuable enterprises – had shifted to a greater sense of ambivalence: the goals of exploration and explorers had come under scrutiny if not attack.[7] It is still possible, of course, to elide or avoid the issue; however, the act of elision or avoidance seems a defensive gesture, indicating a change in the public mind. The discourse of "discovery" now belongs to a colonial version of history to which there are alternatives.

One of those alternatives is to be found in the texts of exploration themselves. Germaine Warkentin argues that skilled reading of those texts can reveal previously unrecognized subtexts and allow us to hear the voices of those erased from the official account. No "solitary hero," the explorer is surrounded by people – other Europeans, Natives, women – with whom he has a variety of relationships; his hand may hold the pen, but his record often suggests the ways in which he, too, is viewed by those whom he observes.[8] Although the retrospective teleology and the metropolitan perspective of the published book typically equate the European appropriation of Native territory with the march of progress, an explorer's own depictions of European-Native relations are generally more varied. The official 1784 edition of Cook's third voyage presents Cook as a benevolent, rather dispassionate observer of Natives whose relations with them are hierarchical: he is parent to the Native child, the nobleman who deigns to notice his social inferiors. Cook's own words, however, recount more emotional responses, more reciprocal relations with Natives: he is sometimes fascinated, sometimes infuriated, but always cautious when outnumbered. He shakes hands, rubs noses, and exchanges gifts with them in an intimacy deemed inappropriate by editor Douglas. For example, Douglas transforms Cook's direct statement about the limitations of his ability to communicate with the people of Nootka Sound – "we had learnt little more from their language than to ask the names of things and the two simple words yes and no" – into something more distant, more qualified: "we learned little more of their language, than to ask the names of things, without being able to hold any conversation with the Natives, that might instruct us as to their institutions or traditions" (Douglas III:2, 334). It is characteristic of Douglas's Cook that he "converses" with the Natives and that this conversation, rather than the Natives themselves, is the means of instruction. As this example suggests, tracing the history of an exploration text's transmission reveals its creation by many hands: it is a narrative produced by a culture rather than an individual. Reading exploration narratives as mediated, consciously shaped, and *literary* (rather than as transparent and factual) documents dismantles many of the old stereotypes about exploration and explorers

for those who want to read against the grain of historic inevitability –
an inevitability of which most explorers (and their editors) were convinced.

❀

"Cook's own words." This phrase suggests both a discrepancy between
the words put into Cook's mouth by the editor of the third voyage and
the textual/discursive focus of this book, which examines the texts of
Cook's third Pacific voyage. Its specific focus is the month Cook's party
spent at what is now called Nootka Sound, on the west coast of Vancouver Island, in the spring of 1778. Comparing the portrayal of this
month in the official published text (which first reached the British
reading public in 1784) with Cook's own journal account (made widely
available by J.C. Beaglehole's scholarly edition of 1967)[9] reveals the
degree to which "Captain Cook" is a textual creation.

John Hawkesworth edited the journal of Cook's first voyage – so
badly, in Cook's opinion, that the Lords of the Admiralty selected
another editor for the second: Dr. John Douglas, Canon of Windsor and
St. Paul's (later Bishop of Salisbury). Cook never saw what Douglas had
done with the account of the second voyage; by the time it was published in 1777, he had already returned to the Pacific. When the *Resolution* and *Discovery* returned to England in 1780, the Admiralty asked
Douglas to also edit the third voyage for publication; it appeared in
1784. The five-year delay was due to the length of time it took to produce the eighty-seven engraved charts and plates from the visual materials of the voyage. In 1785, eager to capitalize on the *Voyage*'s
popularity, publishers Nicol and Cadell followed it up with second and
third editions.[10] In all, thirty-five versions – including French, Austrian,
German, Dutch, Swedish, Russian, and Italian publications – appeared
in the ten years following the first edition, attesting to the immense popularity of exploration narratives in general and of Cook's in particular.[11]

In 1967 the Hakluyt Society published a scholarly edition of the third
voyage, edited by the New Zealand historian J.C. Beaglehole.
Beaglehole also produced scholarly editions of the first and second voyages, an edition of Joseph Banks's *Endeavour* journal, and a *Life of
Cook*. Beaglehole's textual history of materials relating to the third voyage is useful, but the most complete bibliography of Cook's voyages is
still M.K. Beddie's *Bibliography of Captain James Cook*. It lists the
locations of the journals and logs produced by Cook and the officers
who served under him on all three voyages, all published versions of the

voyages, and other documents relating to them (letters, drawings, and so on). No authoritative edition appears until 1967, when Beaglehole's scholarly edition for the Hakluyt Society was published. These two editions – Douglas's of 1784 and Beaglehole's of 1967 – are the main texts of Cook's third voyage.

Establishing a base text for the third voyage is unproblematic until January 1779.[12] Cook's own journal, some of which is in his hand and the rest of which is in that of a clerk, is housed in the British Museum. Egerton MS 2177A covers the voyage from 10 February 1776 (the initial planning stage) to 6 January 1779; 2177B is a log fragment dated 7 to 17 January 1779. These manuscripts correspond exactly to the three volumes in the Public Records Office (Adm 55/111, 112, and 113). A significant feature of this correspondence is that the third volume overlaps the second in both documents: Adm 113 begins in the middle of a sentence that is part of the description of Nootka Sound – "the Sea, but has little else to recommend it."

Cook died on 14 February 1779; his last known entry is dated 17 January, although some loose papers, possibly his entries for that time, were lost in late 1780. Beaglehole says that it is "impossible to believe" that Cook wrote nothing for nearly a month.[13] It is at this point that the textual history of the third voyage becomes complex. After Cook's death, Charles Clerke, captain of the *Discovery*, assumed command of the voyage but died six months later of tuberculosis; a few days before he died, Clerke made James King (second lieutenant on the *Resolution*) commander of the *Discovery*. John Gore, who had been first lieutenant on the *Resolution* under Cook, assumed command of the *Resolution* and the voyage. At Joseph Banks's recommendation, James King was asked to finish the narrative when he returned from the West Indies in 1782,[14] and, accordingly, his name is listed, with Cook's, as author on the title page of the first edition. Beaglehole calls King "highly literate";[15] his brothers were intimate with the Burkes, including Edmund Burke, whom King himself knew well enough to write to from the Cape after the ships left England. King studied science in Paris and then Oxford, where he met the professor of astronomy Thomas Hornsby, who recommended him for Cook's third voyage.[16] Cook often relied on the *Resolution*'s surgeon William Anderson (according to Beaglehole, "the intellectual of the voyage," along with King)[17] to supply ethnographic information, sometimes leaving blanks in his own journal that he evidently meant to fill in later with Anderson's contribution. In his scholarly edition, Beaglehole's footnotes make clear the source (and sometimes the extent) of Douglas's borrowings from the journals of Anderson, William Bayly, James Burney, Clerke, Thomas Edgar, George Gilbert, David Samwell, and others. Beaglehole also provides a companion volume of excerpts from the other officers' journals to form a kind of composite account.[18]

Many of these officers' journals were published in various forms before Beaglehole included them in his scholarly edition: for example, Thomas Edgar's *Portion of an Incomplete Journal* (Dublin, 1784; CIHM 18145), William Ellis's *An Authentic Narrative of a Voyage Performed by Captain Cook* ..., often attributed to Rickman (London, 1782; CIHM 37249), the American marine corporal John Ledyard's *A Journal of Captain Cook's Last Voyage to the Pacific Ocean* (Hartford, CT, 1783), John Rickman's own *The Journal of Captain Cook's Last Voyage to the Pacific Ocean* (published anonymously in London, in Berlin [trans. J.R. Forster], and in Dublin in 1781), and the German carpenter Heinrich Zimmerman's *Reise um die Welt, mit Captain Cook* (Mannheim, 1781). These publications violated the Admiralty rule that all journals and logs be handed over immediately upon returning to England. Rickman and Ellis, it seems clear, were desperate for money: Ellis received fifty pounds for his account, but it ruined his career with the Royal Navy, as did Rickman's anonymous version when, after publication, it was attributed to him.

The Admiralty strictures did not apply to the American Ledyard and the German Zimmerman, who published their accounts of the third voyage in their own countries. The influence of their texts in the imperial discourse about Cook in Britain is unclear, although Beaglehole claims that much of Cook's bad image at Hawaii is attributable to Ledyard's portrayal of him. Beaglehole describes Zimmerman's text as being of interest primarily because it provides a sense of how Cook was viewed below decks. However, "it is not much more than a pamphlet – one hundred [and ten] pages only – of what Zimmerman knew or recollected of the Voyage; and he neither knew much nor recollected accurately."[19] In any case, Zimmerman's edition was not available in English until the 1920s, and even then only by way of a French translation, so its influence on the construction of Cook for the British Empire was probably negligible.

Ultimately, I think, the unauthorized published editions have about the same influence on the public construction of Cook and the third voyage as do the log and journal material available in various archives and libraries around the world: those of Anderson, Clerke, Edgar,

George Gilbert, Gore, King, and Rickman in the Public Records Office; William Bayly's in the Alexander Turnbull Library; James Burney's in the Mitchell Library; and David Samwell's in the British Museum. To most practical extents and purposes, Beaglehole makes this material available and apparent for the first time in his edition of the third voyage. Furthermore, even those writers whose unauthorized versions appeared before the official text of 1784 base their own truth-claims on Cook, who is inevitably mentioned in each title: Ellis's *Authentic Narrative of a Voyage Performed by Captain Cook*, Ledyard and Rickman's *Journal[s] of Captain Cook's Last Voyage*, Zimmerman's *Reise um die Welt, mit Captain Cook*. It is the invocation of Cook's name that guarantees these books and authors a reading public; it is what establishes the credibility and importance of the text's content. Would British readers be interested in *An Authentic Narrative of a Voyage Performed by William Ellis, The Journal of John Ledyard's (or Lieutenant Rickman's) Pacific Voyage,* or *Reise um die Welt, von Heinrich Zimmerman*? Given the great public interest in narratives of exploration, perhaps these books would have found a contemporary market; clearly, however, they trade on their connection with Cook to generate interest (for later scholars as well as for their contemporary readers). That the name "Captain Cook" in the title functions as a marker of authority is somewhat paradoxical, given that Cook is not presented as author but, instead, is treated as a character in the narrative.

I.S. MacLaren's work serves as a continual reminder that the published book is at best an ambiguous and at worst a doubtful record of an explorer's actual words. That Douglas's edition is a thoroughly mediated representation of Cook's words about Nootka Sound is not in question – hence its importance for my study: as MacLaren puts it, "for nearly two centuries, Douglas's Nootka, not Cook's, awaited visitors to Vancouver Island."[20] Even when journal accounts are available, and the published text differs markedly from them, the published text reveals what entered the public discourse, what was sayable by an individual and acceptable to a culture.[21] Accordingly, I am interested in reading the journals of Cook's third voyage, particularly the 1784 edition but also Beaglehole's, not as objective descriptions of reality but as a variety of discursive strategies that achieved certain effects.

More than two centuries after the publication of Cook's third voyage, readers have very different understandings of language and its relation to the world from those governing the texts themselves, in Beaglehole's edition as well as in Douglas's. Beaglehole's edition reflects the assumptions governing the production of Cook's *Voyages* for eighteenth-century readers, who expected to be informed about new places and people, and entertained in the process. One such assumption was the referentiality of language. It was Cook's job to describe as best he could the new territories and peoples he encountered; it was the ship's artist's job to provide supporting pictorial material (charts, sketches of flora and fauna, landscapes, drawings of people); and it was the editor's job to unite the whole into a package that communicated not only a sense of the strangeness of the New World but also a form of encounter and engagement with it. The book, meant to allow readers to discover strange people and places for themselves without ever leaving home, mediates Old and New Worlds. If the navigator cannot accurately chart a coastline, if the draughtsmen cannot reproduce its distinctive features, if the landing parties cannot communicate in some way with indigenous peoples, then the scientific mission of the voyage has failed; if these discoveries cannot be conveyed to a European audience, then the cultural mission of the voyage has failed. Both missions depend on an assumption that the world is knowable and that description makes it recognizable. In this regard, Cook's *Voyages* participate in one of the oldest traditions of travel and exploration literature as a genre. That a speech-act can appropriate a territory according to European imperial culture (as in the Spanish *requiremiento*) demonstrates and enacts the desire for a transparent language characterized by the fixity of words and things.

Much twentieth-century critical theory destabilized such assumptions, particularly that influenced by the work of Edward Said and Michel Foucault, which defined discourse in terms of the relationships between power and knowledge: sometimes oppositional, sometimes complicitous, never neutral. A discursive model that views all statements about the world as interested – politics passing themselves off as truth (some with greater success than others) – shifts the eighteenth-century empirical model of disinterested truths about a world carefully observed by a detached, authoritative voice, unaffected by local politics. The marketplace of ideas is not governed by laissez-faire economics: just as some nations are wealthier than others, and act to increase that wealth, so some discourses carry more weight than others at culturally and historically specific moments. Privileging "literature" over "travel" as the operative term – particularly in exploration narratives – inverts the goals and motivations of writers who saw their work as participating in the service of science. The very notion of a text's shaping in language precludes the idea of a fixed relation between words and things. The value of such an approach to travel and exploration literature is immediately obvious because it calls into question the "correspondence theory of truth" upon which the authority of texts such as Cook's *Voyages* rests.[22]

Cook's voyages – both circumnavigations and texts – can function as a "contact zone" of the kind theorized by Mary Louise Pratt. While the old discourse of discovery assumed the view from Europe, the notion of contact indicates the limitations of this viewpoint. Pratt suggests that the contact zone – "the space of colonial encounters"[23] – creates its own context as two parties meet and form relationships that cannot entirely be understood within the framework of either party. Instead, each group must feel its way into interactions with the other, essentially creating a new shared culture in the process. Although one group may have greater power than its partner in the colonial encounter, the process of transformation is not one-directional, nor does it happen only in the literal space of contact. Cook's explorations exemplify this notion of transculturation: just as the arrival of his ships changed Pacific societies, so the reports of his encounters with them changed European ones. Even Douglas's editorial changes cannot eliminate the radical uncertainty with which Cook approached an unknown coast and its inhabitants; the texts of his voyages reveal the work of cultural encounter as two parties struggle to communicate.[24] Considering textual history, however, transports the contact zone from the Pacific coastline to the moment of reading, in the here and now (wherever and whenever that is) as well as in the late eighteenth century. It reveals the process of cultural self-fashioning at work and invites us as readers to also make meanings in relationship to the text. In effect, I see the texts of Cook's voyages as an ongoing contact zone in which there is still much to be encountered.

That said, I must acknowledge that the contact zone I discuss here is the imperial past. My concern is to examine how a variety of eighteenth-century discourses constructed Nootka Sound for European readers. As a result, the view of the Pacific remains predominantly that of eighteenth-century Europe. Clearly, there is much work to be done in considering the contact zone of Nootka Sound in 1778 from the perspective of the people who rowed out to meet Cook's ships.[25] Daniel Clayton looks briefly at Native histories of early contact with Europeans to consider the variety of "disciplinary practices" that constructed Vancouver

Island in the precolonial period.[26] His analysis suggests how shifting the frame of reference expands the field of imperial history in general and Cook studies in particular: "The Native and White texts I have discussed construct truth and reality in different shades. They both push Cook from centre stage and help us to pinpoint his subject position."[27] My study, by contrast, puts Cook at the centre of a series of discourses that constructed both Pacific and British societies as well as Cook himself. Comparing Douglas's and Beaglehole's editions of the third *Voyage* shows how Douglas's changes to the journal account of Nootka Sound shaped how Cook was viewed posthumously. Somewhat paradoxically, doing this pushes Cook to the margins, to be replaced at centre stage by the discourses governing his appearance in print.

Any important literary work is like the Trojan Horse at the time it is produced. Any work with a new form operates as a war machine because its design and its goal is to pulverize the old forms and formal conventions. It is always produced in hostile territory. And the stranger it appears – non-conforming, unassimilable – the longer it will take for the Trojan Horse to be accepted. Eventually it is adopted, and, even if slowly, it will eventually work like a mine. It will sap and blast out the ground where it was planted. The old literary forms, which everybody was used to, will eventually appear to be outdated, inefficient, incapable of transformation.[28]

Constructing Colonial Discourse interrogates the varied and sometimes seemingly contradictory colonial discourses in the texts of Cook's month at Nootka Sound and in the scholarly and critical accounts of Cook's voyages. Chapter 1 contextualizes the third *Voyage*, locating it within the generic conventions of eighteenth-century travel and exploration literature and examining the means by which the journals of an explorer like Cook became published books. Chapters 2 and 3 consider the mutually interdependent discourses of aesthetics and science: based upon assumptions of objectivity, they distance the observing subject from the object observed, in time as well as in space. Chapter 4 traces the development of a discourse of cannibalism and argues that it works in the editions of Cook's third voyage to further distance the people of Nootka Sound from the British by textually establishing their savagery; Chapter 5 examines the discourses of history used to construct Cook as imperial culture hero for eighteenth-century Britain, Western Europe, and the settler cultures that followed in his wake.

The textual corpus of Cook's *Voyages* is vast: I have chosen to look at one moment that expands in other directions, offering this discussion as a beginning in a growing field with relevance for studies of other travel and exploration narratives, eighteenth-century British culture, and postcolonial criticism. Douglas's edition of the third voyage, like the voyage itself, was associated with a larger imperial project, which, if thought globally, was enacted locally. Drawing on critical insights about colonial discourse developed out of other times and places, I have tried both to place Cook's month at Nootka Sound within the larger world of the European imperial project and to link that project with a specific local context – Canada's Pacific coast. Crossing temporal, geographic, and disciplinary lines, this study brings together a cultural history of the eighteenth-century English-speaking world, an intellectual history of European discourses supporting the growth of racism and the birth of British colonies in an expanding empire, and a close reading of a textual encounter with social, political, and economic implications. For the discourses I trace here have currency still – a currency that is sometimes legitimated by its origins in an imperial past.

But having said that, I also want to note the necessary distinction between the historical person, James Cook, and the constructions of Cook that I examine in this book. The first is the construction created by Douglas's composite text, in which the editor's or other officers' words and opinions are attributed to Cook; this version of Cook is "corroborated" by other eighteenth-century versions of the third voyage available in libraries and archives in Europe, North America, and the South Pacific as well as on microfilm through CIHM. If Douglas's Cook is an imperial hero, then it is largely to Beaglehole that we owe the contemporary image of Cook as a benevolent, enlightened explorer whose voyages represent the "contact" model of European relations with the New World – the antithesis of the violent "conquest" model whose goal was the destruction of difference rather than its archival preservation. While Beaglehole's Cook is also a construction, I interrogate it rather less than I do Douglas's Cook since my prime focus is to locate Cook's presentation of Nootka Sound within the intellectual and cultural contexts that shaped both the third voyage itself and the contemporary published account.

Comparing Beaglehole's Cook with Douglas's Cook reveals some of the paradigm shifts that occurred over 200 years: Douglas gave the world an urbane, detached explorer, always aware of his innate superiority as an Englishman and a gentleman. Beaglehole replaced that paragon with a self-made man, whose hard work lifted him from working-class origins to the company of aristocrats; a pragmatic man, who judged things for their utility and fitness rather than for their appearance; a driven man, whose thirst for knowledge expanded the boundaries of the known world. Writing during the period when many former colonies gained their independence from Britain, Beaglehole offered Cook as an early model of the possibilities of Pratt's contact zone, a European who tried to meet Native peoples with the hand of friendship rather than the guns (or Bibles) of conquest. Unlike the many Kurtzes who preceded and followed him to the Pacific, Beaglehole's Cook recognized the humanity of Native peoples. Governed by the scientific ideals of empiricism and objectivity, he tried to describe and understand what he observed of their societies on their own terms. This Cook often represented the best motivations and actions of European explorers: he was committed to preserving the health of the sailors under his command; he demonstrated (frequently if not consistently) that it was possible and desirable for Europeans to communicate with Native peoples peaceably; his voyages introduced thousands of new things from the Pacific to Europe and from Europe to the Pacific. His voyages and their findings suggested the fascinating diversity of the world and the possibilities of empiricism, even as they pointed out the limits of European knowledge. Even Cook's career, moving from shopkeeper's apprentice to the merchant marine to the Royal Navy, rising through naval ranks from able-bodied seaman to circumnavigator and Captain, suggested England's changing social and economic climate, in which it was possible to rise above one's parents' social milieu through hard work, merit, and luck. While this construction of Cook as the humane embodiment of Enlightenment principles predated Beaglehole, his work (one might almost say lifework) in the four-volume *Journals of Captain James Cook on His Voyages of Discovery* for the Hakluyt Society gave scholarly weight and substance to the myth.

This construction governed most twentieth-century Cook scholarship, perhaps until Gananath Obeyesekere's *The Apotheosis of Captain Cook* was published in 1992. Obeyesekere took the postcolonial challenge to the old imperialist assumptions a step further, presenting a violent, irrational Cook, prone to shows of force – beating his men, firing at crowds, and punishing the theft of ship's goods by taking Native chiefs hostage.[29] Although this portrait of Cook might be seen as the logical consequence of a work like Alan Moorehead's 1966 study, *The Fatal Impact*, Pacific scholars were generally underwhelmed by Obeyesekere's portrait. Of course, *my* Cook is a textual construction too, a sign of the processes that produced his voyages and were produced by them in the published texts. As Greg Dening notes, constructions of Cook reveal "a cultural nerve ... [The] myth of hero, discoverer and humanitarian expressed in rituals, monuments and anniversaries, sustains our image of who we are and who we should be."[30]

It is important to disrupt the long-unchallenged construction of Cook – and of the accounts published in his name – by differentiating between what he wrote and what was written for him; it is no less important to acknowledge that this construction appeared so natural for so long. That the foundation of this construction lies in discourse does not change the power it has wielded. Studying the constructions of Cook rising out of his third voyage demonstrates the richness and complexity of Cook's legacy, expanding the sense of his importance for eighteenth-century British (and European) culture as well as for the modern world emerging in his era. As a figure both historical and symbolic, around whom many discourses coalesce, Cook allows all these meanings and more to expand; and they do not necessarily cancel each other out.

If Cook faced the New World from the deck of a ship, his readers encountered it between the covers of a book. For most Europeans reading the journal of Cook's third voyage, this first encounter with the Pacific Northwest was textual, occurring in the act of reading; however, it was clearly also a *colonial* encounter, given that the first fur-trading vessel arrived at Nootka Sound one year after the official account of Cook's third voyage was published in 1784, revealing the astronomical profits to be made selling sea otters furs traded at Nootka Sound in China (up to $120 per skin).[31] This colonial encounter gave Britain both material and spiritual advantages: the wealth of (European) nations who profited from this trade and a sense of identity for British people through the idea of empire. Nootka Sound and its resources were never as thoroughly appropriated as were other parts of the New World: of all the European nations anxious to monopolize the fur trade on British Columbia's west coast, "no country, not even Britain, cared enough to draw the distant land mass into its imperial orbit through a firm, unequivocal assertion of sovereignty."[32] Yet the discourses of empire and colony have nonetheless shaped that space, still distant from political and economic centres of power. Cook's account of Nootka Sound marks the beginning of what Daniel Clayton has called the "imperial fashioning" of Vancouver Island: the representation of the place and its inhabitants in the official edition of his third voyage drew the Northwest Coast into the discursive orbit of the European powers. Although those Europeans who arrived after Cook decided that there were more important territories to annex, rule, and settle, the decisions they made in other parts of the world affected Nootka Sound and its people.[33]

The consequences of this visit to the west coast of Vancouver Island have been far-reaching. Cook's own account of Nootka Sound differed quite dramatically from the version that entered public circulation in the official edition of the third voyage. Editor John Douglas used Cook's words as raw material, shaping them according to the conventions of travel and exploration literature, the expectations of his readers, and some of the discourses important to eighteenth-century British culture. After Cook's death, Douglas was aware that he was not simply editing yet another exploration account: he was constructing Cook as a national and imperial hero and, by extension, justifying Britain's presence in the Pacific. Douglas's account profoundly influenced his European contemporaries as well as the imperial and colonial cultures that followed in Cook's wake. Even as the book brought far-off shores into European readers' lives, Douglas's changes ensured that they were continually reminded of the distance between there and here, presented at least in part in terms of the distance between savagery and civilization.

I consider the texts of Cook's third voyage as source documents in the intellectual history of colonial discourse. I examine the kinds of changes Douglas made in editing Cook's journal of the third voyage for publication. These changes were not made in a vacuum; they were influenced by the intellectual contexts of the time. Exploration literature was a popular genre in eighteenth-century Europe, and Douglas drew on some of the imaginative and generic structures established by his predecessors. With the text of Cook's third voyage, however, he also transformed the genre, establishing new conventions for his followers. He used concepts drawn from contemporary aesthetics to "improve" Cook's descriptions; he used the discourse of natural history to present the people of Nootka Sound as Linnaean specimens. Perhaps the most drastic change Douglas made to Cook's journal account of Nootka Sound was to claim that its inhabitants were cannibals. And in his handling of Cook's death, Douglas turned history into a tableau. By representing the New World for European readers, the European discourses governing the context of Cook's voyages became colonial discourses.

CHAPTER ONE

Travel and Exploration Literature: Constructing the New World

A central question for Cook's *Voyages* – that is, one of the main tasks faced by Cook and his editors – was this: how to bridge the gap between the summit of civilization and the ends of the earth? Cook had to write about his experiences in the far-off Pacific in a way that made them intelligible to British readers. His editors, entrusted with turning Cook's journals into a book celebrating his accomplishments, faced a similar task. Armchair travellers themselves, they took the material of Cook's journals and shaped it for European readers, making it intelligible by using the familiar narrative patterns for writing about travel and exploration. All these models (both fictive and actual) handled the problem of representing the new, offering a master narrative, a philosophy of cultural encounter, and a rationale according to which details could be given greater or lesser priority. Some variables remained relatively constant: most models, for instance, were organized predominantly along the axes of time and space, taking the journey's trajectory as the plot line. Such models help to contextualize the project of the published accounts of exploration (even if, sometimes, by negation or opposition) by demonstrating the kinds of connections British writers and readers found between the centre and margins of the world they knew.

The oldest models for narratives of the New World came from antiquity: the writings of Herodotus and Tacitus. The first of these, Herodotus's fifth-century BCE *The Histories*, chronicled the attempt by the powerful Persian Empire to conquer Greece and the surprising Greek victory. In many ways *The Histories* offers an excellent model for the kind of writing Cook had to do: Herodotus "constructs a huge road-map of the known human world, past and present, in which everything is linked through story to everything else."[1] Spanning more than a century (557–479 BCE) and depicting the reigns of four successive Persian kings, *The Histories* uses the Persian Empire's expansion to organize the narrative while Herodotus occasionally steps away from that story to "seek out digressions": "no matter where in his ongoing story Herodotus finds himself, he is always willing to pause to note interesting and astonishing phenomena that occur almost as afterthoughts, or parenthetical remarks only tangentially related to the topic at hand."[2] Although he records a variety of marvels, his tone is generally matter-of-fact and relativistic as he attempts to depict other cultures on their own terms. In the intellectual and methodological descendant of Herodotus's *Histories*, Tacitus's *Germania* (CE 98), the marvels to be found in far-off lands become increasingly savage and monstrous as the writer travels further from the centre of the known world. Tacitus ends his account of Germania, already a wild and savage place on the fringes of the Roman Empire, with a portrait of the wildest, most savage tribes on the fringes of Germania: "what comes after [the Fenni] is the stuff of fables – Hellusii and Oxiones with the faces and features of men, but the bodies and limbs of animals."[3]

From the fourteenth to the seventeenth century, exploration was most often understood in terms of the marvellous and fantastic in accounts of the wonders of far-off lands. In one famous example Othello enthralls Desdemona with his tales "of the Cannibals, that do each other eat, / The Anthropophagi, and men whose heads do grow beneath their shoulders." Such tales mark Othello with the dangerous exoticism of his experience as well as his person and reveal the assumptions that shaped fantastic exploration. Another notable and influential example, the fourteenth-century *Travels of John Mandeville*, presents a salmagundi of exotica bound together loosely by the structure of the journey, which encompasses the known world (providing a useful guide to the city of Jerusalem) as well as the absolutely strange and unfamiliar (e.g., the land of the Amazons). The *Travels* begins in a world that can be known at many levels: for example, Jerusalem is a city whose streets can be mapped; it is also the centre of Christ's body and, therefore, the heart of a map that cannot be completely known by humans. It follows that the farther one travels from the Holy Land into the unknown, the greater the barbarity and bloodiness of customs to be found. "The people here where I am now," Mandeville typically notes, "do not eat human flesh, nor do they have one great eye in the middle of their foreheads, nor have I entered the land of the Amazons; but such people are to be found over the mountains or across the river, somewhere in the distance – or so I have heard."[4] Far-off regions of the world were so distantly incomprehensible that their imagined populations signified that very distance and incomprehensibility as well as a fascination marked equally by fear and desire.

Written accounts of Renaissance exploration were organized by myths and dreams of the riches of Cathay, by the fantasies and marvels thought to be found beyond the limits of the known world thanks to works such as Mandeville's. Sometimes these marvels were fabulous forms of humanity (people with the heads of dogs or with one great eye in the middle of their foreheads); sometimes they were fabulous places (El Dorado or the land of Prester John). Ultimately, such myths offered a means of bridging the gap between here and there; they functioned as a kind of mental passage allowing unimpeded travel from Europe to the mythical East. Over time, these marvels dwindled and diminished as Europeans found more tangible sources of amazement in the customs of indigenous peoples all over the globe. However, certain notions proved difficult to dislodge. Long after they had given up on meeting sea-serpents or Amazons, explorers and sailors eagerly looked for signs of cannibalism, for instance, and readers of exploration were willing to believe that the Patagonians were giants.[5] Theories based on Ptolemaic geography, which hypothesized the presence of a Great Southern Continent to balance the land mass of the northern continents and a Northwest Passage linking the Atlantic and Pacific Oceans, were cherished well into the eighteenth century. El Dorado and the land of Prester John had been given up, but more prosaic fantasies could still be activated to fund a voyage of exploration.

By Cook's time, the model of fantastic exploration was being displaced by the model of empirical science, a change that is visible on the maps he produced. By 1779, the year of Cook's death, the most notable features of Renaissance maps had practically disappeared. No longer did coastlines suddenly stop at the limits of European knowledge; the outlines of the continents had been mapped.[6] The monsters inhabiting unknown territories and oceans vanished, as did the words "Terra Incognita" and "Mare Incognita." For example, in 1726 the North Pacific was a blank space where Jonathan Swift could locate Brobdingnag; by 1795, George Vancouver's meticulous charting of the coast had destroyed the notion of a Pacific entrance to a navigable northwest passage. Accounts of the marvellous, banished from the world of scientific exploration, found a home in fictive travels, where they continued to function as imaginative structures. Often they served the same purpose: in both sentimental and satiric travels, the British self is revealed by contact with the Other. *Gulliver's Travels*, for instance, offers images of marvellous faraway lands and creatures such as the Lilliputians and the Brobdingnagians (not to mention the Yahoos) who comment on English society; an early example of sex tourism, Laurence Sterne's *Sentimental Journey* (1768) constructs British identity within an oppositional web of gender, class, and nationality.

Accounts like those by Swift and Sterne play out against other fictive and actual travels, notably Defoe's *Robinson Crusoe* (1719) and the Grand Tour tradition.[7] Swift's satire records Gulliver's encounters with exotically different people in places far from Britain, satirizing the tropes of marvellous exploration in the process. Defoe's novel offers the dream of a desert island, an empty, uninhabited New World that can be possessed without displacing any original inhabitants. *Robinson Crusoe* thus comments both on marvellous travel and the notion of disinterestedness. By contrast, the Grand Tour tradition, which produced a seemingly endless stream of observations and reflections on the sites of classical antiquity visited by upper-class Britons,[8] also functioned as a social safety valve. Those men were encouraged by the practice to sow their wild oats abroad, with minimal disturbance to British society. Sterne's *Sentimental Journey* is as much a sexual as a sentimental tour; Yorick's observations and reflections are produced not in response to the monuments of Western culture but in response to such potential sexual partners as pretty chambermaids.

Mary Louise Pratt argues that two main changes in the genre of travel and exploration writing in the mid-eighteenth-century, the growing importance of natural history as a means of knowing and representing the world and the shift from charting coastlines to mapping continental interiors, "register a shift in what can be called European 'planetary consciousness.'"[9] She takes as her example two significant and related events in 1735: the publication of *Systema Natura* by Carolus Linnaeus (the Swede Carl Linné) and the launching of the first major international scientific expedition, which aimed to determine conclusively whether the earth was round or spherical. Just as Linnaeus chose Latin for his system of universal classification precisely because it was "nobody's national language," so the European nations aimed to overcome national prejudices in order to produce knowledge about the globe.[10] This shift from imperial possession of knowledge about the non-European world to scientific cooperation had tremendous consequences. European nations had long defined themselves against foreign "others"; throughout much of the eighteenth century, for example, a sense of British national identity was constituted largely in opposition to France.[11] This process of identity formation in opposition to difference was easily transported to the non-European world, helping to define the European nation against its colonized subjects. The shift from nationalist to internationalist perspectives, however, did much to contribute to a sense of a European self defined against a Native "other." The European world remained fractured by oppositional national identities, but the sense of Europe emerging in opposition to a non-European other came about through the new internationalist, global, universal perspectives of eighteenth-century scientific exploration.

Of course, old rivalries between European nations remained; even the shift to international cooperation could become a competition to be (or to be seen as) most cooperative. Similarly, the old ambivalencies over the disinterested pursuit of knowledge and the very interested pursuit of wealth in the form of New World territories and their produce also remained. Two examples from Cook's voyages illustrate this shift from national rivalries to internationalist scientific community. When the *Endeavour* arrived at Rio de Janeiro in November of 1768, on its way to Tahiti to observe the Transit of Venus in 1769, the Portuguese viceroy treated ship and crew with considerable suspicion; he could not believe that a ship would sail so far from home simply to make scientific observations, whether these were botanical or astronomical in nature. "Why sail thousands of miles to dig up plants? Why sail thousands more miles to study a planet?"[12] This suspicious attitude surprised and rankled Cook, the more so since Britain and Portugal were allies. By contrast, his third and last voyage coincided with the American War of Independence. While a major part of that war was fought at sea, American warships and their French allies were instructed not to interfere with Cook's voyage; the commercial implications of the discovery of a northwest passage were deemed more internationally important than were the kinds of political points that could be made by harassing or impounding his vessels.[13] So, although the old rivalries over imperial and colonial possessions continued to play a role on the international scene, as the conflict between Britain and Spain over rights to Nootka Sound in the 1790s demonstrated, in particular instances the internationalist claim of advancing scientific knowledge about the world overrode local and nationalist claims.

Each of Cook's voyages had a scientific mission of international significance. The first voyage was the least influenced by commercial considerations: Cook and the *Endeavour* were sent to Tahiti as part of the international project to observe the transit of Venus. This voyage's secondary aim, to search for the Great Southern Continent, became the purpose of the second voyage. Like the second voyage, the third, in search of the Northwest Passage, was marked by commercial and imperial as well as by scientific considerations. For example, the Admiralty instructed Cook to promote friendly relations with Native peoples by "making them Presents of such Trinkets as you may have on board, and they may like best; inviting them to Traffick" (Beaglehole III:1, ccxxiii). Trade with Native peoples had many purposes: it ensured contact between ships and shore, contact which brought "Native peoples [and the products of their lands] within close range of Cook's artists and scientists."[14] The commercial and scientific missions of the voyage were thus intertwined from the start. Somewhat ironically, only the first voyage managed to accomplish its primary goal: the transit of Venus at Tahiti was indeed observed. By sailing around New Zealand, the *Endeavour* voyage proved that that land mass could not be the Great Southern Continent. It was left to the second voyage to prove that there was no continent greater than Australia to be discovered in the South Pacific. Not only did Cook fail to discover the Northwest Passage (or to disprove the theory entirely) on his third and last voyage, but, because of fog, he also missed the opening (now called Juan de Fuca Strait) that separates Vancouver Island from the Mainland. Many of the other global scientific expeditions also failed to accomplish their stated goals. But these failures could only be viewed as such in political or financial terms; for the scientific community, what looked like failure could in fact open the door to new possibilities by disproving faulty hypotheses about the natural world.

Cook's task as writer and explorer was defined in relation to some of these models, most obviously the scientific model of empirical exploration. But some of the writers under him (the officers under his command, notably the third voyage's surgeon, David Samwell) were seemingly influenced by Sterne's sentimental/sexual tourist model. The men who deserted Cook's ships, particularly at Tahiti, may not have read *Robinson Crusoe*, but the cultural fantasy of a Pacific paradise, a desert island where an ordinary Briton could order all things to his own satisfaction, was probably part of their cultural baggage some decades after the publication of Defoe's novel. Within this context, the writing of the New World by scientific and empirical exploration comes into focus.

In Cook's time, travel narratives of all kinds were immensely popular, in part because, as a genre, travel literature seemed to satisfy the Horatian requirement of *utile dulci* (pleasurable instruction). Accounts of voyages of exploration to distant lands, like accounts of tours to the sites of classical antiquity, offered readers both instruction and delight. Information about the world, its inhabitants, and its histories provided instruction; the novelty of the material and the vividness with which it could be described provided entertainment. Although it may seem that accounts of continental travels would differ considerably from accounts of maritime exploration in the distant Pacific, for eighteenth-century readers they differed primarily in degree rather than in kind. Eighteenth-century travel literature "achieved a generic blending of factual information and literary art. A 'thirst for knowledge' now joined a lust for gold in motivating the typical traveler in his search through foreign lands, and this traveler could now return home with the notes for an entertaining and instructive travel account, a prize of more value to some than the rarest gem."[15] A good deal of the pleasurable instruction to be found in both kinds of narratives came from their use of a structure based on observations and reflections. Observations were specific and detailed descriptions of what the traveller actually saw, while reflections suggested thoughtful responses to these sights and their cultural significance.[16] By definition, a travel book necessarily offered observations; the purpose of the form was to present the many scenes of faraway places for the instruction and diversion of readers. Observations were necessary to furnish the material for reflections, but the genre also demanded that observations not become so standardized as to lose their novelty. A steady stream of new observations was necessary to entertain travel readers; novelty was essential to the pleasure of instruction.

Cook's *Voyages* were synonymous with such novelty. His pivotal place in the history of exploration is a truism, but noting his importance as a writer shifts the focus from the content of exploration narratives to their form, to the rhetoric or discourse shaped by the written text. Although travel and exploration narratives took many forms,[17] the ideological and generic supports were generally the same. A sense of the inevitability of European expansion and the progression of European civilization provided ideological supports essential to the creation of an exploration narrative. This ideological apparatus necessarily transformed the record of exploration into a narrative with a teleology. However, in exploration accounts, any "discovery" is not just an event to be recorded: it is bound up with "the economic and political contexts in which journeys were planned and accounts written. The verb 'to discover' thus implies anticipation, and later knowledge, of an object that has already been defined or allowed for in the contemporary discourse about where the traveller has been."[18] The explorer's purpose of making known to Europeans the strange new place gives meaning not only to the narrative itself but also to the very process of exploration, often marked by a singular lack of discoveries.[19] In the case of Cook's *Voyages*, long periods at sea provided few observations to record beyond comments about shipboard life, weather conditions, and navigational details. Even seemingly momentous events are not necessarily connected: Cook's "discovery" of Australia bears no intrinsic relationship to his "discovery" of Nootka Sound beyond that which can be constructed in writing. Because Cook recorded parts of the world previously unknown to his readers, however, even a list of mundane details had scientific value. The expectation of discoveries to come makes reading about months at sea worthwhile and significant; the fact of publication suggests that the voyages actually discovered something worth writing a book about. The published text is thus a retrospective that transforms the random events of daily activity into significant patterns supporting a narrative teleology. The story of discovery thus comes to stand for the discovery itself.

Exploration literature is a profoundly public discourse: explorers (or their editors) emphasized their role as representatives of corporation, Crown, or even civilization over any individual goals or aspirations. Paradoxically, doing this allowed them to assert their personal importance, their willingness to sacrifice themselves for the growth of knowledge, trade, or imperial territory. The popularity of the genre indicates that the reading public who purchased accounts by explorers were willing, even eager, to see them in that light. Douglas's edition of Cook's third voyage is probably not typical, but it provides a suggestive example nonetheless: priced at four and a half guineas (a high price – the *Voyage* was pitched at an elite audience),[20] the first printing in 1784 sold out in three days.[21] Some were so eager to buy it that they offered ten guineas, more than double the listed price.[22] A second edition was printed and sold out in 1785, followed that same year by a third (as well as by pirated and abbreviated editions and a French translation). By 1801 the total profits were £4,000 (half of which went to Mrs Cook), but sales were slow: copies of the third edition still remained. Prices were lower than the market would have borne, the publisher George Nichol suggested in a letter to Joseph Banks on 14 January 1801: "I have often calculated what the profits of the Book would have been, had it been published at such a price, as any fair Dealer could have put upon it – and I found, they would have amounted to about £12,000!"[23] While Nichol may very well have exaggerated the profits he might have made, the figures attest to the popularity of this work and suggest the popularity of the genre.[24] The public was willing to pay high prices for Cook's last *Voyage* because of its sensational content, especially its accounts of the "murder" of Captain Cook at Hawaii. The supposed authority of Cook's depictions of the Pacific was another incentive.

Like other published exploration accounts, Cook's third *Voyage* had multiple markers establishing authority: the appeal of the eyewitness created by a first-person speaker and the sanction of the Lords of the Admiralty, for example. Further, the well established conventions of travel literature, by providing a generic framework familiar to readers, helped to make the radically new seem familiar. The very power of the form to incorporate the new had serious consequences for representing it, however, and the process by which travels became a book is a complex one.

In "Exploration/Travel Literature and the Evolution of the Author," I.S. MacLaren outlines the process by which an explorer's journal account became a published book. Understanding this process is crucial to understanding the text, the foundation of which must be laid before the work of analysis proceeds. This is especially the case for exploration literature: no reliable claims about what any explorer actually thought or wrote can be made without an understanding of the relation between his journal account and the published text. MacLaren identifies four distinct stages in the process. The field note or logbook entry puts the explorer's experience in writing for the first time; often a record of the day's activities, it is usually close in time or place to the events described. After this initial expression comes the journal, a retrospective account written after the voyage (or at least a portion of it) has been completed. This journal material is then worked into a draft manuscript, which in turn is edited to produce a published text. The effects of hindsight on this process cannot be overestimated: a narrative teleology is shaped retrospectively, determined by the results of the voyage, as the writer (not necessarily the explorer himself) and/or editor arranges events to lead up to and conform with those results, usually taking into consideration an anticipated audience.[25] Cook's death at Hawaii in 1779, for example, gave Douglas an obvious narrative climax as he edited the journals of the third voyage.

Clearly, Douglas's edition of the third voyage is a fourth-stage document, but even Beaglehole's edition is not a first-stage account. It consists not of field notes or daily logbook entries but, rather, a retrospective rewriting of such entries, as the fact that some of it is in the hand of a clerk suggests. Cook's standard practice was to narrate the day-to-day activities at a given landing-place, writing a more detailed account when the ships left. While Douglas's edition follows this quality of Cook's second-stage journal, this very preservation calls attention to the process by which the book was crafted. For example, the description of Nootka Sound in Douglas's edition occurs in Book Four (Chapter 2) of the second volume, a backward glance while the narrative of the journey freezes in its tracks. Cook has already exchanged parting gifts with one of the chiefs (with what Douglas, if not Cook, presents as a standing invitation to come back and trade for pelts) at the end of the previous chapter, which concludes: "Such particulars about the country, and its inhabitants, as came to our knowledge, during our short stay, and have not been mentioned in the course of the narrative, will furnish material for the two following chapters" (Douglas III:2, 287). The forward movement of the ships is textually suspended, the discussion of Nootka Sound taken out of chronological time. The chapter heading on the next page promises an "Account of the adjacent Country. – Weather. – Climate. – Trees. – Other vegetable Productions. – Quadrupeds [...] – Sea Animals. – [...] – Birds. – Water Fowl. – Fish. – Shellfish,&c. – Reptiles. – Insects. – Stones,&c. – Persons of the Inhabitants" (Douglas III:2, 288). Douglas's edition thus puts readers at two removes from the narrative. He presents a Cook who divides his journals into books and chapters since the title page of this edition does not mention an editor. Volumes I and II, it promises, are "written by Captain JAMES COOK, F.R.S." In conjunction with his transformation of Cook's journal, Douglas's replication of Cook's past tense thus creates the sense that the first-person narrator, Cook, looks back at Nootka Sound to catalogue its particulars, almost as if describing an emotion recollected in tranquillity.[26]

It is impossible to overestimate the importance of the textual stages producing a published exploration account: they effectively standardized both observations and reflections about far-off places and people. Explorers educated in the navy (as was Cook) or in the school of experience might not be best prepared to present their findings to a sophisticated and demanding audience, well versed, as Batten demonstrates, in the generic conventions of travel literature. They might well have taken other published accounts as their models; certainly the men who edited explorers' journals for publication tended to follow the formula once it was established. Editors like Hawkesworth and Douglas altered the description of particular observations, but, more frequently, they inserted reflections designed to demonstrate the wealth of learning – often in such new fields as comparative ethnography – which made the published account of exploration so valuable. And they did so primarily as ghostwriters whose names rarely appeared on the title page.

The fact that there are considerable discrepancies between what Cook observed and recorded (as revealed in Beaglehole's edition of the third voyage) and what Douglas offered to posterity has been well documented. Indeed, this fact created the need for Beaglehole's scholarly edition for the Hakluyt Society, which often differs so significantly from Douglas's as to raise the question of who speaks in the 1784 edition. Comparing the month at Nootka Sound in Douglas's edition with Beaglehole's reveals the kinds of changes Douglas typically made in editing the third voyage. Some of these changes should pass without comment; they are merely what one would expect of an editor who clarifies and corrects individual sentences. Others transform what Cook wrote, in some cases very significantly. The most important of these lift Cook from a self-made man "employ'd as a discoverer"[27] into a kind of gentleman-traveller; put another way, the changes transform Cook from himself into someone more closely resembling Joseph Banks. Douglas amplified Cook's journal (even his copy-editing tends to make Cook's sentences slightly longer) and used a variety of rhetorical devices to ennoble the representative of the Enlightenment in the New World.[28] In descriptive passages about events on board ship, Douglas simply subjected Cook's journal to a careful copy-editing. Similarly, he tended to follow the *content* of Cook's observations relatively closely, although he typically amplified them, changing words and sentence structures to heighten the formality of Cook's expression and so elevate the explorer. It is in the reflections on those observations, especially the descriptions of land and people, that Douglas took the greatest editorial liberties, positioning Cook within contemporary discourses of gentility and learning.

For example, Beaglehole's edition records Cook's comments on approaching Nootka Sound:

> S U N D A Y 29th. At length at 9 oclock in the Morning of the 29th as we were standing to the NE we again saw the land, which at Noon in our Latitude was 49°29'33" N, longit. 232°29' East, extended from NWBN to ESE the nearest part about 6 leagues distt. The Country had a very different appearance to what we had before seen, it was full of high Mountains whose summits were covered with snow; but the Vallies between them and the land on the sea Coast, high as well as low, was cloathed with wood. The SE extreme of the land formed a low point off which are many breakers, occasioned by sunken rocks, on this account it was called *Point breakers.* (Beaglehole III:1, 294)

Douglas produced that passage from Cook's journal in his edition as follows:

> At length, at nine o'clock in the morning of the 29th, as we were standing to the North East, we again saw the land, which, at noon, extended from North West by West to East South East, the nearest part about six leagues distant. Our latitude was 49°29' North, and our longitude 232°29' East. The appearance of the country differed much from that of the parts which we had before seen; being full of high mountains, whose summits were covered with snow. But the valleys between them, and the grounds on the sea coast, high as well as low, were covered to a considerable breadth with high, straight trees, that formed a beautiful prospect, as of one vast forest. The South East extreme of the land formed a low point, off which are many breakers, occasioned by sunken rocks. On this account it was called *Point Breakers.* (Douglas III:2, 264)

Clearly, Douglas amplifies Cook's passage: three sentences and 122 words in the original become six sentences and 147 words in Douglas's version. Douglas did not merely break Cook's sentences into smaller units as the doubling suggests, however: the amplification is not distributed evenly across sentences. Douglas makes only the most basic editorial changes to the first and last sentences of the passage. He inserts commas to set off modifiers, breaks one sentence packed with navigational detail in two, and expands navigational abbreviations into words without significantly lengthening the original (Cook's first sentence goes from forty-seven to fifty-four words, the last from twenty-seven to twenty-eight). Douglas's changes to Cook's second sentence describing Nootka Sound go considerably further, however, swelling it by almost half (forty-six words become sixty-five) and altering both syntax and meaning. He turns a subject complement, "a very different appearance," into the subject, and the subject of Cook's sentence into a modifier; thus "The Country had a very different appearance" becomes "The appearance of the country." The effect is to heighten the formality of the expression as the immediacy of Cook's conversational style becomes more gentlemanly.[29] It also heightens the sense that readers are seeing this new place through Cook's eyes, looking with him from the deck of the *Resolution* to the shore. Douglas emphasizes Cook's reliability as a reporter in his account of the countryside, comparing it with other parts of this coast and the world that readers have already encountered in this book. His editorial changes remind readers that not only are they seeing something entirely new but also that this account is a trustworthy one. This writer, ostensibly Cook, has seen many different countrysides and the mountains of many parts of the world: his qualified opinion is worth having.

It is in the description of the forest that the editorial intrusion becomes apparent: Douglas has gone beyond editing Cook's journal for clarity to "improving" it with an inserted aesthetic evaluation. While Cook notes that mountains are covered with snow and valleys "cloathed" with trees, Douglas deletes this homely metaphor and turns the scene into a "prospect." This one word sums up Douglas's approach to the editing of Cook's journals, which he "improved" with the judicious application of cultured terms. A conventional word in eighteenth-century topographical poetry and landscape painting, the word "prospect," like the word "view," refers both to what was seen and to a way of seeing it. In landscape painting "prospect" indicated what the observer actually saw when looking at a landscape. But when used in topographical poetry, "prospect" took on another, related meaning, suggesting a vantage point oriented in time as well as space. In this double meaning of the word, "looking *out* becomes looking *ahead*."[30] The word "prospect," therefore, encompasses both observations and reflections: it not only describes the physical features of a place but also suggests its historical associations and future possibilities. By using this word, Douglas simultaneously anticipates a happy future for the place Cook claimed for Britain and locates it within a familiar aesthetic vocabulary. He also turns Cook's observation into a reflection by calling to the reader's mind the wealth – and weight – of topographical poetry like Sir John Denham's *Cooper's Hill* (1665, 1668), Alexander Pope's *Windsor-Forest* (1713), and James Thomson's *The Seasons* (1730), effectively locating Nootka Sound within a literary landscape.

Douglas's use of rhetorical devices such as *litotes*, a form of understatement in which something is said by denying its opposite, provides another example of how he gives the hard-working (and working-class) navigator, son of a day-labourer, the air of a gentleman on the Grand Tour. Cook's description of the manner of preserving fish at Nootka Sound, and the result, appears in Beaglehole thus:

> They hang them on small rods at first about a foot from the fire, afterwards they remove them higher and higher to make room for others till they get to the roof of the house; when dryed they are made up into bales and covered with Mats; thus they are kept till wanting and *eat very well, but there is but little meat upon them*. In the same manner they cure Cod and other large fish, and some are cured in the air without fire. (Beaglehole iii:1, 303–4, my emphasis)

The edited passage is a little longer, but Cook's observations on the manner of preserving fish at Nootka Sound are basically unchanged – except for one phrase:

> They hang them on small rods, at first about a foot from the fire; afterward they remove them higher and higher, to make room for others, till the rods, on which the fish hang, reach the top of the house. When they are completely dried, they are taken down and packed close in bales, which they cover with mats. Thus they are kept till wanted; and *they are not a disagreeable article of food.* Cod, and other large fish, are also cured in the same manner by them; though they sometimes dry those in the open air, without fire. (Douglas iii:2, 280, my emphasis)

Fish which for Cook "eat very well, but there is but little meat upon them" are transformed by Douglas into "not a disagreeable article of food." A Captain's prosaic concern with provisioning his crew as efficiently (and, in Cook's case, as healthfully) as possible is recast as a mini-meditation on the pleasures of the table. In Douglas's edition of the journal, rhetorical devices establish the qualities of gentility and discernment deemed essential in a Cook who was carefully being elevated into an imperial hero. The rhetorical figures that Douglas puts in Cook's mouth highlight the hierarchical nature of Cook's relationship with these (or any other) Natives. Douglas's editing thus ensures and establishes the distance between a Native "them" and a European "us."

Comparing Beaglehole's scholarly edition of Cook's third voyage with the official text published in 1784 reveals the role of the editor in shaping the official account of a national hero. The kinds of editorial changes made in the published text of the third voyage differ from those made in the first two in degree rather than in kind: Cook's own journal accounts were polished by editors in all three circumnavigations. His first voyage was published in 1773 with the voyages of Byron, Wallis, and Carteret in *An Account of the Voyages undertaken by order of his present Majesty for making Discoveries in the Southern Hemisphere, And successively performed by Commodore Byron, Captain Wallis, Captain Carteret, And Captain Cook. in the Dolphin, the Swallow, and the Endeavour: drawn up from the Journals which were kept by the several Commanders, And from the Papers of Joseph Banks, Esq.,* edited by Dr. John Hawkesworth. This volume made a considerable and disgraceful splash on publication: Hawkesworth's editorial liberties with the account of the first voyage offended not only many of its readers but also Cook himself, who was not pleased by the misrepresentation of Pacific societies (particularly Tahiti) and of his work. James Boswell recorded meeting Cook and his wife in April 1776, and he recorded Cook's comments on Hawkesworth's editing: "Hawkesworth made in his book a general conclusion from a particular fact, and would take as fact what they had only heard. He said it was not true that Mr. Banks and he had revised all the book; and in what was revised Hawkesworth would make no alteration (I think he said this too)."[31] Accordingly, the work of editing Cook's second voyage went to someone else – Dr John Douglas, Canon of Windsor and St Paul's – who presumably could be trusted not to shock readers with blasphemy and immorality as Hawkesworth had done. Douglas's task was perhaps somewhat easier than that of Hawkesworth since, after the publication of his first voyage, Cook became increasingly concerned with his own presentation in writing of the events of a voyage. Douglas's editorial task was to shape the text of the journals in accordance with mid-eighteenth-century notions of decorum and propriety so as to present and confirm Cook's status first as a gentleman and then as a national hero.

This raises the question, however, of whether Douglas's editing for elegance and rhetorical flourish extends beyond the language of description to alter that which is described. The short answer is "yes," which raises another question: does the official edition of 1784 present what *Cook* saw at Nootka Sound (and elsewhere) or *Douglas's* beliefs about what Cook saw and what a British audience expected to see? MacLaren considers this issue to be central to an understanding of the exploration genre, suggesting that the publisher's desire to produce a marketable commodity could affect the narrative of a travel journal as much as does the traveller's own perceptual baggage. He argues that the potential profits to be realized from volumes of travel and exploration encouraged publishers to standardize "formats and sentence structures," thus simultaneously meeting and shaping the expectations of their readership.[32] These revisions, especially those meant to elevate the workday prose of an explorer into the refinements expected of an imperial hero, reveal a discourse of *class* at work in addition to one of empire.[33]

Douglas's comments reveal that he took seriously the responsibility of shaping the raw material of Cook's journals into an acceptable public discourse. In the "Textual Introduction" to his edition of the third voyage, Beaglehole quotes a letter from Douglas to an anonymous correspondent, in which Douglas seemingly complains about his lack of recognition as ghostwriter: "The Public never know, how much they owe to me in this work. The Capt's M.S.S. was indeed attended to accurately, but I took more liberties than with his Acct of the second Voyage; and while I faithfully represented the facts, I was less scrupulous in cloathing them with better Stile than fell to the usual Share of the Capt – Anderson's M.S. was also a fruitful Source of important Additions, & by being perpetually before me, enabled me to draw up a much more interesting Narrative than could have been extracted from Capt. Cook's M.S. alone. My Introduction to the Voyage, & my Notes, still added more to ye value of the publication."[34] The contradictions in this passage are instructive – Douglas "attended to" Cook's manuscript "accurately" but in so doing "took more liberties than with his Acct of the second Voyage." He could do so because Cook was dead. Significantly, the reading public did not realize the extent of Douglas's changes. In an irritated letter in 1783, Douglas wrote to an unnamed correspondent

"'I am announced to the Public as employed in *finishing grammatically* Capt Cook's Voyage. After all my Care & Study to have my name kept back, it equally mortifys & surprizes me, to be thus made the Sport of News Papers.'"[35] Evidently Douglas thought it better to go unrecognized than to have his role diminished.

The extent of Douglas's changes to Cook's journal seems all the more surprising in light of Beaglehole's theory that Cook approached the journal of the third voyage as a writer as well as an explorer; rather than merely transcribing events, Beaglehole argues, Cook was intent on shaping his experiences in language. Cook was determined "to write a book – or at least an account of the voyage that would need the minimum of editing by another hand, or of rewriting by his own, before it appeared as a book … it is a far cry indeed from the journal of the first voyage to this sophisticated document. The log entries for the long days at sea are remorselessly compressed to a sentence or two of narrative [… In general,] he seems to have reached virtual finality on what he wanted to write, in general shape, proportions, and detail. This finality is obviously the result of careful thought."[36] In this context, Douglas's stylistic liberties seem all the more intrusive, especially his ascription of cannibalism to the people of Nootka Sound. The ships visited Nootka Sound in the spring of 1778, almost a year before Cook's death at Hawaii; the journal account would thus have been part of what Cook himself revised to near "finality" without once mentioning cannibalism. Douglas's portrayal of cannibalism at Nootka Sound goes well beyond "cloathing [the facts] with better Stile than fell to the usual share of the Capt." It demands analysis of why Douglas would put such words into Cook's mouth. The question is explored more fully in Chapter 4, but in light of Douglas's general use of strategies of elevation designed to rhetorically lift Cook above the people he describes, it suggests two things: (1) that the text of Cook's third voyage should be read as a case study in the construction of the explorer as national hero and (2) that Douglas's changes are designed to turn Cook, posthumously, into a mirror showing British readers their own reflection as enlightened and rational observers of the Pacific.

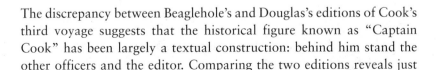

The discrepancy between Beaglehole's and Douglas's editions of Cook's third voyage suggests that the historical figure known as "Captain Cook" has been largely a textual construction: behind him stand the other officers and the editor. Comparing the two editions reveals just

how much Douglas altered Cook's description of the month at Nootka
Sound by adding, if not his own opinions and edification, then the opinions of the other officers as if they were Cook's. Indeed, the act of reading Beaglehole's scholarly edition of the third voyage makes the extent
to which Douglas borrowed from the journals of the other officers visually explicit: Beaglehole's footnotes outlining Douglas's sources often
take up almost as much space on the page as do Cook's own description
of the place and its people.

For example: Douglas's version of the first contact at Nootka Sound
goes as follows:

We no sooner drew near the inlet than we found the coast to be
inhabited; and at the place where we were first becalmed, three
canoes came off to the ship. In one of these were two men, in
another six, and in the third ten. Having come pretty near us, a
person in one of the two last stood up, and made a long
harangue, inviting us to land, as we guessed, by his gestures. At
the same time, he kept strewing handfuls of feathers toward us;
and some of his companions threw handfuls of a red dust or
powder in the same manner. The person who played the orator,
wore the skin of some animal, and held, in each hand, something
which rattled as he kept shaking it. After tiring himself with his
repeated exhortations, of which we did not understand a word,
he was quiet; and then others took it, by turns, to say something,
though they acted their part neither so long, nor with such
vehemence as the other. (Douglas III:2, 265–6.)

Beaglehole presents a rather different scenario.

We no sooner drew near the inlet than we found the coast to be
inhabited and the people came off to the Ships in Canoes without
shewing the least mark of fear or distrust.* We had at one time
thirty two Canoes filled with people about us, and a groupe of
ten or a dozen remained along side the Resolution most part of
the night. They seemed to be a mild inoffensive people, shewed
great readiness to part with any thing they had and took
whatever was offered them in exchange, but were more desireous
of iron than any thing else, the use of which they very well knew
and had several tools and instruments that were made of it.
(Beaglehole III:1, 295–6)

In contrast to Douglas's ethnographic descriptions of a moment that evidently has some cultural or ceremonial significance for the people of Nootka Sound (as if they already realize the importance of this encounter to the history of their coast), Beaglehole's edition offers a more prosaic and limited description of behaviour meaningful to and understood by Europeans: the desire to trade. A footnote at the word "distrust" in Beaglehole, a reference to the log of Edward Riou, midshipman on the *Discovery* and later on the *Resolution*, provides a possible source for Douglas's version:

When we first Entered this Sound at about 5 PM several Canoes came off to the Ships and In them a set of the dirtiest beings ever beheld – their faces and Hair being a lump of red and black Earth and Grease – Their Bodys covered with the Skins of Animals or a kind of garment made Exactly like the *Hahoo* (or Cloth) of New Zealand but of a Quality very inferior and differently shaped. In the Canoe that first came Along side was a Man that stood up and held forth a long while – at the same time pointing to the Sound as if the ship should go further Up – his oratory did not seem to be the best in the world and he appeared to Utter with much difficulty; on his head he wore a kind of hat made of Cane and in shape resembling a buck's head; after having finished his harangue he presented it to Sale as well as several other things, which at once convinced us they were no novices at that business, in return for his hat he had a large Axe and left us quite Content. – Riou, 30 March. (Beaglehole III:1, 295–6)

It may be to Riou, then, that Douglas owes his vivid description of this first encounter. If so, this is somewhat surprising for it counters one of the general patterns of Douglas's borrowings. His greatest debts are to William Anderson (surgeon on the *Resolution*), whose journal had been "perpetually before him" throughout the revising process,[37] and James King (2nd lieutenant on the *Resolution*), listed with Cook on the title page as the author of Volume III, the portion of the third voyage following Cook's death. Not coincidentally, Anderson (whom Beaglehole called "the [Sir Joseph] Banks or [William] Wales of the third voyage")[38] and King were the officers most capable of producing the reflective, gentlemanly material valued by Douglas.

Beaglehole's "Textual Introduction" to the third volume of the *Voyages* discusses the nature and extent of Douglas's borrowings from the other officers' journals: "Douglas makes great use of Anderson, who might also go on the title page as a third author. He is quoted where Cook quoted or made provision for quoting him; and elsewhere, often for pages at a time, is worked skillfully in sentences and paragraphs, with or without attribution, has separate chapters allotted to him, or is given large parts of other chapters with some such introduction as 'observations ... combined with those of Mr. Anderson, who was a very useful assistant on all such occasions.'"[39] One such interpolation is found in the description of Nootka Sound (pages 288–340 in Douglas's edition), which begins: "In drawing up the preceding account of the people of this Sound, I have occasionally blended Mr. Anderson's observations with my own; but I owe everything to him that relates to their language; and the following remarks are in his own words" (Douglas III:2, 334). Douglas – for nothing remotely resembling this paragraph appears in Beaglehole's edition at the same juncture – then proceeds to quote Anderson for two pages. Unfortunately, the part of Anderson's journal that would contain his account of Nootka Sound is lost, so the extent to which Douglas borrowed from Anderson, and the nature of those borrowings, remains unclear, although the correspondences between the existing two-thirds of Anderson's journal and Douglas's edition makes Anderson's contribution to the published *Voyage* generally apparent.

Subsequent chapters discuss specific borrowings in more detail, but the general pattern is clear: Douglas uses the words of other officers not only to supplement Cook's account, as in Riou's more vivid image of the ships' arrival at Nootka Sound, but also as part of his strategy of elevation. Plainly put, Douglas borrows more from the higher-ranking officers like Anderson and King – unless borrowing from the lower-ranking officers allows him to create the desired effect. James King produced an account similar to Riou's of the first contact between Britons and the people of Nootka Sound:

> The first men that came would not approach the ship very near & seemed to eye us with Astonishment, till the Second boat came that had two men in it; the figure & actions of one of these were truly frightful; he worked himself into the highest frenzy, uttering something between a howl & a song, holding a rattle in each hand, which at intervals he laid down taking handfulls of red Ocre & birds feather & strewing them in the Sea; this was follow'd by a Violent way of talking, seemingly with vast difficulty in uttering the Harshest & rudest words, at the same time pointing to the

Shore, yet we did not attribute this incantation to ... any ill intentions towards us. (Beaglehole III:1, 393–4)

For sheer drama, this scene rivals if not surpasses Riou's description. Why did Douglas not choose it over the midshipman's version? King's description of "frenzy," and the animalistic connotations of "something between a howl & a song," support some of Douglas's own beliefs about Pacific "savages," yet these images do not make their way into his initial description. The reason for this is to be found in King's use of the word "frightful."[40] Douglas's editing works relentlessly to remind readers of Cook's superiority to the peoples of the Pacific; to portray a Cook frightened at first meeting by their appearance would accord them a kind of power that the rest of the account consistently suppresses. By contrast, Riou's description of people wearing garments made of cloth inferior even to that made by Maori can be worked into a passage conveying a sense of bemused incomprehension at the sight of this strange ritual.

The first-person "I" who speaks in the official edition of the third voyage is thus more of a "we." Douglas not only changes some of Cook's own descriptions quite drastically but he also supplements Cook's journal with the words of other officers to convey impressions not recorded by Cook. Of course the explorer's logbook or journal and the published account of his exploration are documents with different purposes. The logbook and journal record events both boringly ordinary (fumigating the ship, disciplining the crew, painstakingly charting miles of shoreline)[41] and exotically strange (brewing beer out of spruce needles, eating walrus meat, observing the customs of non-European peoples); the published book narrates those events to an enthusiastic audience. Unlike Cook, Douglas is concerned not only with transmitting the geographical and navigational observations of the moment but also with providing suitable reflections on those observations, instructing his readers in how they ought to perceive far-off shores. For – unlike the oft-described sites of classical antiquity upon which every British traveller to Italy felt obliged to comment – Cook and his editors had to write a kind of verbal cartography. Descriptions of the South Pacific and the Northwest Coast of North America had to give European readers a feeling of being there, but before that they had to chart the way there, preparing readers for the observations and reflections of a place and its inhabitants by locating that place within the context of the known world.

To further complicate matters, Douglas uses "the first-person singular, which voices all the published descriptions as ultimately and solely the explorer's own" and gives his edition an apparent eyewitness validity.[42] The fact that we cannot know without reference to Beaglehole when the "I" that speaks is Cook and when it is Douglas means that Douglas's role is as complex as is Cook's. The captain of a voyage of discovery, a de facto scientist, and the writer of an official document, Cook was also an icon, a symbol of Britain and its representative in the Pacific. This construction was made possible in part by that first-person narration, which, by ostensibly allowing readers to see the New World through his eyes, encouraged them to identify both personally and nationally with the project of his voyages. As editor, Douglas functions as a tour guide to Cook's voyage: out of a bewildering variety of new information (arranged chronologically and spatially), he chooses for readers the highlights of the tour, provides reflections where necessary to supplement Cook's detailed observations, and makes connections between one experience and another. Douglas points out the similarities and differences between Pacific and European societies and often provides footnotes, citing another explorer, for example, to ensure that readers get as much as possible out of our armchair travels with Cook.

However, Douglas himself was an armchair explorer whose experience of the Pacific, like that of other readers of Cook's account, occurred between the pages of a book. Thus his editorial changes to Cook's description, discussed more fully in the following chapters, can be seen both as making Cook's journal conform to the generic conventions of late eighteenth-century travel and exploration literature and as indicating what might interest stay-at-home readers. The textual authority created as a result was so great as to shape those expectations and conventions in turn.

This brings us to the issue of influence – not just Cook's influence on later explorers, or the third voyage's influence on later European exploration of the Pacific, for those are unquestionable,[43] but the influence of Douglas's editorial changes on later writers and editors of exploration accounts. Looking at two later accounts by officers who had sailed with Cook suggests the nature of Douglas's influence. This may, of course, be due as much to the sensational manner of Cook's death as to Douglas's editorial style; we should perhaps think of the official edition of Cook's third voyage as a publishing phenomenon whose influence extended beyond what anyone, including Douglas, could have anticipated.

The first example is that of George Vancouver, who had sailed as a midshipman on Cook's second and third voyages. In 1791 Vancouver returned to the North Pacific on a voyage motivated by Britain's need for more precise knowledge about the territory in the aftermath of the Nootka Crisis and the signing of the Nootka Convention between Britain and Spain.[44] Vancouver's negotiations with the Spanish representative, Don Juan Francisco de la Bodega y Quadra, were inconclusive, but the fact-finding mission of his voyage was an unqualified success. He demolished the myth of the Northwest Passage by meticulously charting every tiny bay and inlet along the Northwest Coast.[45] Vancouver's attempts to render his findings accurately in print were as conscientious as were his attempts to chart the Northwest Coast, but the published account of his voyage conspicuously failed to make a splash. While the voyage itself was clearly important for both the science and commerce of navigation, readers were underwhelmed by Vancouver's painstaking accuracy. One of Vancouver's own midshipmen called his account "one of the most tedious books I ever read."[46] While some readers today might find Douglas's edition of Cook's journals as dull and ponderous as Vancouver's *Voyage*, no one could accuse Douglas of choosing mere accuracy over rhetorical flourish.

The second case suggesting the influence of Douglas's edition on later writers and editors is William Bligh's account of the ill-fated *Bounty* voyage, which left England in December of 1787 (the mutiny occurred in April 1789; Bligh returned to England in March 1790). Bligh had continued the ship's log after the mutiny and, not surprisingly, his published account changed the logbook's description of the mutiny to justify his own behaviour.[47] Edwards's analysis of some of the ways Bligh transformed his log accounts for publication suggests that Bligh learned from Douglas. For example, Bligh's log entry for 20 May 1789, nearly one month after the mutiny, reads "Our appearances were horrible, and I could look no way but I caught the Eye of some one" becomes "the patronizing 'caught the eye of some one in distress.'"[48] The speaker's self-presentation as a humane noticer of others' greater distress is textbook Douglas. Edwards argues further that Bligh worked so furiously on his account because "he knew the importance of monopolizing the public record, or at least the importance of getting in first, establishing an official version and investing it with authority. His own vituperative disagreements with the official version of Cook's last voyage, especially what James King recorded, remained quite literally marginalized."[49]

Bligh objected to the official edition of Cook's third voyage for a number of reasons, including the crucial issue of the accuracy of navigational description. Bligh claimed that many of his own maps and surveys were credited to a copyist, Lieutenant Henry Roberts. Worse, the charts of the Northwest Coast presented somebody's supposition as geographical fact.

> I wish also particularly to take notice of an error in the Map published with C. Cook's works last voyage, where in the latd. of 63.00 N near Bearings Streights is placed an Island not existing. It is called Anderson's Island, laid down to the Eastward of Clerks Island, whereas the east part of the latter was the land seen ... This unaccountable error arose only from sheer ignorance, not knowing how to investigate the fact, and it is a disgrace to us as Navigators to lay down what does not exist. I know it does not, from a perfect knowledge of the lands, and it requires no great skill to show I am right even by the Common Ship Logs. This very Isld may hereafter be said to have sunk into the sea relying on the authority of Capt. Cook – I therefore wish to have it said that I declare no such island can be found.[50]

When it came time to produce for publication an account of a voyage almost as sensational as Cook's last, Bligh might well have learned from Douglas's edition that strict accuracy matters less than does the power to control what enters the public record. His book, Edwards argues, shows "that all published voyage-narratives are exercises in public relations"[51] – or at least all *successful* published voyage-narratives. By contrast, the public dismissal of Vancouver's book may have stemmed in part from his refusal to use his writing in such a fashion.

Douglas's edition of Cook's third voyage showed later writers and editors that, whether or not a voyage of exploration discovered what it set out to, it could still become commercially successful: a well received publication could turn a considerable profit. Bligh seemed to have learned this lesson, while Vancouver did not. Of course, Douglas's edition of Cook's third voyage was more than a publishing phenomenon: it was not just that Douglas changed Cook's journal accounts but, rather, that the kinds of changes he made influenced later explorers and their editors. The following chapters examine in more detail the specific nature of these changes.

CHAPTER TWO

Approaching Sublimity: Aesthetics, Exploration, and the Northwest Coast

The *Resolution* and *Discovery* arrived at Nootka Sound on 29 March 1778. Over the course of three Pacific voyages and more than a decade of exploration, Cook, the officers and crewmen under him, and his audience had gained some familiarity with the South Pacific, which created the impression of cumulative knowledge. They read the Northwest Coast of North America through a double filter, through perceptions formed first in Europe and then in the South Pacific. The North Pacific, however, required a reorientation. The transition from the inviting environment of the South Pacific (symbolized for European readers by the Islanders' near-nudity, a fact which became a trope) to the more forbidding North Pacific is demonstrated by the sailors' need to trade for fur clothing at Nootka Sound.[1] A sense of the newer newness of the North Pacific, and the way in which it represents for Cook another unfamiliarity that must be accommodated and incorporated, is provided by Beaglehole.[2] As if to rebuke or counter those surprised that Cook missed Juan de Fuca Strait and thus failed to realize he was not on the Mainland, Beaglehole writes:

Vancouver Island is built on vast proportions: no one approaching it from the sea, or even flying down its coast, would take it for an island – the scale of hills behind hills is too great, the snowy mountains inland recede too far, the line of breakers is too long; the very clouds are almost too immense. The spruce and hemlock and cedar of the forest cover it, to within a few feet of the sea; the flat points reaching a short way into the ocean are covered; the islets off-shore are crowned with trees, like grave barbaric princesses pacing up the coast to some remote festival;

trees spring, it seems, from each individual solid rock. The sides
of the sound and of the minor islets that run off it, north, east,
and south, fall precipitous to the water, with only here and there
a narrow strip of land marching with it, or a larger ledge.[3]

The phrase "vast proportions" in Beaglehole's first sentence suggests
the vocabulary of the Sublime and its companion term, the Picturesque.
Together these aesthetic discourses suggest a whole variety of responses
to landscape among eighteenth-century Britons. Notions of human
relation to the land, notions of disinterest and "objectivity," notions of
property and ownership: all these issues are raised by the aesthetic
vocabulary of the Sublime and the Picturesque in eighteenth-century
exploration in general and in Cook's third voyage in particular.
The language of Cook's own journals exemplifies Thomas Sprat's
notion of scientific writing, defined against the metaphoric style he
abhors: "the only Remedy, that can be found for this Extravagance ...
[has been] a constant Resolution, to reject all the Amplifications,
Digressions, and Swellings of Style; to return back to the primitive
Purity and Shortness, when men deliver'd so many *Things*, almost in an
equal number of *Words*."[4] Douglas inserts those "Amplifications,
Digressions, and Swellings" so as to elevate Cook's plain style into a
more leisurely periodic prose. Using eighteenth-century aesthetic conventions that constructed the aesthetic subject as a landowning male,
Douglas amplifies Cook's description of Nootka Sound. In the process,
he transforms Cook from a working-class pragmatist into the kind of
gentleman whose eye takes in and possesses all he sees.

In the previous chapter I discussed how Douglas uses the word "prospect" to turn land into landscape and thus to locate Nootka Sound
within a literary landscape. Seeing New World landscapes through
European aesthetic conventions such as the prospect, the Sublime, and
the Picturesque made them intelligible to explorers; describing them in
these terms made meaningful communication with European readers
possible. "Just as the determination of longitude and latitude told the
traveller/explorer where he was in relation to Greenwich, so the habitual description of terrain by means of the Sublime and the Picturesque
told him where he was relative to the landscapes roundabout Greenwich and the rest of England and Scotland."[5] Both conventions articulated human responses to and relationships with landscape and so

conveyed an explorer's experience far from home; descriptions using these conventions also allowed readers to respond emotionally to the worlds they encountered in a book.

The Sublime and Picturesque suggested different kinds of relationships between humans and the natural world. While the Sublime had long been defined as a feeling of awe in response to a product of culture (the rhetorical Sublime), Edmund Burke extended its application to the natural world in his *Philosophical Enquiry into the Origin of Our Ideas on the Sublime and the Beautiful* (1757).[6] Burke defined the Sublime not in relation to the Picturesque but in opposition to the beautiful, aligning the terms with oppositional gender values. In Burke's formulation, the Sublime was supremely masculine, associated with power, immensity, roughness, darkness, or obscurity; it produced in the viewer feelings of awe and terror proportional to the sense of danger raised by his inability to take it all in. This danger was not immediate or personal but psychic or epistemological as the viewer realized his insignificance relative to the grandeur of the Sublime. The beautiful, by contrast, was associated with femininity, understood as weak, small, smooth, and light; the beautiful sight, like a beautiful woman, produced in the viewer feelings of love proportional to his sense of power over it. The aesthetic object is aligned with gender in this formulation, but so is the viewer. Clearly, Burke's definition of the beautiful rested on notions of male power over women; the beautiful constructs the aesthetic subject – the viewer – as male in relation to feminine beauty. Conversely, the immensity of the Sublime made the male viewer feel like a woman, smaller and weaker than the object viewed, perhaps the cause of psychic terror.[7]

John Webber's drawing of Kerguelen Island, *A View of Christmas Harbour*, provides an example of a Sublime landscape from Cook's third voyage (see Figure 1). After passing the Cape of Good Hope, the *Resolution* and *Discovery* spent the Christmas of 1776 at Kerguelen Island before sailing on to New Zealand. The island itself seems to consist of barren rock with patches of spiky grass, and the drawing is dominated by the huge rock of the middle ground, its shape imposing even on the clouds that highlight it. The rock towers over both ships (part of one is just visible at the drawing's left edge), the boats and landing parties, and the apparent inhabitants of the island – a flock of penguins Webber added to give life to the drawing. The immensity of the scale is suggested by the fact that the penguins are at least as large as the men landing on shore. "The contrast between humans and animals could not more explicitly evoke an atmosphere of desolation";[8] nothing less Christmaslike could be imagined. Indeed, the name of the harbour seems to emphasize its isolation and inhospitability. There is awe here – an awe tempered not by wonder but by fear.

By contrast to the dangerous singularity of the Sublime demonstrated in Webber's drawing of Christmas Harbour, the Picturesque landscape was characterized by a pleasing variety. Moderating the Sublime's jagged rocks to rough and irregular terrain, the Picturesque did not invite a response of awe or terror; it seemed diminished or contained, allowing the male viewer the pleasure of emotional response without the psychic threat of disintegration or feminization (no doubt part of the source of its appeal). But the most significant quality of the Picturesque landscape was its "paintability." This term did not in fact suggest that a landscape evoked in the viewer the desire to turn it into a painting; rather, "paintability" implied the degree to which a landscape already resembled a painting – especially the landscapes of Salvator Rosa, Poussin, and Claude Lorrain, which presented "idealized versions of the countryside around Rome [and] established an intricate relationship of water, distant hills, buildings (especially the effect of ruins or the formal contrasts of square and round temples), bridges and trees."[9] These works influenced the way Britons saw both paintings and landscapes. The wealthy landowners who collected the paintings of Claude and Poussin for their country houses also transformed their grounds into landscapes resembling those paintings, employing celebrity gardeners like "Capability" Brown, who spent a great deal of time (and their employers' money) making estates look untouched and wild. The degree of artifice necessary to create a landscape that looked "naturally" picturesque is suggested by the fact that these landowners occasionally demolished or moved entire villages in order to improve the views from their country houses.[10] So the Picturesque landscape evoked a sense of order and control, a cultivated wildness already framed as if ready for painting.

Throughout the late eighteenth and early nineteenth centuries, British explorers employed the prevailing conventions of landscape appreciation, as MacLaren's work on various overland travel accounts of British North America demonstrates.[11] In recording their responses using the discourses of the Sublime and the Picturesque, British explorers were not only unable to see the difference between familiar and New World landscapes without positing difference as inferiority, but they were also unable to see beyond what their educations, experiences, and

cultures had taught them to see. Nor was this process necessarily conscious. By the late eighteenth century the principles of landscape composition were so central to landscape appreciation that they could be
unconsciously applied to New World territories.[12] Many British explorers not only described but also viewed the landscapes of discovery as if
through a Claude glass or camera obscura, devices that transformed
nature into landscape pictures. Their tendency to privilege Picturesque
over Sublime landscapes goes beyond a sense of cozy familiarity to psychological orientation; Britons *felt* lost in Sublime environments precisely because of the qualities that made them Sublime – their immensity
and the resulting sense that they were beyond human control. The
result, MacLaren argues, is a linguistic failure in response to Sublime
landscapes.[13] By contrast, Barbara Maria Stafford locates the Sublime
within a different psychological framework. She argues that the vocabulary of the Sublime (awe, terror, psychic danger) provides a way to
communicate the excitement generated by the challenge of a threaten-
ing landscape.[14] These different perspectives on the Sublime as an aesthetic vocabulary in the service of exploration suggest some of the ways
that European aesthetic expectations shaped perceptions of place in the
so-called New World.

Some blurring of the boundaries between these terms occurred
towards the end of the eighteenth century; by 1786, for example, William Gilpin conflated two terms in the phrase "picturesque beauty." In
doing so, he did not so much replace the Beautiful with the Picturesque
as the antithesis of the Sublime as shift from an oppositional to a rela-
tional meaning. As the Picturesque lost its sense of novelty and excitement and came to seem somewhat tame and ordinary, appreciators of
landscape increasingly looked for Sublime scenes to stimulate in them
the feelings no longer raised by the Picturesque.[15] Because both aesthetic
discourses allowed for an emotional response to landscape, the desire
for one kind of landscape could shift into a greater appreciation for the
other. By the early nineteenth century, for example, travellers and immigrants to Canada expected to find scenes of sublimity and were disappointed when nature seemed inadequately grand or terrifying. In two
famous examples, Catharine Parr Traill complained about the lack of
sublimity in the area of her Peterborough bush farm in her *Backwoods
of Canada* (1836); more unusually, Anna Brownell Jameson's *Winter
Studies and Summer Rambles* (1838) recorded not the awe she expected
to feel at the magnificence of Niagara Falls but, rather, her disappoint-
ment that they had not lived up to their reputation.[16] The Sublime, with

its emphasis on pleasurable feelings of terror and awe, provided a way to visit and appreciate landscapes that would previously have been avoided as unpleasantly frightening.

European aesthetic discourses like the Picturesque and the Sublime helped to make New World territories seem familiar and knowable, both to explorers and to readers of exploration texts. The emotional response to landscape generated by these discourses located explorers and readers psychologically. But the very familiarity of this way of see-ing set up another relationship between humans and landscape: if land is viewed according to the conventions of landscape painting, then the person seeing the land is separated from it, positioned outside the paint-ing's frame as an observer.

This distancing effect was not incidental to the landscape painting's composition; rather, it was the foundation of eighteenth-century aes-thetics. Writers like Addison, Shaftesbury, Hume, Burke, Reynolds, and Kant posited a "generic perceiver," whose "disinterested contempla-tion" decontextualized an aesthetic object from its material surround-ings and so maintained "the autonomy of the aesthetic domain from moral, political, or utilitarian concerns and activities."[17] Only a certain kind of person is capable of seeing a work of art "universally," perceiv-ing its scope and achievement without getting lost in its particular details, contemplating it with the disinterest that comes from freedom from the need to work to produce the necessities of life, and from enjoy-ing autonomy, the ability to cut oneself off from everyday economic and political concerns. That person is a gentleman.[18] Eighteenth-century aesthetic theorists imagined the aesthetic subject as a property-owning man in terms that figured the object of aesthetic scrutiny – landscape or woman – as a possession. Hence the appeal of landscape gardening. The property owner intent on "improving" his estate (highlighting its beauty as attention to dress and toilet could improve the beauty of a woman) simultaneously demonstrated his possession of both land and taste, and confirmed his status as a gentleman: male in relation to the feminized land, gentle by contrast to the vulgar working man.

If the aesthetic discourse producing the British spectator of continen-tal and domestic landscape constructed him as its gentleman-owner, then what happened when he turned his gaze to the non-European world? A postcolonial reading of this aesthetic vocabulary has called attention to the exercise of what Pratt has called the "imperial eye," but the issue is more complex than visual appropriation alone. The notion of disinterest was also built into the popular understanding of discov-

ery, especially with the rise of scientific travel in the late eighteenth century. Joseph Banks's comment to Mrs Cook after the death of her
husband – "His name will lie forever in the remembrance of a people
grateful for the services his labours have afforded to mankind in general" – suggests that "Cook's scientific non-partisan achievement
should stand on its own merits even at a time when the strategic importance of colonial exploration could not fail to be recognised," as if
Cook stands for this disinterested pursuit of knowledge.[19] The British
used the trope of curiosity implied by discovery to separate the disinterested pursuit of knowledge from the implications of discovery for the
"interested" processes of imperialism and colonialism.[20] By suggesting
the excitement naturally associated with learning something new, the
notion of curiosity disassociated the desire to go and find out about
other places, other people, and other customs from the desire to claim
those places, to trade with those people, and to change those customs,
by force if necessary. Aesthetic discourses claiming universality, disinterestedness, and autonomy as basic assumptions brought together
seemingly mutually exclusive projects, the disinterested pursuit of
knowledge and the very interested pursuit of economic and political
power. For European powers, rapidly becoming imperial (and soon to
be colonial) powers, discovery equalled a claim to possession of New
World territories.

Bernard Smith has argued that "European experience of the Pacific ...
challenged the supremacy of neo-classical values in cosmological theory
as it had helped to challenge those values in the theory and practice of
landscape-painting."[21] In similar fashion, Barbara Maria Stafford
argues that the very difference of the New World necessitated new verbal and visual conventions, free of centuries-old associations with classical knowledge and traditions. Against the tendency to privilege the
form and content of the knowledge of the Ancients, Stafford links
Locke's notion of the tabula rasa with the project of exploration and
discovery: in the representation of a New World, she identifies not a
problem but an opportunity for representation – an opportunity to
avoid habitual metaphors and old ideas. Cook's voyages, like other voyages of exploration, were dangerous; there was every chance that men
or indeed ships would be lost, destroyed on the Great Barrier Reef (as
the *Endeavour* nearly was in June 1770), or trapped in pack-ice in the
high southern latitudes (as the *Resolution* and *Adventure* could have
been when they crossed the Antarctic circle in January 1773). Cook
himself, of course, never returned from the third voyage. "What is

appealing about these innumerable and dangerous adventures is the
intensity of pleasure they convey. The enjoyment and evident relish mir-
rored in these narratives is based on the idea that the scientific traveler is
usefully, not trivially, engaged."[22] The importance of Cook's voyages to
this sense of the new, the unfamiliar, and the unknown (not to mention
the "intensity of pleasure" that resulted from reading, as well as leading, such "dangerous adventures") cannot be overestimated. However,
these are not fantastic voyages: Stafford argues that plain-language
accounts of a world explored using the methods of empirical science
took on aesthetic status, privileging content over form – against established representational conventions in which new matter was endlessly
injected into old forms, resulting in something like too much "art," or
artifice, and not quite enough substance.

   Now it is time to turn to the texts of Cook's third voyage, especially
the month at Nootka Sound. What effects did aesthetic disinterestedness, based on assumptions of possession understood in class and gender terms, have on Cook's depiction of Nootka Sound? Are there
differences between how Cook perceived this coast and how it was represented in the published text? What aesthetic conventions influenced
the artists? In considering these questions, we will have to look at both
visual and verbal accounts of Nootka Sound.

All three of Cook's voyages carried artists as well as scientists – artists
whose job was to supplement, with images, the written account of
strange new lands and peoples. These images (nearly 3,000 drawings of
Pacific plant, animal, bird, and sea life; coastlines and landscapes; people and societies) were an important part of the voyages' contribution
to knowledge, shaping Europeans' encounter with the Pacific. In the
case of the third voyage, the delay in publishing an official text (from
1779, when the ships returned to England, to 1784) was caused by the
length of time it took to turn several drawings into engraved plates.

   On the third voyage, as on the first and second, the representative
function was paramount in the secret instructions given Cook by the
Admiralty: "you are ... to survey, make Charts, and take views of such
Bays, Harbours, and different parts of the Coast, and to make such
Notations thereon, as may be useful to Navigation or Commerce. You
are also carefully to observe the nature of the Soil and the produce
thereof; the Animals & Fowls that inhabit or frequent it; the Fishes that
are to be found in the Rivers or upon the Coast, and in what plenty;

and, in case there are any peculiar to such places, to describe them as minutely, and to make as accurate drawings of them, as you can."[23] The North Pacific environment, radically different from the relatively familiar South Pacific, necessitated an even closer attention to detail than usual. One of the artists employed to produce this visual record was John Webber, a professional artist trained in Berne and Paris as a landscape and figure draughtsman. Recommended by Daniel Solander, Webber was asked to join the third voyage after organizers saw his Royal Academy exhibition. Webber was "pitched upon ... for the express purpose of supplying the unavoidable imperfections of written accounts, by enabling us to preserve, and bring home, such drawings of the most memorable of our transactions, as could be expressed by a skilled and professional artist" (Douglas III:1, 5). The other artist was the surgeon's second mate, William Ellis, who produced mostly drawings of plant and animal life.

Much more than the artists of Cook's previous voyages, Webber documents life in the contact zone. Trained primarily in history painting rather than in botanical drawing, Webber produced a series of set pieces for most major landfalls: "encounter" and "entertainment" paintings, head and shoulder studies of at least one man and woman, and often full-length portraits as well as ethnographic drawings to provide visual support for Cook's written descriptions. Bernard Smith argues that Webber's encounter and entertainment paintings "constitute a new kind of history painting ... a new visual source for the study of history, and not as in academic history paintings, the retrospective illustration of a traditional text."[24] Smith and Rüdiger Joppien support this claim in their analysis of one of Webber's encounter paintings:

There is a complexity of action and movement which only unfolds itself after a close examination. Many studies were necessary to build up a comprehensive scene like this ... [A]t all major ports of call, in Nootka Sound as much as in Kealakekua Bay, Webber observed similar scenes, vignettes of daily life. Though he may not have drawn these regularly at all stations, the fact that occasionally they are encapsulated in his pictures shows he was aware of them. By them, Webber reflected the expedition as a history-making event in itself. To have noticed and understood this is a new element among the body of visual representations from Cook's voyages ... Furthermore each incident depicted is given much the same weight in Webber's drawings, indeed his presentation is so impartial we cannot be sure which of the two British officers in the foreground is Cook. Webber's tendency to demonstrate the complexity of action is historical in an eventful and documentary sense but it is also anti-heroic.[25]

Much of this commentary is applicable to the encounter painting Webber produced at Nootka Sound, which also narrates events typical of landing.

Webber's use of the codes of history painting has profound consequences for the encounter scenes in particular, constituting an ideological claim more potentially transformative of both European and Pacific societies than either portraits or engravings. History painting occupied the top of the hierarchy of art forms established by the Royal Academy. Since it valorized heroic or noble deeds by its form as well as its content, history painting created a rhetoric of virtues for a public sphere constructed as male. Like the aesthetic discourses of the Sublime and Picturesque, history painting assumed the universal, disinterested, and autonomous gentleman viewer; just as viewing a landscape came to stand for imaginatively possessing it, so understanding the values at work in a history painting came to stand for possessing them. Such an emphatically public mode not only visually states the historical, economic, and moral importance of the events portrayed but it also locates them in the kind of power relations established by a landed elite.[26]

This understanding of history painting is essential to locating the concerns of Webber's "encounter" painting from Nootka Sound, *The Resolution and Discovery in Nootka Sound* (see Figure 2). Joppien and Smith's analysis of the drawing – the largest Webber produced on the third voyage – puts it in the context of European examples of paintings uniting historical and topographic genres, in which the "geographical and commercial components of both land and sea are drawn together into a hub of human activity."[27] The problem facing Webber was not the depiction of standard landfall activities (which, two years into the voyage, he must have witnessed many times, after all) but, instead, that of locating these activities in a strange landscape. This drawing, like many of the encounter paintings, is "complex and anti-heroic" in that the viewer cannot identify Cook as the hero and central figure who gives the narrative meaning, in contrast to paintings such as Benjamin West's famous *The Death of General Wolfe* (1770) (see Figure 3). West initially seems to emphasize reportage of a historical event because he clothes the British soldiers in uniforms instead of in the classical draperies Reynolds thought appropriate to heroic subject matter. In fact, however, many of the officers wearing those uniforms and surrounding the dying Wolfe were not present at his death but paid West £100 each to paint them into the scene, a powerful endorsement of the cultural importance of history painting.[28] The presentation of this apotheosis – General Wolfe's death almost at the moment of England's victory over France on the Plains of Abraham in 1759, a victory that ended the Seven Years' War – as a history painting imparts a sense of heroism and nobility to a war of colonial expansion.

Because Webber fuses the topographic genre with the historic, the effect in *The* Resolution *and* Discovery *in Nootka Sound* is the opposite of both West's painting and Douglas's edition of the text. While the text presents Cook as a hero, Webber's drawing is dominated not by Cook the hero but by the ships; the puny human figures of the foreground are dwarfed by the irregular rocks and lofty pines of the middle ground. Landfall activities are discernible, but the figures engaging in them are not: a Briton, presumably but not explicitly Cook, extends his hand towards a group of Natives, while the crew is occupied with such activities as wooding, watering, and trading. In this drawing the voyage itself becomes the hero, as signalled by the enormous flag almost the size of the ship's hull, and the potential economic profits to be realized by European traders as a result of this voyage. The Native canoes may not equal the size of the European ship, but there are many of them, filled with people presumably eager to trade.

The contrast between Douglas's construction of Cook as an imperial hero and Webber's anti-heroic landing-paintings thus suggests the occasionally competing discourses governing the third voyage.[29] While Douglas's Cook is a gentleman-scientist engaged in the disinterested pursuit of knowledge, Webber's paintings point to the commercial considerations governing voyages of exploration. The Northwest Passage was, after all, not sought for centuries merely for the sake of adventure and the advancement of knowledge; the commercial value of a quick sea route to the East was the prime incentive. Webber's paintings also suggest a greater sense of equality and reciprocity between Europeans and Natives than Douglas can manage. The fact that both groups are overshadowed by the bulk of the ships indicates that the process of cultural change caused by the encounter was, in fact, beyond the power of either to control entirely.

Maria Tippett and Douglas Cole describe the movement of ships north-
wards along the western coastline of North America as a movement
from the Picturesque to the Sublime landscape; the similarity of the
Oregon and Washington coastline to English landscaped parks meant
that its beauty could easily be recognized.

> Moving further up the coast, however, no such artful
> arrangements were evident. The foreshore of today's British
> Columbia disappeared as the mountains rose directly from the
> sea, creating steep cliffs around deep inlets. No longer were there
> gently ascending hills chequered with varied woodlands, but only
> conifer-clad mountains rising precipitously above the snowline.
> The scene lacked all the qualities of the familiar and beautiful.
> No greater departure from the sensitively arranged nobleman's
> park could be imagined.
>   The British Columbia coast loomed silent and desolate,
> enveloped by huge and rocky mountains, filled with raging
> waterfalls and tempestuous weather and frequently obscured by
> mists and fogs. While this shoreline appeared neither pleasing
> nor beautiful to the early explorers, it could provide the refined
> mind of the age with a suitable setting for a study of the sublime
> in nature.[30]

With the notable exception of Joseph Banks, "the refined mind of the
age" was less likely to be found on the quarter-deck of a voyage of
exploration than to be reading the published account of the voyage
from the safety of home. There, in its aristocratic guise it was creating
(and in its middle-class guise touring) Picturesque landscape gardens, in
addition to collecting or admiring the paintings of Claude, Poussin, and
Salvator Rosa, or gazing in awe at the Alps.

But how real or important were these aesthetic questions to Cook?
Did he perceive Pacific shores according to such aesthetic notions as the
Sublime or the Picturesque? The first description of Nootka Sound in
Douglas's edition of the third voyage presents it as a Sublime landscape:

> The land bordering upon the sea coast is of a middling height
> and level; but within the Sound, it rises almost every where into
> steep hills, which agree in their general formation, ending in
> round or blunted tops, with some sharp, though not very
> prominent, ridges on their sides. Some of these hills may be

reckoned high, while others of them are of a very moderate height; but even the highest are entirely covered to their tops with the thickest woods; as well as every flat part toward the sea. There are sometimes spots upon the sides of some of the hills which are bare; but they are few, in comparison of the whole, though they sufficiently point out the general rocky disposition of these hills. Properly speaking, they have no soil upon them, except a kind of compost, produced from rotten mosses and trees, of the depth of two feet or more. Their foundations are, therefore, to be considered as nothing more than stupendous rocks, of a whitish or grey cast, where they have been exposed to the weather; but, when broken, they appeared to be of a bluish grey colour, like that universal sort which were found at Kerguelen's Land. The rocky shore are a continued mass of this; and the little coves, in the Sound, have beaches composed of fragments of it, with a few other pebbles. All these coves are furnished with a great quantity of fallen wood lying in them, which is carried in by the tide; and the rills of fresh water, sufficient for the use of a ship, which seem to be supplied entirely from the rains and fogs that hover about the top of the hills. For few springs can be expected in so rocky a country, and the fresh water found further up the Sound, most probably arose from the melting of the snow; there being no room to suspect, that any large river falls into the Sound, either from strangers coming down it, or from any other circumstance. The water of these rills is perfectly clear, and dissolves soap easily. (Douglas III:2, 289–90)

Douglas's description of the Sound reads almost like a description of a painting: he begins by noting the middle and background, the forest that overwhelms the eye as the consciousness is overwhelmed not so much by the height of the hills as by the "rocky disposition" and the wildness of the scene. Then he moves down through the middle ground, noticing the "bare spots" on the hills (a contrast that serves to highlight that they are mostly covered with trees) towards the foreground, where particulars of the soil, rocks, and trees can be distinguished. The reference to Kerguelen's Island, another landscape of barren slopes and rocks of primarily geological interest (as in Webber's drawing of Christmas Harbour), highlights the sublimity of Nootka Sound in the image of rocky mountains, bristling with trees almost down to the water.

But quite possibly this is Douglas's impression rather than Cook's. The passage from Beaglehole's edition of Cook's journals gives little sense of an aesthetic response to Nootka Sound as a Sublime landscape on Cook's part. Douglas considerably expanded Cook's description of the Sound as produced in Beaglehole's edition: "The land bordering upon the Sea coast is of a middling height and level, but about the Sound it consists of high hills and deep Vallies, for the most part cloathed with large timber, such as Spruce fir and white Cedar. The more inland Mountains were covered with Snow, in other respects they seemed to be naked" (Beaglehole III:1, 309). Evidently, Douglas has rewritten and expanded Cook's description using the vocabulary of the Sublime, probably borrowing from the journals of other officers. The previous chapter noted Douglas's frequent borrowings from William Anderson, whose journal account of Nootka Sound was lost; it may be to Anderson that Douglas owes his description of Nootka Sound as Sublime. Certainly, of the remaining officers' accounts, only James King's hints at such an aesthetic response, using such emotionally loaded adjectives as "melancholy" and "wild & savage" to characterize the scene as repellently Sublime.

> The land round the Sound is very much broken into high precipices & deep Chasms; all parts of which are wooded, & continue so down to the water side, where the shore is steep & rocky; the few level spots one meets with, are only bogs & swamps, & the whole has a melancholy appearance; not even the noise or mark of Animals or birds are here either to be seen or heard to give some little animation to the woods of King Georges Sound. The high mountains which rise on the back & far inland are many of them bare, & serve to heighten & finish the Picture of as wild & savage a Country as can be well drawn in so temperate a climate.[31]

King's description is much like Douglas's in its focus on the emotional associations prominent in eighteenth-century landscape aesthetics, a tendency apparent in the place names given by explorers like Cook: Christmas Harbour is so named for the date of the *Resolution*'s arrival at Kerguelen Island, King Georges Sound (Cook's original name for Nootka Sound) for the monarch, a possessive if unimaginative name Cook bestowed liberally throughout the Pacific. The fact that Cook called one of the coves within Nootka Sound "Friendly Cove" suggests that *his* view of the place was informed not by a sense of inhospitable sublimity but of comfort.[32]

The majority of the other officers' accounts echo Cook's description of Nootka Sound as presented in Beaglehole's edition, emphasizing not aesthetic but pragmatic considerations and revealing more about the concerns of the writer in question than about the landscape. For example, the American marine corporal John Ledyard describes Nootka Sound by listing the products of the country. He concludes with a sentence presumably motivated by his desire to return to this coast and his anxiety to convince possible sponsors of the profitability of such an expedition: "The light in which this country will appear most to advantage respects the variety of its animals, and the richness of their fur."[33] The Captain of the *Discovery* and second-in-command of the voyage, Charles Clerke, concentrates on the "vast abundance of excellent Timber": "indeed, the whole face of the Country is cover'd with it, both Hills & Dales. The wood in general is Fir, there are different kinds of it, and such a variety of sizes, that in going a very inconsiderable distance, you may cut Sticks of every gradation, from a Main Mast for your Ship, to one for your Jolly Boat; and these I suppose as good as any as are to be procur'd in any part of the World."[34] Clerke sees not a gloomy, silent forest but, rather, a do-it-yourself lumberyard in the fine stands of timber, there for the cutting and certainly cheaper than masts "procur'd in anypart of the World." In similar fashion, Cook's description in Beaglehole's edition also reflects an eminent practicality. The previous chapter having recounted the difficulties of replacing a rotten mizenmast, it is impossible for Cook to see the forest only as desolate and forbidding: it also must represent a useful stand of timber. The water of the rills may not be as plentiful as desired, the source might be unsure, but even so, it is "perfectly clear," unlike rain water collected in barrels in the middle of the ocean, with an unpleasant taste from the tar of the rigging, and soft, since it "dissolves soap easily."

In Douglas's edition, Cook sees "woods"; in Beaglehole's, he sees "timber." Cook's own description of Nootka Sound, as Beaglehole's edition reveals, is marked primarily by common-sense rather than aesthetic discourses: looking to replace the main and mizen-masts, Cook sees an uncommonly fine stand of timber likely to produce many possible choices. Douglas, however, produces the landscape of Nootka Sound for European readers using the aesthetic discourse of the Sublime.

Douglas presents his own particular vision, imposing the distance not only between ship and shore but also between his library in England and this unknown coast, and he presents this vision as if it were documentary. With Cook's name on the title page of the published edition as the guarantor of credibility, Douglas's metaphoric and rhetorical description of Nootka Sound is received by his audience as mimetic or transparent. Later writers followed Douglas's lead in portraying the Northwest Coast as a Sublime landscape. The journal of George Vancouver's voyage to the Northwest Coast some fifteen years later makes clear that he used the discourses of the Sublime and Picturesque. Because the Puget Sound region reminded him so strongly of picturesque landscape paintings and gardens, Vancouver "confidently asserted its suitability for British settlement and prophesied its evolution into a landscape mecca. It was to him what James Cook had designated the region generally – a New Albion." However, north of present-day Vancouver, British Columbia, Vancouver's crew moved abruptly from the Picturesque to the Sublime, signalled by such place names as "Desolation Sound" and "Burke's Inlet" (for Edmund Burke): "thus, in a single season's surveying, Vancouver and his men had run the gamut of eighteenth-century British landscape aesthetics."[35]

If the published account presents Douglas's Sublime colouring of Nootka Sound, what about the drawings meant to serve as visual correctives to the written account? Although the west coast of Vancouver Island could easily be viewed as a Sublime landscape, Webber does not portray it as such: "if awe-struck or melancholy when contemplating the landscape, he does not convey this emotion onto paper. He is too busy with Nootka types, with interiors of Yuquot houses, with the variety of exotic artifacts, even with a captured sea otter, to concern himself with an essentially forlorn and repellent landscape."[36] Perhaps the codes of history painting allow him to present the narrative details of the time spent at the Sound (a month encapsulated into one painterly moment) and to "discharge his documentary and topographical responsibilities as voyage artist" as painting a Sublime landscape would not.[37] Compare, for example, The Resolution and Discovery in Nootka Sound (Figure 2) to the more obviously Sublime landscape represented in A View of Christmas Harbour (Figure 1). Clearly, there is a wealth of activity and productivity to be found in the drawing of Nootka Sound that dramatically contrasts the lonely desolation of Kerguelen Island. Webber's history painting of Nootka Sound achieves, in his "ability to present people not as heroes but as members of communities who take on the colour and mood of their environment," a new kind of "art as information": he represents the newness of the New World in a new way.[38] While Douglas's editing continually asserts the distance between Britain and the Pacific expressed in the construction of Cook as an imperial hero deigning to notice Natives as social inferiors, Webber's encounter paintings present Cook as a representative of Britain and empire, but one virtually indistinguishable from other such representatives.

The drawing of Nootka Sound depicts the activities common to landing – cutting wood, repairing barrels and filling them with fresh water, setting up observation tents, trading with Natives – and in so doing locates the voyage within the context of the work needed to maintain it. The distance between ship and shore is crossed in several ways: the sailors leave their ships for the shore, and the Natives leave their land for the ships; the two parties shake hands; they trade goods; they communicate. Webber's art dismantles some of the distance established by Douglas's editing. Consider, for instance, Webber's drawing of the interior of a house (Figure 4), which also contains a wealth of information. It portrays many of the things described by Cook (the racks of drying fish, the figures called "Klumma," woven baskets, capes, and hats) and also gives some sense of social organization in the family groups gathered around a central fire. But producing this drawing required Webber to relinquish the artificial distance between ship and shore, between civilization and "savagery," that Douglas's text is so careful to maintain. One inhabitant protested Webber's attempt to draw this interior, particularly the "two large images, or statues placed abreast of each other and 3 or 4 feet asunder, they bore some resemblance to the human figure, but monstrous large" (Beaglehole III:1, 319). Unlike Beaglehole's Cook, Douglas noted that the Natives required offerings "as we interpreted their signs, to give something to these images, when they drew aside the mats that covered them" (Douglas II, 317). Of course, after only a month at Nootka Sound, no one on the ships had learned enough of the language to communicate about matters of belief systems; perhaps the Reverend Doctor takes the image of offerings (to graven images!) from Cook's comment that "some of our gentlemen think they were their gods" (Beaglehole III:1, 319). In a footnote, however, Douglas indicates the specific nature of the offering required – which, it turns out, is not for a European to view the statues but, rather, for Webber to draw them:

It should seem, that Mr. Webber was obliged to repeat his offerings pretty frequently, before he could be permitted to finish his drawings of these images. The following account is in his own words: "After having made a general view of their habitations, I sought for an inside, which might furnish me with sufficient matter to convey a perfect idea of the mode in which these people live. Such was soon found. While I was employed, a man approached me with a large knife in his hand, seemingly displeased, when he observed my eyes were fixed on two representations of human figures, which were placed at one end of the apartment, carved on planks, of a gigantic proportion, and painted after their custom. However, I took as little notice of him as possible, and proceed; to prevent which he soon provided himself with a mat, and placed it in such a manner as to hinder my having any longer a sight of them. Being pretty certain that I could have no future opportunity to finish my drawing, and the object being too interesting to be omitted, I considered that a little bribery might probably have some effect. Accordingly I made an offer of a button from my coat, which, being of metal, I thought they would be pleased with. This, instantly, produced the desired effect. For the mat was removed, and I was left at liberty to proceed as before. Scarcely had I seated myself, and made a beginning, when he returned and renewed his former practice, continuing it till I had parted with every single button; and when he saw that he had completely stripped me, I met with no further obstruction." (Douglas II, 317–8)

While Beaglehole quotes Webber as having "disposd of my buttons" (Beaglehole III:1, 320), Douglas uses a somewhat ambiguous phrasing that leaves the reader uncertain of whether Webber is in fact "completely stripped" or stripped of his buttons.[39] It should be noted that, if Webber had had to trade away all his clothes, Douglas would have used exactly the kind of phrase he did above to conceal that fact. The image of a European man naked in the presence of a group of Natives (who are themselves clothed, according to the drawing) is certainly an unusual one, but even if Webber is stripped only of his buttons, to produce this drawing he has had to cross the line of aesthetic disinterestedness and interact with the aesthetic objects.

Webber's written account of the context within which he produced the drawing flies in the face of eighteenth-century aesthetic discourse: the "objects" of his drawing refuse to stay put and insist on being subjects. In Douglas's edition, however, the objects stay objects; the inhabitants of Nootka Sound are merged with and subordinated to the landscape, described only after the region's vegetables, animals, and even minerals have been catalogued.[40] It may be that this revising of Cook's description of Nootka Sound to conform with notions of the Sublime was part of Douglas's editorial purpose of elevating Cook into a gentleman, the kind of man who perceives not land but landscape, and in so perceiving implicitly possesses it. This brings me back to the assumptions of universality, disinterest, and autonomy in eighteenth-century aesthetic discourse, especially as they apply to the Picturesque and the Sublime and the kinds of connections they posited between people and landscape. The Sublime landscape did not commonly include humans; one of its characteristics was its presumed inhospitability to human presence. Increasingly, towards the end of the eighteenth century the Picturesque landscape did include humans but in circumscribed roles. According to Gilpin's theory of the Picturesque, human figures were ornamental, roughly equivalent to the groups of cattle that served the same formal function. Although a landscape painting generally required that human figures be rural workers, Gilpin's aesthetic demanded that they not be portrayed working. The focus of such a landscape is not the productivity of the land or the people who work it, but the disinterested and autonomous perception of its aesthetic appeal. "Work is unpicturesque."[41]

I have already noted the tendency of explorers to describe landscape as if they viewed it through a Claude glass. To see land as a landscape painting through the Claude glass, the viewer turned his back to it, detaching both himself from the scene and the scene itself from its surroundings. The distancing effect of such a transformation, meant to characterize the relation between viewer and landscape as one of ownership, possibly reflects the change from a moral economy to agricultural capitalism at a time when landowners increasingly disassociated themselves from the agricultural source of their wealth and divested themselves of any responsibility beyond paying a wage towards those who produced it.[42] Cook, after all, was not born into the aristocratic or even the middle classes; he was the son of an agricultural day-labourer, the kind of person whose presence in a landscape painting as a "faceless ornament" served a formal function that divested him of his livelihood.[43] These concerns are not incidental to the portrayal of Cook in Douglas's edition: not until he had been constructed as a gentleman by Douglas's editing and public commendation for his service to his country was Cook given the promotion from commander to captain.[44]

Not only in his account of the forest as "timber" but throughout his journal Cook is relentlessly focused on pragmatic concerns. Douglas's editing consistently transforms those pragmatic concerns into aesthetic ones, meant to elevate Cook from a plain-speaking, plain-dealing man into a gentleman and to demonstrate Cook's superiority to the peoples he encountered on his voyages. When Douglas's narrative turns from a relatively benign, though slightly suspicious, description of trade relations to the statement that the nearly unspoken assumptions about the nature of "savages" everywhere apply in Nootka Sound as much as in the South Pacific, the distancing function of these aesthetic discourses comes more fully into play. In the imperial or colonial context of Cook's voyages, this distancing function implies mastery or possession. While Nootka Sound remained an outpost of empire, Britain was quick to assert a claim to the territory against competing claims by Spain, particularly during the Nootka Crisis of 1790. "Nootka Sound was transposed into this European setting and reconstructed as an object of both national and imperial concern."[45] Ultimately, Britain wanted to draw Nootka Sound within the imperial orbit less than it wanted to maintain, however sporadically, the right to trade for furs there. To the extent that Nootka Sound, a place accessible only by air and water, ever became a European settlement, it did so as a trading post.[46] Even if Britain acted as a kind of absentee landlord, however, it wanted occasionally to collect the rent. Clearly this establishes a kind of colonial relationship that differs from that involving occupation and settlement, which displaces the original inhabitants. But Britain's claim to the rights of resource extraction, of profiting from the products of a distant territory, nonetheless drew Nootka Sound into the network of colonial possessions.

CHAPTER THREE

Science and Ethnography: The Field of Vision

In the preceding chapter I discuss how Douglas amplified and improved Cook's plain non-metaphoric style using eighteenth-century aesthetic discourses. This chapter considers the discourse and language of natural history as they influenced the third voyage – particularly the global classification project of the Swede Carl Linné, or Carolus Linnaeus, as he called himself, using Latin to emphasize the universality of his system. Natural history and exploration shared an aim: description of the new and unfamiliar. Just as the travel genre provided a narrative format for the description of new peoples, places, and products, so natural history provided a method, rhetoric, and context for the description of the New World. The two modes of writing also shared observation as the essential method. While travel writers depended on observations and reflections upon foreign places and customs, natural historians observed the natural world, collecting specimens when it was possible to do so and recording observations when it was not (as in the case of natural phenomena). From its beginnings as a method for the descriptive classification of plants, natural history came to be seen as a "logical guide to exploring" their New World habitats.[1] In consequence, both the form and the content of travel writing were transformed: "the observing and cataloguing of nature itself became narratable. It could constitute a series of events, or even produce a plot. It could form the main storyline of an entire account."[2] Natural history moved from a supporting to a central role in exploration narratives, signifying a shift in the focus of discovery from new territories to their constituent elements. It is as if the central image for this project of exploration and discovery changed from a map with blank spaces denoting unknown, uncharted territory to a display case rapidly being filled with distinctive specimens. But the process also worked the other way: exploration itself became a scientific and epistemological process, a metaphor for the arrangement as well as the advancement of knowledge.

Linnaean natural history began by classifying plants according to their reproductive parts. As published in Linnaeus's *Species Planatarum* (1753), the system consisted of a one-page chart. The process by which a plant was identified and labelled was revolutionary in its simplicity: it consisted essentially of counting the number of stamens and pistils, then noting the shape and distribution of leaf, flower, and fruit, and differences from other plants in the same locale. In Linnaean botany, discovery amounts to an act of naming: within the closed system, the plant is the name, and all significant features that distinguish one plant from another are contained within the name.[3] The authority according to which an identification was accepted lay in the methodology, which was in turn laid out in the name. One specimen is understood to be the representative of its species; the name given that specimen refers to that species only, anywhere in the world. With a New World full of unfamiliar, unknown, often seemingly unknowable data coming increasingly into the purview of the old, the unquestionable authority of the Linnaean name reassures by establishing an apparently transparent bond between a specific name and a corresponding thing. Unlike European plants, for example, known for centuries and by many possible names across time and space, the flora of the Pacific were unknown to and unnamed by Europeans. Naming them using the Linnaean catalogue meant that they could be recognized by anyone familiar with the system, whether or not he had ever seen the plants in question.[4] The discourse of natural history thus offered a means to represent as well as to perceive the New World.

The implications of such a classifactory system are profound: fixing names and plants so irrevocably "made the conception of the Great Chain of Being completely rational. After Linnaeus, the binomial label pointed both to a species or kind unique from all others, and to a link on the Chain. It evoked, at once, the very specific and the whole order of the universe."[5] The metaphor of the Chain of Being itself suggested that new discoveries were not unrelated bits of information but, rather, were necessarily linked to what was already known.[6] In other words, knowledge is not random but cumulative: identifying individual specimens, whether plant, animal, or human, from any part of the Chain, adds up to a composite picture of the world, knowable through the relationships between its constituent elements. Out of a chaotic mass of detail comes

clarity: "the New World of exotic mystery, of distance-shrouded indis-
tinctness, gives way to a sharp-edged, delineated, concrete description
systematically and rationally related to the Old World."[7]

As a field of inquiry, eighteenth-century natural history included those
disciplines now known as botany, ethnology, geology, meteorology, and
zoology; it excluded only what was made by humans. Natural historical
discourse did not differentiate between plants and humans, but Europeans in the New World were not often described as if they were just
another natural production. In North America such portrayals were
reserved first for Native peoples and then for Africans. The same methods that natural historians applied to the classification of strange plants
were applied to the non-European peoples they encountered in scientific
exploration, producing so-called manners-and-customs descriptions. In
his *Systema Naturae* (1735), Linnaeus had included humans in his list of
animals, listing different human groups as different links in the Great
Chain of Being. The effects were far-reaching: "the division of man into
separate races began the speculation that would culminate, as early as
1766, in Hume's claim that non-white races were of a different species
than the white race."[8] In theory, it is not so surprising either that the
Linnaean method of classification on the basis of similarities and differences should emphasize racial distinctions or that "observations would
proceed along racial lines." In practice, however, because the New World
of colonial possession was the field for the fieldwork of natural history,
"men of other races [i.e., non-Europeans], perhaps of other species,
became the natural objects of this scrutiny."[9]

Culture and nature, often divided along gender lines in Western
thought, are divided in natural history discourse along racial lines: "culture" (civilization) is the province of Europeans who define "nature" as
everyone else. This objectification has had serious consequences: the
appropriation of territory is erased in the moment of definition, for
things (products) are there to be exploited. As Carolyn Merchant has
argued in her account of the mechanization of the scientific worldview,
the European metaphors based on the association of the natural world
with women (nature as a nurturing mother and nature as disorder) were
transformed by the Scientific Revolution. Mechanistic metaphors
replaced organic ones, and domination, mastery, and control replaced
nurturance and dependence as explanations for the human relationship
with the natural world.[10] This transformation of metaphors explaining
the relationship between humans and the natural world not only provided a justification for exploiting its resources – as men exploited the

labour and reproduction of women – but also provided further legitimation for the exploitation of those humans (women, non-European peoples) associated with nature.[11]

✳

Linnaean classification clearly influenced the development of race theories and racism.[12] The gendered metaphors on which the system depends are much less studied but equally crucial to the knowledge-building project that flourished using Linnaeus's system. The association of non-European peoples with wild, chaotic nature is built upon centuries-old European associations of women with nature. The presentation of information in the Linnaean specimen entry, although designed to be non-metaphoric and precise, in fact relies on an entire structure of metaphor borrowed from eighteenth-century concepts of gender.

The assumed transparency of botanical descriptions calls to mind Thomas Sprat's language project as articulated in his *History of the Royal Society*: "to return back to the primitive Purity and Shortness, when men deliver'd so many *Things*, almost in an equal number of *Words* ... a close, naked, natural way of speaking ... bringing all things as near the Mathematical plainness, as they can."[13] The history of scientific discourse is a history of language as passive, a copy of some reality that exists independently of language and that is never quite adequately grasped by it. The paradox of the scientific revolution's dream of a transparent language lies in the fact that writers like Sprat must resort to metaphor to convey the idea of a purely mimetic language, often imaged as a clear windowpane or glass unobstructed by the garments, veils, or curtains of rhetoric.[14] Such a desire for unity of content and form, the absence of a gap between name and thing, is also, however, part of a masculine enterprise, or of a knowledge-building enterprise defined as a masculine endeavour by a language that itself is becoming increasingly masculine.[15] Perhaps the use of such figurative language is unavoidable, yet scientific discourse presents itself as mimetic, a transparent pane of glass unobscured by a curtain of rhetoric. It is as if scientific writing was not writing at all, as if the content of scientific writing was mediated by neither form nor the human agent.[16]

Like eighteenth-century aesthetics, natural history rested upon assumptions of distance and objectivity; it was also deeply influenced by European concepts of gender, of masculinity and femininity as well as relationships between men and women. As a result, the kinds of knowledge about the New World produced by natural history are bound up in gendered concepts of mastery and possession. Linnaean botany, the foundation of eighteenth-century natural history discourse, breaks the theoretically mimetic structure of scientific language at the very moment of its construction. Grammatical gender is the culprit here: "in Latin and the romance languages of medieval and early modern Europe, nature was a feminine noun, and hence, like the virtues (temperance, wisdom, etc.) personified as female."[17] Thus the relationship between the natural world and the words used to describe it is the metaphoric one of women and men, wives and husbands, submission and domination. A similar metaphor (from the sixteenth century onwards) explains Europe's relationship to the New World by imaging the European explorer (and later settler) as the appropriate husband for the New World territory personified as a woman. The irony is that the supposedly dispassionate discourse of science sexualizes not only human interaction with the world, thus personifying the world of things, but also non-human relationships between elements of the world of things.

Two further points about the Linnaean system are worth making here. One is that the fixity of natural objects, their similarity and knowability on a global scale, is heightened by their presentation in a list. The Linnaean list uses a shorthand derived from medieval Latin, in which verbs are conspicuously absent, resulting in a deliberate stasis; by creating a fixed image of the thing described, the list enacts rhetorically the human control of the chaotic, disordered natural world.[18] The other point is that, although the predicate of reproduction is eliminated along with any others, the *Species Planatarum* sexualizes plants by identifying them according to their reproductive parts in the one-page chart. More important, the accompanying written description uses the vocabulary of human relationships to explain the classifications. For example, the first class (A on the Chart, 1 in the "Characters of Classes"), Monandria, is described as follows:

ONE MALE.
One husband in marriage.
One stamen in an hermaphrodite flower.[19]

Further down the chart, Class x (number 22), Dioecia, is described thus:

ONE HOUSE.
Husbands live with their wives in the same house, but have different beds.
Male flowers and female flowers are on the same plant.[20]

The metaphoric structure used to describe the Linnaean classes is not the only element of these descriptions that bears scrutiny. In my sentences introducing these quotations, the passive voice is required to erase the agent, the subject who describes. The result is a discourse that replaces the persuasive, rhetorical style of centuries past with a clear, unambiguous, expository style appropriate to description that aims for transparency and objectivity. In erasing the subject and agent of the sentence and of an experiment, however, such a conception of language transforms not only the individual writer but also the social world of that writer: the "I" who might be subject and agent is reduced to and conflated with the "eye" observing and recording an event as dispassionately as possible. The scientist no longer participates in the world; instead, he observes and records it. The application of such a system of classification to humans, particularly non-Europeans, heightens the process of objectification: it is not that plants are moved up the Great Chain of Being closer to humans but, rather, that some humans – women, non-Europeans, and other socially marginal groups – are moved down the Chain closer to plants.

The growing cultural influence of the science of natural history is obvious in Cook's voyages, notably in the participation of Royal Society member Joseph Banks and the Forsters (father-and-son Johann Reinhold and Georg) on the first and second voyages, respectively. Daniel Solander on the first voyage and Anders Sparrman on the second were both students of Linnaeus. Although John Webber, the artist of the third voyage, had been recommended to Cook by Solander, there were no professional scientists on the third voyage, perhaps because the scientists had aims and methods not always compatible with Cook's assessment of nautical realities. For example, Banks had planned to go on the second voyage and ordered so many structural changes to the *Resolution* that, when they were completed, Cook stated he would not put out to sea in a ship so unfit. Banks's greenhouse and laboratory were dismantled, and Banks himself resigned in a fit of temper, to be replaced by the Forsters. Relations between Cook and the second voyage's scientists were as strained as those between Cook and Banks had been, however, and, as a result, the third voyage left without an independent scientist or professional botanist – or certainly none of the calibre of Banks or the Forsters. Cook planned instead on using the knowledge of William Anderson and James King.

In Douglas's edition of Cook's journal, the discourse of natural history can be seen in the occasional use of binomial labels and other Latin plant and animal names as well as in specific reference to Linnaeus. Although Douglas does not follow the Linnaean *Methodus* in all its scientific exactitude, he does provide descriptions that compare the object under scrutiny with its known counterpart, either in Europe or the South Pacific, noting differences more particularly than similarities; and he tries to locate it in the lists relative to other known types, often providing footnotes to support his claims. For example, Douglas notes of the deer skins traded at Nootka Sound that they "were scarcer [than bear skins], and they seem to belong to that sort called the fallow-deer by the historians of Carolina; though Mr. Pennant thinks it quite a different species from ours, and distinguishes it by the name of Virginian deer," providing the footnote to Pennant's text for the benefit of readers interested in pursuing the question – or, better yet, for those learned readers already familiar with Pennant's work (Douglas iii:2, 293).

As always in Douglas's edition, textual authority is questionable: it is necessary to compare specific passages with their counterparts in Beaglehole's edition before making any claims regarding Cook's use of Linnaean methodology.

The trees which chiefly compose the woods, are the Canadian pine, white cypress, *cypressus thyoides*, the wild pine, with two or three other sorts of pine less common. The two first make up almost two-thirds of the whole; and, at a distance, might be mistaken for the same tree; as they both run up into pointed spire-like tops; but they are easily distinguished on coming nearer, from their colour; the cypress being of a much paler green, or shade, than the other. The trees, in general, grow with great vigour, and are all of a large size. (Douglas iii:2, 291)

In this passage, the Linnaean name halts the descriptive flow of the observing eye moving across the forest; it halts and fixes the narrative (as indeed it is meant to fix meaning). The passage in Beaglehole's edition is considerably shorter: "The land bordering upon the Sea coast is of a middling hieght and level, but about the Sound it consi[s]ts of high hills and deep Vallies, for the most part cloathed with large timbers, such as Spruce fir and white Cedar*" (Beaglehole iii:1, 309). At that last word, "Cedar," however, Beaglehole provides a footnote bristling with Linnaean nomenclature (the asterisk in this quotation, as in those following, indicates a footnote in the original). "[O]ur Botanist found here the Sipherous wood in great plenty.' – Edgar, f. 152v. – Cook's 'Spruce fir', the European 'Norway Spruce', *Picea excelsa*, is perhaps here the White Spruce, *Picea glauca*. 'White Cedar' must be the 'white cypress, *cypressus thyoides*' (*Cupressus thyoides* Linn.) of *Voyage*, II, p. 291, and is the Yellow Cypress or Cedar, *Chamaecyparis nootkatensis*. It was earlier known as *Cupressus nootkatensis*" (Beaglehole III:1, 309). Beaglehole's footnote makes far greater use of Linnaean labels than did Cook's journals, suggesting that Douglas is again engaged in supplementing – without attribution – Cook's account with material from other sources, either the logs of the other officers or other works entirely.

In its account of birds of the Sound, Douglas's edition specifically mentions Linnaeus.

There are also some [birds], which, I believe, are not mentioned, or at least vary, very considerable, from the accounts given of them by any writers who have treated professedly on this part of natural history. The two first of these are *species* of wood-peckers. One less than a thrush, of a black colour above, with white spots on the wings, a crimson head, neck and breast, with a yellowish olive-colourd belly; from which last circumstance it might, perhaps, not improperly be called the yellow-bellied wood-pecker. The other is a larger, and much more elegant bird, of a dusky brown colour, on the upper part, richly waved with black, except about the head; the belly of a reddish cast, with round black spots; a black spot on the breast; and the under-side of the wings and tail of a plain scarlet colour though blackish above; with a crimson streak running from the angle of the mouth, a little down the neck on each side. The third and fourth, are a small bird of the finch kind, about the size of a linnet, of a dark dusky colour, whitish below, with a black head and neck, and white bill; and a sand-piper, of the size of a small pigeon, of a dusky brown colour, and white below, except the throat and breast, with a broad white band across the wings. There are also humming-birds; which yet seem to difer from the numerous sorts of this delicate animal already known, unless they be a mere variety of the *trochilus colubris* of Linnaeus. These, perhaps, inhabit more to the Southward, and spread Northward as the season advances; because we saw none at first, though, near the time of our departure, the natives brought them to the ships in great numbers. (Douglas III:2, 297)

Although it fulfills the *Methodus*'s requirement for detailed description, this lengthy passage from Douglas is conspicuous in its failure to give Linnaean names and labels to these species, presumably variations on those already named. However, perhaps this failure is not so surprising when the passage is compared to the same moment in Beaglehole's edition: "Of land Birds we saw but few, nor are Water Fowl in any great plenty and all sorts except ravens and crows* were extremely shy and fearfull, probably from being often hunted by the inhabitants. Amongst the land birds is a very beautiful huming bird, amongst the Water Fowl are Swans*..." (Beaglehole III:1, 309–10). Beaglehole's footnote at "Swans" provides the Latin binomials for the birds in question. As usual, Douglas's description is several times longer than is Cook's; however, more curious than the difference in length is the fact that Beaglehole, more than either Douglas or Cook, feels compelled to provide the Linnaean names to identify the species found at Nootka Sound. Often, he does so in footnotes that follow the Linnaean *Methodus* more clearly than the passage they annotate, so that the form in which this material is presented, the scholarly appendage as well as the content (names, theory, genus, species, attributes), solidifies the impression of a scientific text of a scientific expedition.

The way that each editor uses science reflects the scientific discourses of his time. For Douglas, natural history – the work of Linnaeus and his followers – was the realm of the gentleman scientist. While the form of the Linnaean specimen entry, the list, had a democratizing effect[21] (in that an awareness of grammatical rules and stylistic niceties was not required to produce it), the fact that Linnaean lists were written in Latin meant that this knowledge-building endeavour was limited to those possessing a classical education. In England, this meant primarily men of the upper classes. Linnaeus's internationalist choice of Latin as the language of natural history thus constructed the field as the province of the gentleman scientist.[22] In similar fashion, using scientific discourses helps Douglas elevate Cook to the status of honourary gentleman. Nearly 200 years later, when Beaglehole was editing the texts of Cook's third voyage, scientific discourses had changed considerably; Beaglehole uses them to portray Cook as a man governed not by a sense of his own innate superiority as an Englishman but, rather, by objectivity and rationality. Instead of looking back to antiquity, Beaglehole's Cook looks forward to a world in which everything can be known empirically. What both editors have in common is the way that each use the scholarly apparatus of the text (including footnotes) to validate the content and to communicate an agreeable expansion of knowledge.

Just when it seems that natural historical discourses are not quite as crucial in the journal of Cook's scientific voyages as might be expected, whether in Beaglehole's edition or in Douglas's, the narrative turns to a variation on this theme: ethnography. The Native inhabitants of Nootka Sound are subsumed under the general narrative heading "products of the country," coming immediately after minerals, with only a paragraph break to signal the switch in Douglas's account. That more is not made of this transition is puzzling, since fully half of the account of the month at Nootka Sound is devoted to an ethnographic description of its inhabitants, beginning with their "persons." Unlike Douglas's edition, which uses paragraph breaks to signal changes in topic, Beaglehole develops the narrative by using the classificatory norms of science, highlighting changes in ethnographic subject matter with headings such as *"Animals," "Inhabitants their Persons and Habits," "Manufacture,"* and *"Ornaments, Songs"* in the margins of the text.

In the ethnographic accounts of the inhabitants of Nootka Sound, the discourse of natural history comes most fully into play and the Linnaean *Methodus* is most fully achieved. The people, as much as their material culture or their physical environment, are treated as natural objects, as just another type of natural production – a treatment characteristic of natural historical discourses in the New World. In Douglas's edition, far more footnotes and scholarly or scientific additions append descriptions of the people at Nootka Sound than of the area's animals, vegetables, and minerals. A discussion of hair, or, more properly, the lack of facial and body hair, provides the editor with an opportunity to footnote what seems an extraordinarily long (virtually all of one page) discussion of, to paraphrase Swift, "a General History of Beards among Americans."[23] A description of facial hair among the people of Nootka Sound introduces this learned digression:

They have either no beards at all, which was most commonly the case, or a small thin one upon the point of the chin; which does not arise from any natural defect of hair on that part, but from plucking it out more or less; for some of them, particularly the old men, have not only considerable beards all over the chin, but whiskers, or mustachios; both on the upper lip, and running from thence toward the lower jaw obliquely downward.* Their eye-brows are also scanty, and always narrow; but the hair of the head is in great abundance. (Douglas III:2, 301–2)

Plainly, further inquiry is necessary to explain this state of affairs: why should these people have an abundance of hair upon their heads but very little upon their faces? According to Beaglehole's edition, this discrepancy went unnoticed by Cook as well as by the other officers whose comments on hair are footnoted at this juncture (III:1, 311). Douglas's footnote provides an explanation, with reference to no less than four other sources: *Recherches sur les Americains* by Cornelius de Pauw (whom Douglas calls "M. de Paw"), William Robertson's *History of America* (published in 1777 by Strahan and Cadell, the London publishers of Douglas's edition), Jonathan Carver's *Travels through the Interior Parts of North America* (1778), and Marsden's *History of Sumatra* (Douglas III:2, 302).

Douglas's use of these sources in his footnote is interesting for several reasons. Perhaps the most important is that he has cited one book that it was impossible for Cook to know, Carver's *Travels Through the Interior Parts of North America, in the years 1776, 1777, and 1778*, which was published in 1778, the year Cook visited Nootka Sound. While it is not impossible that Cook could have been aware of Carver's expedition, it seems unlikely that he could have been aware of his findings since the two set off in the same year. By including such a work in his own footnote, Douglas may mean to indicate the range of learning that has gone into the text of Cook's *Voyage* as the footnote is signed "- Ed." Then, too, these works not only treat different areas of North America but also refer to Mexico and Sumatra – other parts of the world entirely. By invoking them, Douglas highlights the breadth of knowledge that informs the text of Cook's *Voyage*, as if establishing the Genus and Species of the people of Nootka Sound by noting their similarities to, and differences from, not only Europeans (and that comparison is always at least implied) but also other New World peoples, according to the Linnaean *Methodus*. Such a comparison between cultural groups as specimens of natural history, however, has an essentializing and ultimately dehumanizing effect. The result of such typologies "was to give 'a mental abstraction an independent reality,' to make it real or 'reify' the idea of racial type when in fact the type was a social construct which scientists then treated as though it were in fact 'in nature.'"[24]

The footnote on beards depicts some of the bizarre positions that ethnographic discourse creates in its attempt to determine, or posit, meaning in particular practices.[25] It begins with the assertion that "one of the most curious singularities in the natural history of the human species, is the supposed defect in the habit and temperature of the bodies of the American Indians, exemplified in their having no beards, while they are furnished with a profusion of hair on their heads." It ends with a quotation from *Marsden's History of Sumatra* in which the author "must confess, that it would remove some small degree of doubt from my mind, could it be ascertained that no such custom [as the plucking or tweezing of hair] prevails" (Douglas III:2, 302). What better proof of scientific credibility could be offered than such a lengthy, considered, and annotated discussion of a matter as apparently trivial as the presence or absence of beards? Less attention is paid to colour in Douglas's edition: "Their colour we could never positively determine, as their bodies were incrusted with paint and dirt; though, in particular cases, when these were rubbed off, the whiteness of the skin appeared almost to equal that of Europeans; though rather of that pale, effete cast which distinguishes those of our Southern nations" (Douglas III:2, 303).

Two points are worth noting about this passage. One is Douglas's (characteristic) use of the possessive pronoun "our" to describe southern Europeans; the patronizing effect again portrays Cook as a gentleman both unconscious and aware of his ownership of his presumed inferiors. The other is the connection to Swift's *Tale of a Tub* (1704): the satiric context of the list of the Grub Street hack's other self-important literary endeavours leaves no doubt that *A General History of Ears*, like *A Modest Defense of the Proceedings of the Rabble in all Ages*, is ridiculous. In the context of travel writing or explorers' accounts of the New World, however, no detail regarding the peculiar or exotic nature of the inhabitants is too minute to escape notice and (pseudo) scientific consideration. (In a later section, describing the "extravagant masquerade ornaments" of masks and skin costumes covering the entire person, Douglas remarks in a footnote that this "reflection in the text may furnish the admirers of Herodotus, in particular, with an excellent apology for some of his wonderful tales of this sort" (Douglas III:2, 307). The New World, in short, is the appropriate field for such ethnographic fieldwork, and, once again, knowledge is cumulative: Douglas's text presents itself as participating in, and advancing, a scholarly tradition that stretches back to antiquity.

But these comments apply to Douglas's edition. Beaglehole's scholarly edition of 1967 presents, as usual, a much different perspective on the question of hair. "Their hair is black or dark brown, straight, strong and long, in general they wear it flowing, but some tie it up in a bunch on the crown and others twist it into large locks and add to it false hair, so that thier heads looks like a swab. But when they are full drissed, they powder their [hair] with the white down of birds, which for the most part they carry about with them in thier Canoes, either in a box or bag.* Some have pretty large and long beards and others very little, the difference proceeds from their plucking more or less out of it" (Beaglehole III:I, 311–2). This passage reveals a focus not on theories regarding immutable characteristics of nature but, rather, on the external, observable aspects attributable to culture. At the asterisk in my quotation, Beaglehole provides a footnote that compares Native with European modes of hairdressing: "'they blow the feathers of the head with a machine similar [to] the machines used for powdering hair in Europe.' – Bayly JT, p. 104."[26] The scientific method here consists of the scholarly apparatus providing corroboration in the form of supplementary observation from another source.

This treatment of facial hair, however different in focus, simultaneously reveals what Douglas's and Beaglehole's editions have in common: the invisibility of women. Presumably this account of beards applies only to the men, yet the unqualified "they" gives no indication that the crucial questions of hair, hairlessness, and hair removal applies only to men – until a new paragraph in Douglas's edition signals that this is indeed the case: "The women are nearly of the same size, colour, and form, with the men; from whom it is not easy to distinguish them, as they possess no natural delicacies sufficient to render their persons agreeable; and hardly any one was seen, even amongst those who were in the prime of life, who had the least pretensions to be called handsome."[27] In one sentence, Douglas summarizes the appearance of women (in contrast to the two long paragraphs in the footnote concerning beards). The description of the women in Beaglehole's edition provides more specific details about their appearance: "And they as also all others who visited us are, both men and Women, of a small Stature, some, Women in particular, very much so and hardly one, even of the younger sort, had the least pretensions to being call'd beauties. Their face is rather broad and flat, with highish Cheek bones and plump cheeks."[28] In this comment, the women may be seen alternatively as either sandwiched between general comments about the universal male or as referred to specifically. The difference in reading depends upon the assumed antecedent of the pronoun "their": does it refer back to the women and thus continue talking about them or does it refer further back to the presumed universality of male experience? Beaglehole's footnotes tend to support the latter view and suggest that the pronouns are being used as if gendered. "They" refers always to the general, or male (as in the French *ils*), while references to the women are always specific (*elles*), referring to their difference from the men.

As is often the case, Beaglehole's footnotes reveal more than the main text, as this example, a rather lengthy comment from Bayly on the subject of the women's appearance, demonstrates:

> "The women appeared to be much less in stature than the men, not so well featured having high cheake bones & otherwise very ordinary – which together with them being smeared over with grease & dirt rendered them not very desirable but rather the reverse – so that our Seamen seemed quite easy about them. Indeed some of the officers whose stomachs were less Dillicate purchased the favours of some of them, but at a high price to what was generally given at any other place we have been at, for the men seemed rather unwilling to let them out except for something they wanted, which they could not otherwise get at, & even this was practised only among the lower class of them. The better sort would not hear anything of the kind." With which compare Samwell, p. 1095 below. (Beaglehole III:1, 311)

The reference to Samwell puts a rather different spin on Bayly's account since the account of the ship's surgeon (in part two of Beaglehole's third volume) describes in much greater detail the sexual traffic between the ships and the people of Nootka Sound (the men, as Bayly notes, negotiating with the Britons wishing to purchase the favours of Native women).[29] Indeed, Samwell's account of the "ceremony of purification," the bathing of young women aboard ship as a prelude to sexual encounter, clarifies a rather oblique statement made by Cook above, that "in particular cases, when [paint and dirt] were rubbed off, the whiteness of the skin appeared almost to equal that of Europeans." While the other officers, especially Samwell, explicitly sexualize aboriginal women, mentioning them only in sexualized contexts, Cook and Douglas do not sexualize women but, rather, render them invisible in the account of the voyage. Women at Nootka Sound are, it is true, present in the scholarly edition of Cook's third voyage, but they are quite literally marginalized – brought in from the margins of other officers' accounts through Beaglehole's citations in the footnotes.

This invisibility of women at Nootka Sound and indeed throughout the third voyage must be seen in light of Hawkesworth's portrayal of Pacific peoples, especially his frank depiction of the "public amours" of Tahitian women.[30] Such descriptions created a shock wave throughout English society. Those who read Hawkesworth's depictions might have been reminded of John Cleland's pornutopic novel *Fanny Hill* (1749); sailors were willing to sign on for long and dangerous voyages in hopes of enjoying the infamous sexual hospitality of Tahiti. Others, John Wesley for instance, simply condemned the whole work as immoral. Douglas, a clergyman, was brought in as editor for the second voyage in order to avoid such scandal. Indeed, Cook wrote to him while Douglas was preparing the journals for publication, asking him to purge anything that suggested indecency.[31] The contrast between the presence of women in Hawkesworth's edition of Cook's first voyage and the absence of women in Douglas's edition of the second and third voyages suggests another way that Douglas as editor influenced subsequent exploration accounts. For better or worse, the official publications of Cook's first and third voyages were publishing sensations – the first for Hawkesworth's presumed immorality, the third for Douglas's portrayal of savagery in the form of cannibalism at Nootka Sound and the "murder" of Cook at Hawaii. While Douglas freely borrowed from the accounts of other officers in order to depict Pacific peoples as savages in various ways, he did not incorporate accounts of the sexual traffic between ship and shore. In attempting to eliminate any potentially offensive material from Cook's account, Douglas virtually eliminated women in his descriptions of Native peoples; instead, he focused on *trade* as the primary form of contact between ship and shore, and a safely masculine one at that.

This contrast is worth highlighting. My Introduction notes the long-standing trope that personified the New World as a woman awaiting possession by the masterful European – a sexual/territorial possession which would make her "fruitful." Peter Hulme's analysis of Jan van der Straet's 1600 engraving "America" provides a case in point. The new land is depicted as a Native woman, naked and surrounded by the exotic products of the country; the explorer Amerigo Vespucci claims the continent just as a man claims a woman in marriage, not only by sexually possessing her but also by giving her his name.[32] Hulme argues further that the invisibility of women, except in a sexual context, is part of the process by which the whole enterprise of European encounter with the New World is sexualized: "the novelty of America was always perceived in overtly sexual terms. To speak of the 'maidenhead' of Guiana or Virginia was to condense into one potent image the absence of significant native agriculture and the joyful masculine thrust of Elizabethan expansion."[33] Since North America was personified as female, territorial possession could be enacted locally by Englishmen enjoying sexual possession of Native women. This line of reasoning would see the sexual traffic between ship and shore on Cook's voyages as both the sailors' and officers' response to the sexual (or at least heterosexual) deprivation of months at sea and a means by which ordinary Britons could lay claim to imperial possession of the New World.

It is impossible that Douglas was unaware of these tropes, or indeed of the extent to which the men who sailed with Cook enjoyed the sexual favours of Native women in the Pacific. Indeed, Cook himself recorded his sorrow about the "corrupting" influence of his ships and crews, which both brought venereal disease to Pacific societies and seemed to "teach" Native peoples about prostitution or the sale of sexual favours.[34] Such sentiments are noticeably absent in Douglas's edition of the third volume. By eliminating such references, Douglas has eliminated women almost entirely (a few references to Pacific women's physical inferiority to Englishwomen in terms of beauty remain). No doubt this elimination was motivated by Douglas's larger strategy of elevating Cook into a hero and a gentleman: nobody else would be allowed to kiss and tell under his imprimatur. It may be to Douglas, then, that ethnographic discourse owes its customary focus on what Pratt has called the "the standardized adult male specimen,"[35] and it may be that one of his greatest innovations and influences was this erasure of Native women from the pages of exploration literature.

This feature of the scientific discourse of ethnography – the erasure of women, due to the universalization of male experience, from every aspect of a society except that related to their sexual role – leads me back to the question of aesthetics. In Douglas's edition of the *Voyage*, the women of Nootka Sound merit one short paragraph comparing them to Native men and European women; the relation on both counts is one of inferiority. Their "persons," possessing neither "natural delicacies" nor "the least pretensions to being called handsome," fail to meet European standards of feminine beauty. Their invisibility in the text is clearly demonstrated in the weight Douglas accords the women relative to the weight he accords beards.

At the aesthetic or visual level, this female insignificance is represented in Webber's portraits of a man and a woman at Nootka Sound (figures 5 and 6), reproduced in Lionel Kearns's *Convergences* and accompanied by the following meditation:

> The manipulation of words and images on the page is the manipulation of audience, and you know who that is. Yet this is never done without a purpose. John Webber, in turning his sketches into engravings for publication with the authorized version of the voyage, removed the conical shaped cedar hat with the little bulb on top from the head of the Nootka man and put it on the head of the Nootka woman, though he had never seen a Nootka woman wearing a hat like that. Notice the woven images of the whales and the harpooners' canoes. It is a nobleman's hat. Webber has made the change for us, so that we may be able to view both the hat and the tattooed design on the man's forehead. Such textual liberties, even when taken by me, are entirely for your edification, I assure you.[36]

The difference between "to see" and "to view" is crucial here: the verb "view" recalls the distancing effect of landscape appreciation. Perceived as tableau, landscape is something to look at rather than a place to be in. Similarly, viewing the particulars of the individuals in Webber's portraits establishes a distance between viewer and viewed, a relationship not of interaction but of observation. (Scientific naming sets up a similar distance: unlike Doctor Doolittle, who talks with the animals, the scientist talks about them.) Presumably this woman is not tattooed, or, if she is, her tattoos are considered to be of less consequence than are those of the man whose hat she wears since she has already been accounted for by the generalized male specimen.

Webber in fact imported the nobleman's hat on the woman's head from another drawing, a full-length portrait called *A Native prepared for Hunting* (not reproduced here); although Webber saw bows and arrows during the month at Nootka Sound, he did not see anyone hunting.[37] The visual quotation from his own work reveals some of the problems of ethnographic discourse. The expectation of mimesis in ethnography as a scientific discourse breaks down: the totality of the drawing, image and title, presents Webber's assumptions as if they were documentary. The original sketch of the woman wearing the nobleman's hat "had shown her wearing a hat with a flattened top, Webber not knowing 'that only chiefs wore these hats.' This is the more ironic, since it was the ethnographic element that constituted the *raison d'être* for the engraved portraits."[38] However, just as Douglas transformed the text of Cook's journal to conform with his own expectations and assumptions about Native peoples, so Webber transformed his drawings of the people of Nootka Sound to corroborate the verbal descriptions.[39] Joppien and Smith apparently feel that the portraits of men convey ethnographic information more accurately than do the portraits of women, maybe as the result of the sexual politics affecting the contexts in which the portraits were developed. They suggest that the woman's "clean and bright" face, absent of any of the ochre markings described in the text, might be a result of the "ceremony of purification," or washing, that the sailors gave the Native women who came on board ship.[40] Perhaps that context – prostitution and the corresponding demotion of the women so engaged from human being to object – affected Webber's decision to give the woman the hat with the bulbous instead of the flattened top. Or perhaps he wanted to give a visual example of the variety of clothing worn at Nootka Sound and the skill that produced it.[41] Whatever the reason, readers who are promised a transparent account of the people of Nootka Sound instead receive one that is coloured by the artist's (and editor's) other considerations and designs.

The visual, like the verbal, representation of the empirical observation of land and people is knowledge with a purpose: it is "a normalizing discourse, whose work is to codify difference, to fix the Other in a timeless present where all 'his' actions and reactions are repetitions of 'his' normal habits."[42] The language and conventions of scientific objectivity remove the subjects (or objects) of discussion from any context that might make their observable qualities meaningful as well as from any interaction that would bring them out from under the watchful gaze of the recording subject. This distance creates the notion of the primitive in the colonial context: ethnographic discourse often describes indigenous peoples as somehow still living in a mythic past.[43] A notion of time that equates Western European history with such culturally specific values as "progress" problematizes much writing about contact between Europeans and non-European peoples, erasing the fact that European describer and Native described occupy the same time and place. And, when European realities are taken as the norm, the result is often the implication that Natives are inferior to Europeans, given their failure to move in the same directions, ways, and speeds as European civilization. Karen Ordahl Kupperman's study of early English settlers in what eventually became the United States presents another picture, documenting European dependence on Native technology for survival. In fact, Kupperman states, only the armchair expert who had never been to America or seen Americans assigned them "to a place outside the ranks of full humanity."[44] Dr Douglas, who had never travelled to any part of the Pacific, was one such armchair expert.

In consequence, the comments attributed to Cook in the first published edition regarding the inferiority of Native technology stress European superiority – a superiority that the descriptions do not necessarily support:

> The woollen garments ... have the strongest resemblance to
> woven cloth. But the various figures which are very artificially
> inserted in them, destroys the supposition of their being wrought
> in a loom; it being extremely unlikely, that these people should
> be so dextrous as to be able to finish such a complex work,
> unless immediately by their hands. They are of different degrees
> of fineness; some resembling our coarsest rags or blankets; and
> others almost equal to our finest sorts, or even softer, and
> certainly warmer. (Douglas III–2, 325)

Even this compliment is backhanded at best: the people who produce such beautiful work are simultaneously considered too stupid to design a tool to achieve it (they must, of necessity, use their hands, technology being a mark of civilization or "progress"). At the same time, the concerns/assumptions of the reader at home in Britain are priorised: if blankets made by the people of Nootka Sound are "softer, and certainly warmer" than "our finest sorts," then under what conditions could they be said to be only "almost equal"? From a warm armchair by the fire, perhaps; certainly not within a context in which the tightness of a blanket's weave (the degree to which it repels rain) and its softness are crucial to bodily comfort. Even this praise, however tentative or qualified, reveals an assumption of Native intellectual and technological inferiority. Cook, or, more properly, Douglas, continually comments on a variety of things so finely wrought that he thinks no Indian could be capable of making them. (These are evidently Douglas's opinions, for Beaglehole's Cook makes no such evaluation.)

Douglas's edition of Cook's *Voyage* reveals a good deal more about the preoccupations of British culture in the eighteenth century than it does about the peoples and customs observed and recorded. As the descriptions of the people come after those of the physical characteristics of Nootka Sound, from flora and fauna down to insects and geological formations, it would seem that British society values objects, products, and profits over people. Douglas describes the human inhabitants of Nootka Sound only after listing the elements (such as timber and furs) that might have some economic value for Europeans. This may also reflect a philosophy arising out of the growing interest in natural history and the attempts to reconcile its findings with traditional beliefs in the veracity of the historical record as recorded in the Bible, situating human experience within the larger context of geological time and space. Douglas's edition also suggests a British society in which women are of peripheral interest to men, on the margins of public life and political concerns, and noticed largely for the degree to which they conform or deviate from accepted standards of appearance and their assigned sexual or reproductive roles. Women are appendages, accounted for and subsumed under generalized male experience; yet they are also markedly different from men, and in that difference lies their recreational function.

What seems to me most crucial, however, is the way that aesthetic and scientific representations of the inhabitants of Nootka Sound, although far from internally consistent, are mutually supportive. Individually, each presents an account of Nootka Sound and its inhabitants that its discursive truth-claims (disinterestedness, objectivity, mimesis) establish as fact by hiding their own creation. Webber's portraits, offered as ethnographic truths, consciously alter what he actually perceived in order to convey ethnographic information. Natural history as a discourse offers a metaphoric version of reality as transparent and mimetic. Taken together, their effect is staggering, turning natural history discourse into colonial discourse. In Douglas's edition, the comments on Native technology construct differences between Britons and the people of Nootka Sound as evidence of European superiority in appearance, in manners, in living arrangements, in religion, in economy, in technology – in short, in everything important to a European sense of identity. Demonstrating, again and again, British superiority to the Native inhabitants of the Sound serves to establish and then to disestablish rights of ownership, which are in opposition even in this first encounter. The real conflict, however, occurs not between Cook and the people he meets at Friendly Cove but, rather, between European readers and the Native population from the other side of world, encountered for the first time in the official edition of Cook's third *Voyage*, as the trading relationships outlined in the journal suggest.

The importance of trade and exchange between ship and shore is structurally highlighted in Douglas's edition through the presentation of an encounter scene that culminates in trading: when the *Resolution* and *Discovery* first entered the Sound, they were immediately surrounded by canoes full of Natives eager to trade. Whereas Douglas's account devotes a great deal of attention to the question of Native thievery (a consistent theme in Cook's accounts of Native peoples), Cook's journal in Beaglehole's edition presents these exchanges as more equal. In his account of the month, based on the journals of Cook and the other officers as they appear in Beaglehole's edition of the third voyage, historian Robin Fisher has argued for a sense of reciprocity that did not emerge in the official published account.[45] Indeed, during the whole month of trading at Nootka Sound there was, according to Beaglehole's edition, apparently only one confrontation. This occurred when a landing party went ashore to cut grass for the domesticated animals on board ship. One officer at least was surprised by the reaction of the Natives: "No people had higher Ideas of exclusive property; they made the Captain pay for the grass which he cut at the Village, although useless to themselves, & made a merit, after being refusd payment for the wood & water we got in the Cove, of giving it to us, & often told us that they had done it out of Friendship."[46] The tone of surprise in this account comes from "the unspoken assumption of the four-stages theory, that is, that the representative of a culture where agriculture and animal husbandry are practised has a more legitimate claim to grass than does the representative of only a hunting/fishing culture, who makes no systematic use of vegetation or the soil which grows it."[47] In Douglas's edition, Cook's account of this incident is much longer:

The Inhabitants received us with the same demonstrations of friendship which I had experienced before; and the moment we landed, I ordered some of my people to begin their operation of cutting. I had not the least imagination, that the natives could make any objection to our furnishing ourselves with what seemed to be of no use to them, but necessary for us. However, I was mistaken; for, the moment that our men began to cut, some of the inhabitants interposed, and would not permit them to

proceed, saying that they must *"makook"*; that is, must first buy
it. I was now in one of the houses, but as soon as I heard of this,
I went to the field, where I found about a dozen of the natives,
each of whom laid claim to some part of the grass that grew in
this place. I bargained with them for it, and having completed the
purchase, thought that we were now at liberty to cut wherever
we pleased. But here, again, it appeared, that I was under a
mistake; for the liberal manner, in which I had paid the first
pretended proprietors brought fresh demands upon me from
others; so that there did not seem to a single blade of grass, that
had not a separate owner; and so many of them were to be
satisfied, that I very soon emptied my pockets. When they found,
that I really had nothing more to give, their importunities ceased,
and we were permitted to cut wherever we pleased, and as much
as we chose to carry away.

Here I must observe, that I have no where, in my several
voyages, met with any uncivilized nation, or tribe, who had such
strict notions of their having a right to the exclusive property of
every thing that the country produces, as the inhabitants of this
sound. (Douglas III:2, 284)

At first glance, the opinion expressed by Cook in Beaglehole's edition
does not differ significantly from that expressed in Douglas's, with the
exception of one crucial word: Beaglehole's Cook does not write
"uncivilized."

The Inhabitants of this village received us in the same friendly
manner they had do[n]e before, and the Moment we landed I
sent some to cut grass not thinking that the Natives could or
would have the least any objection, but it proved otherways for
the Moment our people began to cut they stoped them and told
them they must Makook for it, that is first buy it. As soon as I
heard of this I went to the place and found about a dozen men
who all laid cla[i]m to some part of the grass which I purchased
of them and as I thought liberty to cut where ever I pleased, but
here again I was misstaken, for the liberal manner I had paid the
first pretended pr[o]prietors brought more upon me from others
and there was not a blade of grass that had not a separated
owner, so that I very soon emptied my pockets with purchasing,
and when they found I had nothing more to give they let us cut

where ever we pleased.

Here I must observe that I have no were met with Indians who had such high notions of every thing the Country produced being their exclusive property as these. (Beaglehole iii:1, 306)

A more careful reading, however, reveals a considerable difference in tone: Beaglehole's Cook records a moment of misunderstanding in the contact zone, while Douglas's scatters the loose change in his pockets among the Natives as he would throw coins to begging children.

The difference in tone in the two arises from the markedly different assumptions governing each account. This excerpt from Cook's journal in Beaglehole's edition presents a captain making an observation on the "manners and customs" of the people of Nootka Sound that incorporates his extensive experience in the Pacific. In Douglas's edition, by contrast, the observation highlights the hierarchical relationship between European and Natives. Having established a particular kind of trading relationship based on the exchange of goods and services, no questions asked about the potential use or need for the items exchanged, the Cook of Douglas's edition seems surprised that the people of Nootka Sound expect to continue the established pattern (or even that they fail to read his mind and know the basis of trade on his terms). Accordingly, he assumes that trading occurs on his terms, and he is astonished to learn that the Natives might have their own agenda or rules governing trade relations. Or, as MacLaren argues, Douglas uses this incident to remind readers yet again of Cook's superiority, as a representative of an agricultural economy, over members of a hunting/gathering society. While he would never assume he could walk onto an English field and calmly start cutting its grass without first negotiating with the owner, the haughty and condescending tone with which Douglas's Cook describes the "pretended owners" who seemingly lay claim to every "single blade of grass" denies their right to possess the products of their own country. Ledyard's description also makes the importance of this incident in determining ownership of the land and its resources obvious: "They intimated to us that the country all round further than we could see was theirs."[48]

Of course, Douglas was not alone in his astonishment at this notion of sovereignty voiced during the first encounter between the people of Nootka Sound and the earliest representatives of the nation whose absolute claim to the territory was solidified in the name "British Columbia." More than 200 years later, as the issue of land claims occupies provincial courts, government offices, and the public mind, there are still British Columbians who deny the territorial rights of Aboriginal peoples on grounds very similar to those laid out in Douglas's four-stages theory.[49] While many might invoke the authority of a writer like Cook, and of other European "discoverers" of this part of the world, comparing Douglas's and Beaglehole's editions reveals that Cook himself should not be taken as the unquestioned source for such views. He claimed Nootka Sound for Britain ("The inlet I honoured with the name of *King Georges Sound*"),[50] as his instructions required, but his descriptions generally lack Douglas's possessive quality, noted earlier, which aimed to portray Cook as a gentleman. In similar fashion, the apparent empiricism of the text as scientific discourse is disrupted by editorial changes, as the treatment of cannibalism at Nootka Sound clearly demonstrates.

CHAPTER FOUR

Cook and the Cannibals: The Limits of Understanding

Cook's *Voyages* have elicited scandal and sensation for one reason or another ever since Hawkesworth's edition of the first voyage was published in 1773. While Hawkesworth had tried to portray a Pacific Eden, Douglas, the editor of the second and third voyages, portrayed the Pacific as a distinctly fallen world. The first voyage raised the possibility of cannibalism in New Zealand; however, cannibalism assumed great importance as the defining feature of Pacific societies in Douglas's editorial hands, and Hawkesworth's noble savages were displaced by bloodthirsty ones. Before the second *Voyage* was published in 1777, indeed even before Cook and the *Resolution* returned to England in 1775, news of cannibalism in New Zealand had reached the public; after Cook's third voyage, the story was told that Cook was not only murdered but also eaten by Hawaiians. Douglas's editions of Cook's *Voyages* are associated with a changing image of the Pacific, one that elided the early connotations of the term.

Not all of Cook's cannibals were to be found in the South Pacific, however. The official 1784 edition of Cook's third voyage gives the impression that the party also encountered cannibals on the Northwest Coast of North America. Early in his account of Nootka Sound, the Cook of the official edition writes

> But the most extraordinary of all the articles which they brought
> to the ships for sale, were human skulls, and hands not quite
> stripped of the flesh, which they made our people plainly
> understand they had eaten; and, indeed, some of them had
> evident marks that they had been upon the fire. We had but too
> much reason to suspect, from this circumstance, that the horrid

practice of feeding on their enemies is as prevalent here, as we
had found it to be at New Zealand and other South Seas islands.
(Douglas iii:2, 270–1)

The detail contained in this passage is impressive; however, the image of
cannibalism it creates comes from Douglas's own sense of rhetorical
flourish as he embellishes Cook's description of a collection of trade
articles. Cook's own words are much less sonorous than are Douglas's,
as Beaglehole's edition of the third voyage makes clear: Cook records
"pieces of carved work and even human skuls and hands, and a variety
of little articles too tedious to mention" (Beaglehole iii:1, 296–7). The
anticlimactic effect of this shorter version is more characteristic of
Cook's words than of Douglas's stately and periodic emphasis (I return
to this discrepancy later in the chapter). Cook does not "plainly understand" that flesh from human skulls and hands had been eaten; he does
not notice "evident marks that they had been upon the fire," nor does
he find "reason to suspect ... that the horrid practice of feeding on their
enemies is as prevalent here, as we had found it to be at New Zealand."
In fact, Beaglehole's edition reveals that Cook himself never once mentioned cannibalism at Nootka Sound; it was Douglas who transported
the notion of cannibalism from New Zealand to the Northwest Coast.
Clearly, then, in the account of Nootka Sound at least, cannibalism
reveals as much about eighteenth-century Europe as it does about the
far-off Pacific, as much about discourse as about the simple observation
of "savage" behaviour.

　　To call cannibalism a discourse rather than a behaviour is to enter a
very troubled field. Such assertions, most notoriously William Arens's
Man-Eating Myth (1979), are frequently read as claims that cannibalism has never existed anywhere.[1] Various texts documenting eyewitness
evidence of cannibalism are trotted out (e.g., Peggy Reeves Sanday's
Divine Hunger traces the history and development of the idea of cannibalism among many non-European peoples) in order to dispute Arens's
argument by comparing it with such historical sources as early accounts
by explorers and missionaries.[2] However, readers of *Constructing
Colonial Discourse* should see the problem inherent in that kind of
approach. Leaving aside the fact that, like Douglas, European explorers
and missionaries often assumed they would find cannibalism in what
they viewed as primitive and pagan societies, there is the basic problem
of texts. As I.S. MacLaren and this book demonstrate, published exploration texts are rarely transparent records of the explorer's experience;

rather, they mediate that experience in complex and sophisticated ways, through the editorial process and corporate authors' purposes as well as through the demands of the reading public. Exploration texts document a nation's claim to a territory, thus serving political and economic ends; missionary societies might have some interest in demonstrating both the good work already done and the progress yet to be made by missionaries abroad, thus serving fundraising ends. Especially around an issue as troublingly fascinating as cannibalism, early published accounts of cannibalism in non-European societies cannot be taken at face value.

For the idea of cannibalism, especially after Europe's encounter with the New World, has come to have at least two complex sets of meanings, which might be called literal and metaphorical, respectively. According to the literalist tradition, cannibalism appears in accounts of non-European parts of the world because it was there. Douglas belongs to that tradition: for him, the boundary between civilization and savagery is clear, and cannibalism is a distasteful feature of savagery that civilized authors merely observe and record (and that civilized readers eagerly consume). The metaphorical tradition sees cannibalism as a metaphor, or trope, within colonial discourse. It treats both European assumptions and accounts of cannibalism among non-European peoples with some skepticism, asking how cannibalism as a discourse works and what it reveals. My analysis of cannibalism is informed by that skepticism. I should note, however, my belief that "cannibalism does exist: it exists as a term within colonial discourse to describe the ferocious devouring of human flesh supposedly practised by some savages. That existence, within discourse, is no less historical whether or not the term cannibalism describes an attested or extant social custom."[3] My analysis excludes a discussion of what might be called ritual, or ceremonial, cannibalism[4] because it seems to me quite a different kind of custom, one that the writers on cannibalism on Cook's third voyage – including Douglas himself – were incapable of recognizing. While I might argue that ritual cannibalism could have a social significance similar to that of the Christian communion, Dr Douglas was quite incapable either of making such a distinction or of seeing Christianity as a blood religion.[5]

This chapter examines the discourse of cannibalism at work in the texts of Cook's *Voyages*. After considering the accounts of Maori cannibalism arising out of Cook's second voyage, it focuses on the account of cannibalism at Nootka Sound, viewing it as a case study in the workings of the discourse of cannibalism. I hope to suggest some of the ways in

which this discourse functions not only to shape the European construct of the Northwest Coast and its inhabitants but also to reveal the
world that made it.

❂

In Douglas's edition of Cook's third voyage, a supposed observation of
cannibalism at Nootka Sound is turned into a reflection by way of a
comparison linking its inhabitants to the Maori, who were established
for European readers as cannibals by Cook's second *Voyage*. Douglas
writes: "We had but too much reason to suspect ... that the horrid practice of feeding on their enemies is as prevalent here, as we had found it
to be at New Zealand and other South Sea islands" (Douglas iii:2, 271).
To understand the truth-claim made by Douglas's analogy, we need to
examine the accounts of Maori cannibalism, especially those from
Totaru-nui (Queen Charlotte Sound in Cook Strait, which separates the
North and South Islands of New Zealand) in Cook's first and second
voyages. The fact that the cannibals produced for European readers are
always located near some body of water named for the explorer himself
– Cook Strait in New Zealand, Cook Channel in Nootka Sound –
suggests the degree to which accounts of cannibals feature in his *Voyages*.

   Reports of Maori cannibalism coming from the first voyage had been
doubted at home, but the second voyage's account of New Zealand produced evidence. The *Resolution* and *Adventure* had become separated
in late October of 1773 and did not in fact meet again until both ships
returned to England, the *Adventure* in 1774 and the *Resolution* in
1775. The ships had independent experiences of Maori cannibalism,
each disturbing and revealing in different ways.[6] On 23 November
1773 the men on the *Resolution* actually witnessed cannibalism at
Queen Charlotte Sound: they watched a Maori man eat a piece of
human flesh on the quarter-deck. The experience was recorded by Cook
in a somewhat ambiguous manner:

   Calm or light airs from the Northward so that we could not get
   to sea as I intended, some of the officers went on shore to amuse
   themselves among the Natives where they saw the head and
   bowels of a youth who had lately been killed, the heart was stuck
   upon a forked stick and fixed to the head of their largest Canoe,
   the gentlemen brought the head on board with them, I was on
   shore at this time but soon after returned on board when I was

informed of the above circumstances and found the quarter deck crowded with the Natives. I now saw a mangled head or rather the remains of it for the upper jaw, lip &ca were wanting, the scul was broke on the left side just above the temple, the face had all the appearance of a youth about fourteen or fifteen, a peice of flesh had been broiled and eat by one of the Natives in the presince of most of the officers. The sight of the head and the relation of the circumstances just mentioned struck me with horror and filled my mind with indignation against these Canibals, but when I considered that any resentment I could shew would avail but little and being desireous of being an eye wittness to a fact which many people had their doubts about, I concealed my indignation and ordered a piece of the flesh to be broiled and brought on the quarter deck where one of these Canibals eat it with a seeming good relish before the whole ships Company which had such effect on some of them as to cause them to vomit. [Oediddee] was [so] struck with horor at the sight that [he] wept and scolded by turns, before this happened he was very intimate with these people but now he neither would come near them or suffer them to touch him, told them to their faces that they were vile men and that he was no longer their friend, he used the same language to one of the officers who cut of the flesh and refused to except [sic], or even touch the knife with which it was cut, such was this Islanders aversion to this vile custom. (Beaglehole II 292–3)

In this passage, the context for the first example of cannibalism is not entirely clear; Cook's use of the passive voice ("a piece of flesh had been broiled and eat by one of the Natives") obscures agency: who did the broiling? In this scenario, Maori, even the subject of the verb "to eat," are cast as indirect objects of the action; British officers are presented merely as witnesses. The second example clarifies matters somewhat, providing both a context and an agent: in the interests of empiricism ("desireous of being an eye wittness") Cook "ordered a piece of flesh to be broiled." Like any good scientist, Cook suppresses his own feelings about the content of the experiment, focusing instead on its form. He has the opportunity to prove Maori cannibalism, "a fact which many people had their doubts about." His description, matter-of-fact in tone, is followed by reflections on the Maori's state of civilization.[7] In his account, however, one crucial detail is missing: Cook never names the conductor of the experiment. Filling out this version of events requires some lengthy footnotes in Beaglehole's edition of the second voyage; here it requires some descriptive context and reference to the journals of the other officers.

On 23 November 1773 the *Resolution* was ready to leave Queen Charlotte Sound; Cook, J.R. Forster (one of the gentleman scientists on the second voyage), and the astronomer William Wales went with Hitihiti, a young Tahitian travelling with the ship, to check the gardens they had planted. Another group of officers went to trade for curiosities before leaving the Sound; they found at Indian Cove a scene very different from a garden planted with neat rows of vegetables. Evidently there had been a Maori raid, successful at least in part, for a group of warriors was cutting up the body of a young man. His heart, stuck on a forked stick, was fixed to the prow of the largest war canoe, while his head, intestines, liver, and lungs lay discarded on the ground. One of the warriors picked up a lung with his spear and offered it to Richard Pickersgill (third lieutenant on the *Resolution*), inviting him to taste it. This Pickersgill refused to do; instead, he traded two nails for the head and brought it back to the *Resolution,* having surely obtained the most unusual curiosity possible.

Back on board the *Resolution,* Charles Clerke (on Cook's second voyage, first lieutenant on the *Resolution*) cut a "steak" from the head, a piece of flesh from its cheek; he grilled it in the galley and offered it to a Maori man from another part of the Sound who had not been on the raid that produced the head. Clerke recorded that the Maori "not only eat it but devour'd it most ravenously, and suck'd his fingers 1/2 a dozen times over in raptures."[8] When Cook, Forster, Wales, and Hitihiti returned to the ship, Clerke repeated the demonstration. Some of the crew laughed; others, as Cook noted above, vomited. Hitihiti, the Tahitian, was the most disturbed: Cook wrote that he "was [so] struck with horror at the sight that [he] wept and scolded by turns, before this happened he was very intimate with these people but now he neither would come near them nor suffer them to touch him, told them to their faces that they were Vile men and that he was no longer their friend, he used the same language to one of the officers who cut of the flesh." Such was Hitihiti's repugnance for the whole business that he refused to touch even the knife that had been used.

The *Resolution's* astronomer, William Wales, described the demonstration in detail in his journal, treating it as a scientific experiment and drawing from it a number of conclusions.

I have this day been convinced beyond the possibility of a doubt that the New-Zeelanders are Cannibals; but as it is possible others may be as unbelieving, as I have been in this matter, I will, to give all the satisfaction I possibly can, relate the whole affair just as it happened. After dinner some of the Officers went on shore at a place where many of the Natives generally dwelt to purchase Curiosities, and found them just risen from feasting on the Carcase of one of their own species. It was not immediately perceived what they had been about; but one of the Boats Crew happening to see the head of a Man lying near one of their Canoes, they began to look round them more narrowly, and in another place found the Intestines Liver Lungs &c lying on the ground, as fresh as if but just taken out of the Body, and the Heart stuck on the points of a two pronged spear & tied to the Head of their largest Canoe. One of the Natives with great gayety stuck his spear into the lobe of one of the Lungs, and holding it close to the Mouth of one of the Officers made signs for him to eat it; but he begged to be excused, at the same time taking up ye Head & making signs that he would Accept of that which was given to him, and he presented him with two Nails in return. These Gentlemen saw no part of the Carcase nor even any of the Bones; but understood that the unhappy Victim had been brought from Admiralty Bay, where these natives had lately been on a *hunting Party*; and one of them took great pains to inform them he was the person who killed him.

When the Head was brought on board, there happened to be there several of the Natives who resided in another part of the sound, and who although in friendship with were not of the Party of whom the Head was purchased. These were, it seems, very desirous of it; but that could not be granted: However one of them who was a great favorite was indulged with a piece of the flesh, which was cut off carried forward to the Gally, broiled and eaten, by him before all the Officers & ship's Company then on board. Thus far I speak from report: the Witnesses are however too credible & numerous to be disputed if I had no better authority; but coming just now on board with the Capt and Mr Forster, to convince us also, another Steake was cut off from the lower part of the head, behind, which *I saw* carried forward, broiled, and eaten by one of them with an avidity which amazed me, licking his lips and fingers after it as if affraid to lose the least part, either grease or gravy, of so delicious a morsel.

The Head as well as I could judge had been that of a Youth under twenty, and he appeared to have been killed by two blows on the Temple, with one of their *Pattoos*, one crossing the other; but some were of opinion that the whole might have been done at one blow, and that what appeared to have been caused by the other, was only a cross fracture of the Scull arising from the first.

My account of this matter would be very defective, was I to omitt taking notice of the Behaviour of the young Man whom we brought with us from Uliteah & who came on board with the Captain, &c., in the Pinnace. Terror took possession of him the moment he saw the Head standing on the Tafferal of the Ship; but when he saw the piece cut off, and the Man eat it, he became perfectly motionless, and seemed as if Metamorphosed into the Statue of Horror: it is, I believe, utterly impossible for Art to depict that passion with half the force that it appeared in his Countenance. He continued in this situation untill some of us roused him out of it by talking to him, and then burst into Tears nor could refrain himself the whole Evening afterwards.

From this Transaction the following Corollaries are evidently deducible, viz -

1st) They do not, as I supposed might be the Case, eat them only on the spot whilst under the Impulse of that wild Frenzy into which they have shewn us they can and do work themselves in their Engagements; but in cool Blood: For it was now many Days since the Battle could have happened.

2nd) That it is not their Enemies only whom they may chance to kill in War; but even those whom they meet with who are not known Friends: since those who eat the part of the head on board, could not know whether it belonged to a friend or Enemy.

3rd) It cannot be through want of Animal food; because they every day caught as much Fish as served both themselves and us: they have moreover plenty of fine Dogs which they were at the same time selling us for mere trifles; nor is there any want of various sorts of fowl, which they can readily kill if they please.

4th) It seems therefore to follow of course, that their practice of this horrid Action is from Choice, and the liking which they have for this kind of Food; and this was but too visibly shewn in their eagerness for, and the satisfaction which they testified in eating, those inconsiderable scrapts, of the worst part on board the Ship: It is farther evident what esteem they have for it by the risks which they run to obtain it; for although our neighbours feasted so luxuriously, we had abundant reasons to conclude that they came off no gainers in the Action, since almost all of them had their foreheads and Arms scarrified, which is, it seems, their usual custom, when they lose any near Relation in War.[9]

A greater contrast to Hitihiti's very emotional response could not be imagined.

Wales's account is fascinating in its own right and even more so for its presentation of the empirical evidence in support of Maori cannibalism. Beginning with the assertion that he has "been convinced beyond the possibility of a doubt that the New-Zeelanders are Cannibals," Wales purports to offer the proof that will satisfy those who doubt the matter as he once did. That proof takes the form of a story as Wales sets out to "relate the whole affair just as it happened." The narrative reenacts Wales's own movement from lack of knowledge to the discovery of empirical evidence that confirms Maori cannibalism: not just the sight of Maori "feasting on the Carcase of one of their own species" but also such specific details as "the head of a Man lying near one of their Canoes," "Intestines Liver Lungs &c lying on the ground, as fresh as if but just taken out of the Body," "the Heart stuck on the points of a two pronged spear & tied to the Head of their largest Canoe." The repetition of the word "Canoe," a notable and admirable example of Maori technology, in conjunction with human body parts establishes a connection between cannibalism and canoes as characteristic features of the Maori. The wealth of detail in Wales's account helps to establish its truth-claim: for example, his description of the "great gayety" with which one Maori man offered one of the lungs to a British officer, "ma[king] signs for him to eat it," implicitly suggests that he witnessed the exchange.

But by the second paragraph it is clear that this narrative is not in fact based on Wales's own observations: "Thus far I speak from report," he writes. The head that alerted the British to the possibility of witnessing cannibalism was seen by "one of the Boats Crew," and although "they [presumably the landing-party] began to look round them more narrowly," "[t]hese Gentlemen saw no part of the Carcase nor even any of the Bones; but understood that the unhappy Victim had been brought from Admiralty Bay." While this group of officers had gone to Indian Cove to trade for curiosities, Wales was looking at gardens with Cook, Forster, and Hitihiti in another part of Queen Charlotte Sound. The head and the trading party returned to the ship before Wales and the garden party, so he did not see the Maori who ate a piece of broiled flesh from the head: "the Witnesses are however too credible & numerous to be disputed if I had no better authority." Returning to the ship with Cook, Wales was a witness to the second experiment, ordered by Cook: "another Steake was cut off from the lower part of the head, behind, which *I saw* carried forward, broiled, and eaten by one of them." Wales completes his narrative of the affair by marking Hitihiti's response to the sight of the head and to the man eating a piece of it: first "Terror took possession of him," and then he "metamorphosed into the Statue of Horror."

In his handling of physical detail and eyewitness perspective, Wales's narrative uses empirical evidence to establish credibility. He bases the deductions, developed in four "Corollaries," on this empirical evidence. The cool scientific evaluation of the evidence that produces these deductions helps to distinguish between Britons and Maori in this encounter. According to Wales's description, the Maori are somewhat playful: "One of the Natives with great gayety stuck his spear into the lobe of one of the Lungs, and holding it close to the Mouth of one of the Officers made signs for him to eat it; but he begged to be excused, at the same time taking up ye Head & making signs that he would Accept of that which was given to him, and he presented him with two Nails in return."

This description does two things. First, it establishes a familiar and reassuring distance between civilization and savagery in the persons of Richard Pickersgill and the unnamed Maori, respectively. While the British officer cannot accept a human body part as food, he will accept it as a trade article, a "curiosity" to take home from the margins of the world, proof of the strange cultures of its inhabitants. Second, and more interesting, the description establishes the closeness of the contact zone. This image of a Maori holding his spear close to a Briton's face – let alone a spear with a human lung on it – suggests a potentially dangerous but certainly fascinating proximity. That such an action can be read as a joke rather than a threat suggests a much more complex range of possibilities for relations between European and Pacific cultures than that offered by the old notions of contact and conquest. Perhaps the Briton's response can also be read as playful, given the excessive and self-deprecating formality of "he begged to be excused." The curiously domestic connotations of the scene also suggest a close rather than a distant relationship between Britons and Maori. "These were, it seems, very desirous of [the head]; but that could not be granted: However one of them

who was a great favorite was indulged with a piece of the flesh." Far
from being portrayed as a bloodthirsty savage, the Maori who performs
cannibalism for the crew is akin to a pet, a favourite child or dog singled
out with a mark of special favour. When Wales himself witnesses the
Maori eating a piece of the head, he notes "an avidity which amazed
me, [he was] licking his lips and fingers after it as if affraid to lose the
least part, either grease or gravy, of so delicious a morsel." The tone is
neutral, even indulgent, far from the horror the sight evokes in Hitihiti
(and presumably in readers). Like Cook's account, Wales's account
seems to inhabit a middle ground between horrified condemnation and
detached observation.

A second demonstration of Maori cannibalism arising out of Cook's
second voyage came a few weeks later. The *Resolution* left Queen Charlotte Sound on 24 November 1773; the *Adventure,* which had become
separated from the *Resolution,* arrived only days later, on 30 November, and stayed to make necessary repairs such as mending casks and
rebaking bread. On 17 December 1773 a cutter containing ten men was
sent to Grass Cove to collect greens for the crew. When the cutter had
not returned the next morning, the *Adventure*'s captain, Tobias Furneaux, sent out a search party in the launch. Lieutenant James Burney
commanded ten armed marines and a rowing crew. Near Grass Cove
they saw a double canoe on the beach; two men standing by it ran off
when the launch approached. A search discovered the cutter's rowlocks,
the shoe of one of the missing midshipmen, and what the search party
assumed was fresh dog meat. A further search of the area revealed
twenty food baskets packed with roasted meat and fern root. The discovery of more shoes and a hand marked "TH" suggested the fate of the
cutter's crew: the hand was identified as that of Thomas Hill, who had
been so tattooed in Tahiti. A four-foot circle of freshly dug ground indicated an earth-oven, where the marines began to dig with a cutlass;
Burney began to burn the Maori canoe, but at the sight of smoke from a
nearby hill the men hurried back to their launch, rowing to Grass Cove
where they saw four canoes on the beach and a large crowd (described
somewhat improbably by Furneaux in his account as "not less than
1500 or 2000").[10] Burney ordered the marines to fire at the canoes and
into the crowd at will until the beach was cleared. Then, leaving the
ship's master to guard the launch, he searched the beach with a party of
marines. They found evidence of the cutter – two bundles of wild celery
gathered by its crew and a broken oar stuck upright in the ground – and
behind the beach not the cutter itself but "Such a shocking scene of Car-

nage & Barbarity as can never be mentiond or thought of, but with horror."[11]

Beaglehole does not include what Burney's logbooks described: "Dogs were chewing at the discarded entrails of four or five men, and they found the eyes, hearts, lungs, livers, and heads of their comrades, including the head of Furneaux's black servant, various feet, and Rowe's left hand (identified by its scarred forefinger) roasting on fires or scattered on the ground"; according to New Zealand historian Anne Salmond, the launch party "had evidently interrupted a great whaangai hau ceremony, in which the hau of their comrades (and their ancestors) was being fed to the [Maori] ancestors."[12] While Burney's log account freezes for a moment – "we remained almost Stupefied on the spot" – the possibility of danger restores the narrative: the sound of Maori "gathering in the Valley" reminds Burney that the members of his party are vastly outnumbered, so they destroy the canoes and return to the *Adventure*.[13] The ship was already prepared to leave Queen Charlotte Sound, but Burney's news made leaving even more appealing (although contrary winds caused some delay). Having lost ten men, and with no fixed rendezvous with the *Resolution*, Furneaux sailed southeast in search of the Southern Continent, but cold weather, scurvy, and contrary winds forced the *Adventure* to Cape Horn, then to Cape of Good Hope, and finally home to England by 14 July 1774, a year before the arrival of the *Resolution*.

Dr Douglas was also the editor of the published version of Cook's second voyage, published in two volumes in 1777. Furneaux's narrative of the *Adventure*'s explorations during the time the ships were separated was included as a separate portion of the text.[14] In recording Cook's response to the cannibalism witnessed by the *Resolution*'s crew on 23 November 1773, Douglas is faithful to the original, as comparing the passage from Douglas's edition with the long description by Cook about the "experiment" in Maori cannibalism, quoted from Beaglehole's edition at the beginning of this section, reveals. Douglas's version was published as follows:

Calm or light airs from the North, all day, on the 23rd, hindered us from putting to sea as intended. In the afternoon, some of the officers went on shore to amuse themselves among the natives, where they saw the head and bowels of a youth, who had lately been killed, lying on the beach; and the heart stuck on a forked stick, which was fixed to the head of one of the largest canoes.

One of the gentlemen bought the head, and brought it on board, where a piece of the flesh was broiled and eaten by one of the natives, before all the officers and most of the men. I was on shore at this time, but soon after returning on board, was informed of the above circumstances; and found the quarter-deck crowded with the natives, and the mangled head, or rather part of it (for the under jaw and lip were wanting) lying on the tafferal. The scull had been broken on the left side, just above the temples, and the remains of the face had all the appearance of a youth under twenty.

The sight of the head, and the relation of the above circumstances, struck me with horror, and filled my mind with indignation against these cannibals. Curiosity, however, got the better of my indignation, especially when I considered that it would avail but little, and being desirous of becoming an eye-witness of a fact which many doubted, I ordered a piece of the flesh to be broiled and brought to the quarter-deck, where one of these cannibals eat it with surprising avidity. This had such an effect on some of our people as to make them sick. Oedidee (who came on board with me) was so affected with the sight as to become perfectly motionless, and seemed as if metamorphosed into the statue of Horror. It is utterly impossible for art to describe that passion with half the force that it appeared in his countenance. When rouzed from this state by some of us, he burst into tears; continued to weep and scold by turns; told them that they were vile men; and that he neither was, nor would be any longer their friend. He even would not suffer them to touch him; he used the same language to one of the gentlemen who cut off the flesh; and refused to accept, or even touch, the knife with which it was done. Such was Oedidee's indignation against the vile custom; and worthy of imitation by every rational being. (Douglas ii:1, 243–4)

Clearly, Douglas has changed relatively little from Cook's journal in editing this scene for publication, mostly breaking Cook's strings of independent clauses joined by commas into separate sentences and regularizing his punctuation. He has elevated Cook's language somewhat: Cook's "so that we could not get to sea as I intended" (Beaglehole ii, 292) becomes "hindered us from putting out to sea as intended." The most significant change occurs as Douglas adds a reflection or two regarding Oedidee, or Hitihiti, emphasizing his horror at the sight of cannibalism by enlarging upon it using words from Wales's journal. Cook had noted that the head seemed to be that "of a youth about fourteen or fifteen," but Douglas uses Wales's "youth under twenty"; it is also from Wales that the image of Hitihiti "metamorphosed into a statue of Horror" and the inability of "Art to depict that passion with half the force that it appeared in his Countenance" come (Wales 818; Douglas II, 234). Douglas's embellishment gives readers two points of identification in this scene, encouraging us to identify intellectually with Cook, "desirous of becoming an eye-witness of a fact which many doubted," and emotionally with Hitihiti, horrified at cannibalism. By borrowing Wales's words to turn the Tahitian into "the statue of Horror," Douglas slows down the narrative for a moment, giving readers time to absorb this information and to respond emotionally to it, before "rouzing" Hitihiti and moving on. Douglas closes the scene with a moral reflection, instructing readers on how to respond to this information about the Maori: Hitihiti's "indignation against the vile custom [is] worthy of imitation by every rational being." Portrayed in the language of sensibility in this scene, Hitihiti comes to represent an intermediary between Britons who know that cannibalism is wrong and Maori who practise it, just as Wales becomes an intermediary between the plain-speaking Cook and the man of feeling.

In the published text of Captain Furneaux's narrative, Douglas reproduced Lieutenant Burney's words about the Grass Cove incident in a very carefully structured scene. The suspicion of cannibalism is raised by protestations of doubt, first about the possibility that the cutter's crew met with any violence from Maori – "I had not the least suspicion that our people had received any injury from the natives; our boats having frequently been higher up, and worse provided. How much I was mistaken, too soon appeared"[15] – and then about the possibility of cannibalism: "I still doubted their being cannibals. But we were soon convinced by most horrid and undeniable proof."[16] These protestations culminate in the narrative climax of cannibalism discovered:

A great many baskets (about twenty) lying on the beach tied up, we cut them open. Some were full of roasted flesh, and some of fern-root, which serves them for bread. On farther search, we found more shoes, and a hand, which we immediately knew to have belonged to Thomas Hill, one of our forecastle-men, it being marked T.H. with an Otaheite tattow-instrument. I went with some of the people, a little way up the woods, but saw nothing else. Coming down again, there was a round spot covered with fresh earth about four feet diameter, where something had been buried. Having no spade, we began to dig with a cutlass; and in the mean time I launched the canoe with intent to destroy her; but seeing a great smoke ascending over the nearest hill, I got all the people into the boat, and made what haste I could to be with them before sun-set.

On opening the next bay, which was Grass Cove, we saw four canoes, one single and three double ones, and a great many people on the beach, who, on our approach, retreated to a small hill, within a ship's length of the water-side, where they stood talking to us. A large fire was on the top of the high land, beyond the woods, from whence, all the way down the hill, the place was thronged like a fair. As we came in, I ordered a musquetoon to be fired at one the canoes, suspecting they might be full of men lying down in the bottom; for they were all afloat, but nobody was seen in them. The savages on the little hill, still kept hallooing and making signs for us to land. However, as soon as we got close in, we all fired. The first volley did not seem to affect them much; but on the second, they began to scramble away as fast as they could, some of them howling. We continued firing as long as we could see the glimpse of any of them through the bushes. Amongst the Indians were two very stout men, who never offered to move till they found themselves forsaken by their companions; and then they marched away with great composure and deliberation; their pride not suffering them to run. One of them, however, got a fall, and either lay there, or crawled off on all fours. The other got clear, without any apparent hurt. I then landed with the marines, and Mr Fannin stayed to guard the boat.

On the beach were two bundles of cellery, which had been gathered for loading the cutter. A broken oar was stuck upright in the ground, to which the natives had tied their canoes; a proof that the attack had been made here. I then searched all along at the back of the beach, to see if the cutter was there. We found no boat, but instead of her, such a shocking scene of carnage and barbarity as can never be mentioned or thought of but with horror; for the heads, hearts, and lungs of several of our people were seen lying on the beach, and, at a little distance, the dogs gnawing at their intrails.

Whilst we remained almost stupefied on the spot, Mr Fannin called out to us that he heard the savages gathering together in the woods; on which I returned to the boat, and hauling alongside the canoes, we demolished three of them. Whilst this was transacting, the fire on the top of the hill disappeared; and we could hear the Indians in the woods at high words; I suppose quarrelling whether or not they should attack us, and try to save their canoes. It now grew dark, I therefore just stepped out, and looked once more behind the beach to see if the cutter had been hauled up in the bushes; but seeing nothing of her, returned and put off. Our whole force would have been barely sufficient to have gone up the hill, and to have ventured with half (for half must have been left to guard the boat) woud have been fool-hardiness.

As we opened the upper part of the sound, we saw a very large fire about three or four miles higher up, which formed a complete oval, reaching from the top of a hill down almost to the water-side, the middle space being inclosed all round by the fire, like a hedge. I consulted with Mr Fannin, and we were both of opinion that we could expect to reap no other advantage than the poor satisfaction of killing some more of the savages. At leaving Grass Cove, we had fired a general volley towards where we heard the Indians talking; but, by going in and out of the boat, our arms had got wet, and four pieces missed fire. What was still worse, it began to rain; our ammunition was more than half expended; and we left six large canoes behind us in one place. With so many disadvantages, I did not think it worth while to proceed, where nothing could be hoped for but revenge.

Coming between two round islands, situated to the southward of East Bay, we imagined we heard somebody calling; we lay on our oars, and listened, but heard no more of it; we hallooed several times, but to little purpose; the poor souls were far enough out of hearing; and indeed, I think it some comfort to reflect, that in all probability every man of them must have been killed on the spot. (Burney in Douglas II:2, 257–9)[17]

Burney's account develops two main patterns: it creates a series of nar-rative climaxes and it sets up symbolic contrasts between Maori and Britons. Both of these patterns establish a rationale and justification for violent action in response to cannibalism.

Burney's account recreates the discovery of cannibalism for readers in a series of narrative climaxes. First, the sight of roasted flesh and fern-root (the Maori bread-equivalent), followed by the discovery of the tattooed hand, sets up the initial implication of Maori cannibalism. In consideration of the noun "flesh" (instead of the more generic "meat") and baskets full of bread, the disembodied hand suggests the possibility that the flesh in those baskets is the rest of Hill's body. Then the sight of "a great smoke ascending over the nearest hill" – doubly ominous in light of the roasted flesh – reminds Burney that the roasters themselves are still quite close by: the smoke has come to signify both roasting and Maori. Before this discovery, Maori were seen as friendly;[18] now they have become dangerous, and in the next paragraph Burney recounts firing at the canoes of "the savages" on sight. Significantly, this is the first time during the *Adventure's* stay at Queen Charlotte Sound that the word "savages" has been used to describe the Maori, who have previously been called "inhabitants," "natives," "Indians," "people," and "men."[19] These more neutral terms continue to be used, of course, but "savages" appears later in the passage, once again indicating a crowd of Maori. This pattern of discovery of the signs of cannibalism and violent retribution is repeated again at Grass Cove.

Arriving on the beach at Grass Cove, Burney and the marines once again see food, this time the celery cut by the cutter's crew to supplement the *Adventure's* food stores. The contrast between the sight of innocent, milky celery on the beach and the bloodiness further inland – "the heads, hearts, and lungs of several of our people ... dogs gnawing at their intrails" – evokes another kind of narrative climax. It also establishes a clear distinction between Britons and Maori through the kinds of symbolic associations Burney and his men, and Douglas and his readers, would have been likely to make. The celery gathered by the cutter's crew would have suggested qualities of temperance through being associated with lettuce, a cool, leafy salad vegetable long considered an anaphrodisiac. Celery would also have suggested the scientific principles of the voyage itself, given Cook's emphasis on eating fresh vegetables as a means of helping to prevent scurvy, an innovation in the provisioning of long ocean voyages for which he was famous.[20] The images of human heads, hearts, and lungs, the offal apparently discarded by Maori in favour of flesh, have connotations of their own. The image of these parts strewn along the beach, as well as that of dogs eating the entrails, is graphic and shocking. The discarded heads, hearts, and lungs might also have suggested a rejection of the qualities associated with them – human reason, emotion, and inspiration. The celery-eating British are thus implicitly characterized in this account as cool-headed, scientific, and up-to-date in contrast to the bloodthirsty and primitive Maori. Indeed, in this account Burney remains cool, refusing to be "fool-hardy" and risk losing more men in direct confrontation with Maori, even as he also acts violently, destroying three canoes and firing again into the crowd. But the shocking quality of this sight would also necessarily stimulate the passions among landing party and readers alike, justifying both these actions and hopes of revenge.

This is the textual material regarding Maori cannibalism as witnessed at Queen Charlotte Sound in the fall and winter of 1773. It reveals a multiplicity of responses to cannibalism on Cook's second voyage. Anne Salmond, for instance, sees the demonstration of cannibalism on board the *Resolution* as a parody for both Britons and Maori. Clerke parodied the idea of cannibalism, eyewitness evidence, and scientific experimentation, while the Maori mocked both Hitihiti and Europeans by licking their fingers. Clerke, the first conductor of the experiment, was not above parodying the credulity of armchair travellers: that his account of giants at Patagonia was taken seriously enough to be published in the *Philosophical Transactions* of the Royal Society in 1767 was a source of delight to his shipmates.[21]

Whether we see it as parody or not, in many ways the whole macabre incident reveals more about Europeans than about Maori. Hitihiti's response groups Britons and Maori together: willingness to cut a steak from a human being was, for him, not very different from willingness to eat it. Far from distinguishing the two cultures into civilized eyewitnesses and cannibal savages, the description in Cook's journal suggests a more personal encounter as two groups engage with and reveal themselves to each other. It might also suggest something about the differences between producers and readers of voyages of discovery. The philosophical comments of Cook, Georg Forster (natural historian and son of J.R. Forster), and Anders Sparrman (the Swedish naturalist on the second voyage) refuse to identity Maori cannibalism as the mark of the essential savage. Although he reveals an initial emotional response, Cook ultimately discusses cannibalism dispassionately, arguing that "the custom of eating enemies slain in battle" will disappear with greater tribal unity. Although he uses such value-laden adjectives as "savage" and "civilized," his account gives some sense of how Maori themselves viewed the custom:

At present they seem to have but little idea of treating other men as they would wish to be treated, but treat them as they think they would be treated under the same circumstances. If I remember right one of the arguments they made against Tupaia who frequently expostulated with them against this custom, was that there could be no harm in killing and eating the man who would do the same by you if it was in his power, for said they "can there be any harm in eating our Enimies whom we have killed in battle, would not those very enimies have done the same to us?" (Beaglehole ɪɪ, 294–5)

Such a passage demonstrates Beaglehole's construction of Cook as a man whose cultural relativism indicates his virtues as an observer of foreign cultures. Notwithstanding his own feelings of "horror" and "indignation," and his own cultural values (the "idea of treating other men as [one] would wish to be treated"), Cook tries to present foreign customs not only in comparison to British ones (whether explicitly or implicitly) but also within their cultural context. Indeed, his ability to do so was part of the voyages' contribution to knowledge.

Forster contrasts European brutality, particularly the destruction wrought by warfare, with Maori cannibalism, asking, "is it not from prejudice that we are disgusted with the idea of eating a dead man, when we feel no remorse in depriving him of life?" Sparrman lists examples of European cannibalism.[22] In a brief meditation on the moral issues involved, Forster speculated that the European demand for curiosities caused violence and, possibly, this instance of cannibalism as groups anxious to trade with the *Resolution* in the Sound raided and killed their neighbours.[23] (This latter point may also implicitly question the experiment's methodological validity.) Among the Europeans, Burney alone conveys a sense of outrage and horror in his response. It may be that Cook and Wales describe Maori cannibalism in less emotional language than does Burney because they describe Maori eating other Maori, while Burney describes Maori eating Europeans – altogether a more frightening prospect for British sailors and European readers of the published voyage. At home in Britain, news of the massacre at Grass Cove became proof of the essential untrustworthiness of savages as well as of the corresponding need to use violence when dealing with them.[24] Such an image of ferocity did not, however, keep Europeans away from Queen Charlotte Sound. In spite of encountering cannibalism there, Cook "nominated it as a central port for Pacific explorations." Apparently its advantages as a port (many safe anchorages with good access to the supplies needed by European ships, such as fresh water, fish, vegetables, and wood) outweighed its proximity to cannibals. "Cook's charts and descriptions from his first visit [with the *Endeavour* in 1770] were to bring many European vessels (including his own ships) back to the Sound."[25]

Cook returned to Queen Charlotte Sound in October 1774, almost a year after the Grass Cove incident. Maori, expecting him to take revenge, tried to avoid the Europeans and to conceal what had happened. Although there were rumours and gossip, Cook did not believe them. The *Resolution* had had no contact with the *Adventure* since October 1773, a month before each ship encountered cannibalism at Queen Charlotte Sound in November; furthermore, there were no Polynesians on board the *Resolution* in October 1774, so communication between Europeans and Maori was hampered by language difficulties. However, by the time of his final visit to Queen Charlotte Sound in February 1777, Cook knew what had happened at Grass Cove. Inexplicably, to Maori, Mai (the Tahitian who had travelled to England with the *Resolution* in 1775), and his own men, he did not retaliate, even when a man described as one of the ringleaders of the Grass Cove incident came on board ship. However, Cook's attitude to Maori changed dramatically. On the first and second voyages he characterized them as "brave, open, and honest," but after learning of the Grass Cove killings he described them as "violent and often treacherous" in their desire for revenge. Indeed, Salmond argues that Cook's increasing violence on the third voyage is attributable to his anger and sense of betrayal with regard to Maori cannibalism.[26]

❖

The experience of cannibalism in New Zealand coloured Douglas's, if not Cook's, experience of Nootka Sound, as comparing specific passages from Douglas's edition with comparable moments in Beaglehole's scholarly edition reveals. Beaglehole's edition indicates that Cook himself did not even mention cannibalism in his account of the month at Nootka Sound, let alone portray its inhabitants as cannibals. This discrepancy reveals how the already well established European discourse of cannibalism turned into the expectation that Europeans would find cannibalism in so-called savage lands.

The first suggestion of cannibalism at Nootka Sound in Douglas's edition occurs in the description of the second day in the Sound (30

March 1778). Cook sent three boats under the command of Lieutenant James King to look for a harbour; the inhabitants of the Sound also began investigating, approaching the ships eager to trade.

> The articles which they offered to sale were skins ... weapons ... fish-hooks, and instruments of various kinds; wooden vizors of many different monstrous figures; a sort of woollen stuff, or blanketing; bags filled with red ochre; peices of carved work; beads; and several other little ornaments of thin brass and iron, shaped like a horse-shoe, which they hang at their noses; and several chissels, or peices of iron, fixed to handles. From their possessing which metals, we could infer that they had either been visited before by some civilized nation, or had connections with other tribes on their continent, who had communication with them. But the most extraordinary of all the articles which they brought to the ships for sale, were human skulls, and hands not quite stripped of the flesh, *which they made our people plainly understand they had eaten*; and, indeed, some of them had evident marks that they had been upon the fire. *We had but too much reason to suspect*, from this circumstance, that the horrid practice of feeding on their enemies is as prevalent here, as we had found it to be at New Zealand and other South Sea islands. For various articles which they brought, they took in exchange knives, chissels, peices of iron and tin nails, looking glasses, buttons, or any kind of metal. Glass beads they were not fond of and cloth of every sort they rejected. (Douglas III:2, 270–1, my emphasis)

Beaglehole's edition, however, records this moment in Cook's journal in a much less sensational way:

> Their articles [for trade] were the Skins of various animals, such as Bears, Wolfs, Foxes, Dear, Rackoons, Polecats, Martins and in particular the Sea Beaver, the same as is found on the coast of Kamtchatka. Cloathing made of these skins and a nother sort made, either of the bark of a tree or some plant like hemp; Weapons, such as Bows and Arrows, Spears &ca Fishhooks and Instruments of various kinds, pieces of carved work and even human skuls and hands,* and a variety of little articles too tedious to mention. For these they took in exchange, Knives,

chissels, pieces of iron & Tin, Nails, Buttons, or any kind of metal. Beads they were not fond of and cloth of all kinds they rejected. (Beaglehole III:1, 296–7)

There are a number of interesting discrepancies between these two passages. One is that Beaglehole's version, based on Cook's logs and journals only, is much shorter, primarily because Douglas lists what Cook recorded as "a variety of little articles too tedious to mention." Although these things may have seemed tedious to Cook, or too tedious to note on a daily basis, they could not fail to be of interest to readers, who could see "little ornaments of thin brass, shaped like a horse-shoe, which they hang at their noses" in Webber's illustration (as in Figure 5). Indeed, it was for precisely such details of life in faraway places that readers devoured published voyages of exploration. Another glaring discrepancy between the two texts is that, although *Cook* does not ascribe cannibalism to the people of Nootka Sound, *Douglas* (a ghostwriter whose name does not appear on the title page) does, using Cook's authority to record evidence of cannibalism among them.

The notable similarity is that each version mentions two very distinctive trade articles offered to British sailors by the people of Nootka Sound: human skulls and hands. Each editor's treatment of these curiosities is revealing. Beaglehole simply includes them in the list of trade articles; their emphatic position near the end of the list is reduced by the anticlimactic effect of the "variety of little articles too tedious to mention" that follows. For Douglas, by contrast, these human hands and skulls immediately raise the possibility of cannibalism:

> But the most extraordinary of all the articles which they brought to the ships for sale, were human skulls, and hands not quite stripped of the flesh, *which they made our people plainly understand they had eaten*; and, indeed, some of them had evident marks that they had been upon the fire. *We had but too much reason to suspect*, from this circumstance, that the horrid practice of feeding on their enemies is as prevalent here, as we had found it to be at New Zealand and other South Sea islands. (Douglas III:2, 270–1, my emphasis)

Douglas's inference takes on the status of fact for reasons that have to do with the cultural context of exploration: scientific empiricism, along with the use of the first person and the formal demand for observations and reflections in the published text of exploration, creates a powerful truth-claim. The ambiguous subordinate clause "which they made our people plainly understand they had eaten" is framed by statements invoking evidence of the senses, human skulls and hands actually seen and touched. Sandwiched between empirical statements, Douglas's inference shares in their truth-claim. Douglas also takes the opportunity to move from observation to reflection in his treatment of the list. The analogy comparing the people at Nootka Sound to New Zealand Maori not only satisfies the demand for reflection on the content of observations but also argues in favour of cannibalism at Nootka Sound. Although I have already discussed at length how far removed the explorer might be from the published text of his exploration, editors after Hawkesworth were quick to exploit the ostensible authority of the first-person narrator. Coupled with the growing importance of scientific empiricism, this strategy created a powerful impression of truth – especially when the "I" who spoke was apparently Captain Cook. But, as we have seen, Douglas's edition of the journal is in fact a composite text that borrowed liberally from the accounts of the other officers without necessarily acknowledging them. In Beaglehole's scholarly edition, footnotes indicate Douglas's probable sources from among those accounts and so provide crucial information for any discussion of the textual construction of Captain Cook. The issue of cannibalism at Nootka Sound demonstrates this process at work.

Beaglehole's edition of the third voyage reveals that Cook himself never mentioned the word "cannibalism" during the month at Nootka Sound. Douglas, however, did, thus creating the impression that its inhabitants were cannibals. For Douglas, "human skulls and hands" suggested cannibalism, perhaps because they featured so prominently in the accounts of Maori cannibalism from the second voyage (the "steak" roasted from a human head, the hand tattooed TH). Accordingly, Beaglehole discusses the issue in a footnote after the phrase ("human skuls and hands"*) – a footnote that takes up more space on the page than does the passage it annotates. Beaglehole provides one comment by Cook (about slavery, not cannibalism) together with comments on cannibalism from some of the other officers' journals. The words of these other officers occupy a great deal more space in the footnote than do Cook's. The footnote ends with commentary from a twentieth-century historian and an anthropologist. Beaglehole's footnote represents, in miniature, the development of the cannibal story. Although this story has been attributed to Cook, Beaglehole's edition of the *text* of the journal reveals that Cook was *not* in fact the source. In effect, Douglas has put words from the accounts of the other officers into Cook's mouth, as Beaglehole's footnote reveals:

"One man offered to barter a child of about five or six years of age for a spike-nail; I am satisfied we did not mistake his intention." – [Cook's] Log, 1 April. "We bought 3 or 4 Human hands which they brought to sell, they appeared to have been lately cut off as the flesh was not reduced to an horny substance but raw – they made signs that they were good eating, & seemed to sell them to us for that purpose or at least all of us understood them in that light. They likewise brought on board two or three Human Skuls & offered them to sale – our Surgeon bought one of them." – Bayly JT, 30 March. Edgar was more careful in examining these suspected cannibals. At first there was "all the reason in the World to think they were so. But it was evident we did not understand them or that they did not understand us, for I had this morning a most Convincing Proff of the falsity of our notions." He bought a hand from one man "and then desir'd him to Eat it, which he would not do, I then offered him more Iron & Brass than wou'd have purchas'd one of their most Elegant dresses, if he would eat part of it, all which offers he treated with Great Contempt & departed in Great anger. Yet there are several Gentlemen in the two Ships, who still continue prepossessed of their former opinion." – Edgar, 25 April. Howay writes, in his edition of Zimmerman, p. 72, n. 119, "the better opinion is that cannibalism did not exist save as a ceremonial affair or part of a religious rite." And Philip Drucker, "The situation as to ceremonial cannibalism is not clear; it may have been practiced after successful raids, although modern informants deny it unanimously. If it ever was customary, as so many of the early explorers maintain, it went out of use early in the historic period." – *The Northern and Central Nootkan Tribes* (Washington, D.C. 1951), p. 342. (Beaglehole iii:1, 297)

This footnote offers a wealth of information about the nature of cross-cultural communication and British sailors' assumptions about non-European peoples, all of which deserve a closer look. It contains statements of description and evaluation, observation and reflection, by three journal writers: first Cook himself, then two members of the

Discovery's crew – the astronomer William Bayly and the master Thomas Edgar. Cook's statement is the most straightforward and Edgar's is the most subtle and nuanced, while Bayly's is governed largely by assumption. Bayly and Edgar offer a similar observation – the empirical evidence of human hands brought to the ships as trade articles – but differ in their interpretations of it. What seems most striking, however, is the fact that Cook's comment has nothing whatsoever to do with cannibalism but, instead, records his perception about slavery: "One man offered to barter a child of about five or six years of age for a spike-nail; I am satisfied we did not mistake his intention." Why Beaglehole puts Cook's mention of slavery in the same category as Bayly and Edgar's comments about cannibalism is unclear, but the fact that he has done so suggests that the appearance of human hands and skulls as trade articles left no impression of cannibalism on Cook. This contrasts markedly with Cook's handling of cannibalism from Queen Charlotte Sound on the second voyage, when he "ordered a piece of the flesh [off a head bought as a curiosity] to be broiled and brought on the quarter deck where one of these [Maori] Canibals eat with a seeming good relish before the whole ships Company" (Beaglehole II, 293). Beaglehole records that the whole passage "is one that Cook worked over in B, f 150, a great deal, presumably to get the greatest possible dramatic effect. The page is a mass of correction and rewriting, including the final red ink" (II, 293).[27] The fact that Cook took such pains in his account of cannibalism in New Zealand suggests that he would have treated similar evidence at Nootka Sound with equal care. That he did not even mention the word gives the lie to Douglas's claim, made using Cook's authority, to "understand" that the people of Nootka Sound were cannibals.

Initially, the comment from Bayly seems straightforward enough. Its neutral opening ("We bought 3 or 4 Human hands which they brought to sell") echoes the tone describing trade relations in Beaglehole's edition of Cook's own journal. Indeed, Bayly's presumption that the Natives are cannibals is conveyed in a tone much more scientifically objective than is Douglas's, lacking that gentleman's explicit judgment of the "horrid practice." Bayly deduces from the evidence of recently severed human hands (which he describes in terms that liken them to food; that is, he calls the flesh "raw," as if it were meat) that the Natives will eat them: "they made signs that they were good eating." What he does not provide, however, is a record of the signs themselves, offering instead his interpretation – "or at least all of us understood them in that light" – without the supporting data. Readers cannot follow Bayly's deductive process; we must take his word. This brief account by Bayly, then, demonstrates how a partial account, based on assumption, expectation, and (wilful?) misinterpretation, may become the whole truth. Even his admission of the possibility of mistake ("or at least all of us understood them in that light") strengthens his claim to credibility since he has apparently considered that there might be other viable interpretations of the evidence. One of the main purposes of a voyage of exploration was, after all, its contribution to knowledge and understanding of the world.

By contrast to Bayly's play of assumption masking as deduction, Master Edgar attempted to test the hypothesis of cannibalism empirically. Edgar's account begins where Bayly's ends, with the purchase of human artefacts. Edgar buys a hand and then asks the vendor to eat it, offering to pay him handsomely for doing so. Edgar's transaction, as much as Bayly's, is marked by the difficulties of cross-cultural communication; just as Bayly reads "signs" made by Native traders as evidence that they eat human hands, so Edgar presumably must indicate by signs to the man from whom he bought a hand that he "desir'd him to eat it." What Bayly and Edgar's accounts both reveal is an interest in the possibility of cannibalism that amounts to an expectation that it exists among Native societies – an expectation that proved difficult to dislodge. Although Edgar conducted an experiment disproving cannibalism, at least to his own satisfaction, his evidence was ignored by "several Gentlemen in the two Ships, who still continue prepossessed of their former opinion," as well as by Douglas.[28] The idea, the expectation, and the assumption of cannibalism among the "savages" is so deeply "understood" that physical evidence to the contrary is invisible, is edited out. And, indeed, the one comment by Cook suggesting a similarity between the Natives and Europeans (i.e., participation in a slave economy) is buried under a discussion of a supposed cultural difference – the literal cannibalism of the Natives as opposed to the metaphoric cannibalism of English colonialism (suggested by Swift's *Modest Proposal* earlier in the century). Instead, Douglas likens the people of Nootka Sound (as supposed cannibals) to the people of New Zealand.

This focus on difference, the assumption among some Britons that human hands and skulls are part of the food chain at Nootka Sound, suggests that cannibalism works as a discourse in this encounter. At the very least, it is far more than a matter of simple observation. What these accounts from Bayly and Edgar, taken together, may reveal most clearly about the contact zone is its radical uncertainty, and the grave possibilities of misunderstanding, as the ambiguity of Bayly's phrase "made signs that they were good eating" suggests. While sailors and officers who had spent considerable time in the South Pacific had learned rudimentary or conversational Polynesian, there was no such linguistic or cultural fluency in the North Pacific. Every mention of cannibalism from the journal accounts of the month at Nootka Sound occurs within the context of human hands and skulls brought to the ships in trade. What if Native traders read the British sailors' fixation on those body parts as evidence that the Europeans wanted those specific items, either as trade goods or as food, and offered them articles likely to satisfy that demand? There is only one eyewitness account of actual cannibalism from this time at Nootka Sound, recorded in the journal of the American marine corporal John Ledyard within the context of his description of food at Nootka Sound.

The food we saw them use consisted solely of dried fish and blubber oil, the best that any man among us had ever seen! This they put into skins. We purchased great quantities of it, and situated as we were with respect to butter or suet, it was a very good succedaneum to either, and was constantly used to fry with; besides it furnished our lamps, and answered to many other purposes useful and necessary. Like all uncivilized men they are hospitable, and the first boat that visited us in the Cove brought us what no doubt they thought the greatest possible regalia, and offered it to us to eat; this was a human arm roasted. I have heard it remarked that human flesh is the most delicious, and therefore tasted a bit, and so did many others without swallowing the meat or the juices, but either my conscience or my taste rendered it very odious to me.

    We intimated to our hosts that what we had tasted was bad, and expressed as well as we could our disapprobation of eating it on account of its being part of a man like ourselves. They seemed to be sensible by the contortions of our faces that our feelings were disgusted, and apparently paddled off with equal dissatisfaction and disappointment themselves. We were complimented once before in the same stile, at our first discovery of Sandwich-Islands.[29]

Like Edgar, Ledyard was anxious to conclusively prove or disprove the notion of cannibalism, so he too conducted an experiment with "a human arm roasted": "I have heard it remarked," he writes, "that human flesh is the most delicious, and therefore tasted a bit, and so did many others without swallowing the meat or the juices, but either my conscience or my taste rendered it very odious to me." Apparently, not finding the meat "delicious" is enough to disqualify the Europeans from the ranks of the cannibal savages.

Ledyard's account, independently published in the United States in 1783, makes the most explicit claim for cannibalism – not only among the Natives. Indeed, although he accounts for their supposed cannibalism in one sentence, Ledyard devotes the next three pages (almost half his description of Nootka Sound) to an attempted explication of the origins of the practice of cannibalism, complete with Biblical precedent. For example:

> The circumstance of Abraham's intended sacrifice of Isaac to which he was injoined by the Deity, though he absolutely did not do it, yet was sufficient to introduce the idea that such a sacrifice was the most pleasing to God, *and* as it was an event very remarkable it probably became an historical subject, *and* went about among other tribes, *and* was handed down among them by tradition, *and* liable to all the changes incident thereto, *and* in time the story might have been that Abraham not only offered but really did sacrifice his own son.[30]

Not only is his account riddled with probability and might-have-beens, but it also accepts unquestioningly that Biblical narratives of origin can explain the practices of people who have been described as probably having never seen Christians before. Further, it establishes once again the superiority of Europeans, who know that Abraham did not in fact kill Isaac but, rather, was able to make a more pleasing sacrifice at the last minute. The coordinate structure of Ledyard's explanation, one very long sentence of ninety-six words, betrays a kind of hysteria in the accumulation of phrases beginning with "and" as well as its own tentativeness, which is highlighted by the inability of such structures to establish causality.

Ledyard takes what he reads as the appearance of cannibal practices as proof positive, although his account "proved absolutely nothing about the Nootka and identified only one known cannibal – Ledyard himself!"[31] Other officers, a little more critically minded or perhaps not counting on revenues from book sales, refused to judge on the scanty evidence presented. King writes, "as we cannot be said to converse with the people, we can only judge from outward actions, & not knowing all the Causes that give rise to them, we must be constantly led into error."[32] Similarly, Samwell records "we were led to think that these People are Cannibals, however of this we had no certain proof."[33] But most of the journals of Cook's subordinates were not published until recently, many of them in Beaglehole's two-volume scholarly edition of the third voyage.

In the same year that the official edition of Cook's journal was published, another appeared, claiming to be "a copious, comprehensive, and satisfactory Abridgement" published by John Stockdale, Scatcherd and Whitaker, John Fielding, and John Hardy.[34] If Douglas implied that the people of Nootka sound were cannibals, then this later 1784 edition presents that implication as fact. At a point in his edition that corresponds (roughly) to parallel observations from Cook's journal in Douglas and Beaglehole's editions, Stockdale's Cook states:

> Among all the articles, however, which they exposed to sale, the most extraordinary were human skulls, and hands, with some of the flesh remaining on them, *which they acknowledged they had been feeding on*; and some of them, indeed, bore evident marks of having been upon the fire. From this circumstance, *it was but too apparent*, that the horrid practice of *devouring* their enemies, is practised here, as much as at New-Zealand, and other South-sea islands. (Stockdale III:2, 211, my emphasis)

No longer is cannibalism merely "understood," as in Douglas's edition: Stockdale's edition declares that the Natives are so depraved as to acknowledge readily that they *devour* their enemies (in contrast to Douglas's comparatively neutral "feeding on"). In this later 1784 edition, even Douglas's innocent-sounding chapter heading, "Articles brought to barter," is made much more sinister and incriminating: "Variety of Articles brought to Barter, particularly human skulls" (Douglas III:2, 269; Stockdale III:2, 209). By the end of 1784 the savages of the Pacific are served up for European consumption as cannibals one and all.

Douglas's phrase "we had but too much reason to suspect that the horrid practice of feeding on their enemies, is as prevalent here, as we had found it to be at New Zealand" acquired the status of historical truth in less than one year. However, it was not inevitable that Europe-

ans identify cannibalism as a practice. The Spanish, who first made contact with coastal societies in 1774, made no mention of cannibalism at
Nootka Sound until *after* reading Cook's published journal. Although
the Spanish typically tried to learn as much as possible about Native
societies in order to facilitate their conversion to Roman Catholicism,
the authority of Cook's *Voyage* was so great as to override their own
research and records.[35] In spite of the fact that Cook never once mentioned cannibalism at Nootka Sound, and that the officers' accounts
differ greatly in their treatment of the evidence, Douglas recorded the
suspicion of cannibalism in his edition of Cook's *Journal* in such a manner as to inscribe *both* doubt and certainty, invoking all the authority of
expertise gained by Cook in two previous voyages around the world
among people for whom, Douglas says, the "horrid practice ... is prevalent." John Douglas, not James Cook, gave this label to the peoples of
the Northwest Coast, and it stuck.

Notwithstanding vast differences of culture and geography, some striking similarities emerge from the accounts of cannibalism at Queen Charlotte Sound (New Zealand) on Cook's second voyage and at Nootka
Sound on his third. Most obviously, the British were interested in cannibalism among Native peoples all over the globe, from the South Pacific to
the North Pacific – so interested that Britons like Cook, Wales, and Edgar
deliberately conducted experiments intended to prove or disprove the
hypothesized cannibalism of the Maori and Nuu-chah-nulth. Such
experiments, no less than Banks's botanical specimens or Webber's
ethnographic drawings, reveal the importance of empiricism and the scientific method as the intellectual foundation of Cook's voyages.
    It strikes me as peculiar indeed that writers – and readers – horrified
by cannibalism at Queen Charlotte Sound in the South Pacific and
Nootka Sound in the North Pacific should nonetheless quite readily
accept the appropriateness of these places as bases for further exploration. Indeed, the Nootka Sound Controversy of 1789 occurred because
Spain contested Britain's territorial claim to the Sound, well after
Douglas's account of cannibalism among the Nuu-chah-nulth had circulated through Britain and had been translated into the major languages of Europe. Notwithstanding fear of cannibalism, Europeans
were anxious to lay claim to the area because of its wealth of sea otter
furs, which were traded for astronomical profits in China. Similarly, in
spite of the apparent cannibalism there, Cook proposed Queen Char-

lotte Sound as a base for European exploration in the South Pacific because of its protected harbours and fresh water. Another puzzling point arises from the name Cook gave to the part of Nootka Sound he visited: Friendly Cove. Why give such a name to the habitation of cannibals? The obvious answer is that, since Cook himself found no evidence of cannibalism, there was no paradox for him in so naming the place. Cook's journal suggests that "Friendly Cove" was an appropriate name for Yuquot because, quite simply, the people there had given the ships a friendly reception.

Douglas turned the friendliness recorded by Cook into the suggestion of cannibalism. A firm believer in the four-stages theory, he looked at New World peoples rather differently from the way in which Cook did. Although a product of his time, Cook was able to consider other cultures on their own terms, to some degree at least. His account of cannibalism at Queen Charlotte Sound on the second voyage, for instance, voices the Maori rationale "can there be any harm in eating our Enemies whom we have killed in battle, would not those very enemies have done the same to us?" (Beaglehole II, 295). Douglas, however, was incapable of taking this perspective, seeing cannibalism only as proof of primitive savagery. Another reason for Douglas's presentation of Friendly Cove as the home of cannibals may come from the literary patterning at work in his edition – in this case, the argument from analogy. At Nootka Sound, the analogy that provides a "reason to suspect" that the Natives are cannibals may work to create another kind of proof. It took considerably more evidence than the mere sight of a "human hand, roasted" to convince Cook, his crew, and his readers of Maori cannibalism. Douglas is willing to assume that the people of Nootka Sound are cannibals on much slighter evidence. Hands, particularly, are a staple of the cannibal trope, perhaps because they are so identifiably, so distinctively human. Hands also feature prominently in the most disturbing account of Maori cannibalism at Queen Charlotte Sound. When hands appeared as trade articles at Nootka Sound, they must have called to Douglas's mind the hand of Thomas Hill, the *Discovery* midshipman lost and presumed eaten at Grass Cove in New Zealand. Other body parts might not have created so automatic a suspicion of cannibalism at Nootka Sound. In any case, the inference is Douglas's.

Douglas could also produce "Friendly Cove" as the home of cannibals precisely because cannibalism belongs to two discourses in the colonial and imperial context. I have already identified cannibalism as having both literal and metaphorical meanings within the context of Europe's encounter with the New World. For armchair travellers like Douglas, cannibalism meant, quite unambiguously, the custom of eating human flesh, a feature of life in non-European societies; for contemporary postcolonial critics, cannibalism represents a projection and metaphor for Europe's consumption of those societies through the imperial project. But cannibalism belongs to two discourses in another sense as well, and so it bridges the seeming gulf between the image created by "Friendly Cove" and the cannibal feast: it stands for the fears and desires projected onto Native peoples by European visitors to their shores.

What the European observer regarded as cannibalism in a Pacific culture was frequently accompanied by what he regarded as perverse and excessive sexual appetites. The sexual customs of Pacific societies, so different from those of Britain, were commented on by virtually every European writing about the Pacific. Particularly, the idea that *women* might have sexual agency independent of male ownership or possession and, even worse, the idea that women might have sexual appetites, marked them as whores according to the European mores governing female sexuality. Such a label, and such an understanding of women, cannot be divorced from the power relations of class and race as well as those of sex. In the Pacific of Cook's voyages such tropes are played out in the frequent comments about the wanton and lascivious gestures of Polynesian women and the brief references to the sexual trade between ship and shore. Whether presented as passive or active participants in this traffic, the women are somehow responsible; whether their sexual favours are sold by the men of their community or by the women themselves, on the morals of its women depend the morals of the nation. If the women are sexual, unchaste, unclean, then so, by extension, is the society they represent.

The position of the men is somewhat more ambiguous because the ownership model of heterosexuality does not quite fit. The Native men who brought "their" women to the ships were held in contempt by the ships' crews and officers anxious to buy the favours of other men's sisters, daughters, wives. The notion of the traffic in women conducted between the men on the shore and the men in the ships, on the face of it, defines the men as pimps (according to European standards) as surely as the women's sexuality defines them as whores. But within the colonial context European metaphors of husbandry and the imaging of America as a woman whose arms open to welcome the European explorer require the erasure of the Native men who might reasonably expect to become husbands to Native women. As Hulme argues in *Colonial*

Encounters, the discourse of some "atrocity" perpetuated by Native men is used, in effect, to dispossess them of their territorial right to both land and women – simultaneously, since the land is imaged as female.[36] Paradoxically, the word "husband" both assumes a similarity between European and indigenous cultures (that "marriage" stands as a social institution governing sexual relations between men and women) and functions to divorce Native men from their place in the institutions of their culture.

But Native men are not only erased (or demonized) in colonialist texts; they are also frequently feminized as the power and sexual hierarchies of the ships come into play. This suggests another kind of possible sexual dynamic in Cook's voyages – one governed by desire between men. Certainly homosexual encounters and relationships were neither unthinkable nor uncommon in the all-male environment of the ship; during long periods at sea, homosexual relations were not only possible but, in some instances, unavoidable.[37]

While I have yet to read an account of a sexual encounter between one of Cook's crew and a Native man (or between two men of Cook's crew, for that matter), Beaglehole's edition of the third voyage records evidence of homosexual relationships in Hawaii – not as unusual or remarkable sexual encounters but as socially accepted and significant relationships signalled by the word *aikāne*. Cook himself did not mention it; however, references to *aikāne* by King, Clerke, Samwell, and Ledyard indicate their social, sexual, and political functions. Although the journal writers tended to emphasize the sexual role of *aikāne*, the social acceptance and political importance of these young men are clearly indicated as well.[38] For example, on 29 January 1779 ship's surgeon David Samwell wrote of Kalaniopuu's state visit aboard the *Discovery* that "[a]nother Sett of Servants of whom he has a great many are called Ikany [*aikāne*] and are of superior rank to Erawe-rawe. Of this Class are Parea [Palea] and Cani-Coah [Kanekoa] and their business is to commit the Sin of Onan upon the old King. This, however strange it may appear, is fact, as we learnt from frequent Enquiries about this curious Custom, and it is an office that is esteemed honourable among them & they have frequently asked us on seeing a handsome young fellow if he was not an Ikany to some of us."[39] On 10 February, when Kamehameha came aboard the *Discovery* for an overnight visit, Samwell wrote that among his attendants was "a Young Man of whom he seems very fond, which does not in the least surprize us as we have had opportunities before of being acquainted with a detestable part of

his Character which he is not in the least anxious to conceal."[40]
Kalaniopuu was the highest-ranking chief (*ali'i*) Cook and his officers
met at Hawaii; Palea (like Kamehameha, an *aikāne* of Kalaniopuu)
himself indicated the nature of his *aikāne* relationship to Clerke: "he
call'd himself T'akanee to Terreeoboo [Kalaniopuu], & mentiond the
name of others being the same" (Beaglehole's note at the word
"T'akanee" defines it as "sodomite").[41] Palea's interactions with the
officers indicate the social and political roles of *aikāne*: he acts as
Kalaniopuu's official representative and spokesman. Indeed, one of
Cook's first comments about Hawaii at this time notes that "a well
looking young man nam'd Pareo [Palea], was soon observ'd to have the
most consequence."[42] His status and behaviour confirm and exemplify
the various writers' presentation of *aikāne* as a relationship simultaneously personal (affectionate and sexual: the *ali'i*'s lover) and official
(social and political: the *ali'i*'s counsellor and confidante), that this relationship was shared by several young men at once, and that it was an
accepted part of Hawaiian society, among the chiefly rank at least.

     Although King condemns the practice as depriving Hawaiian women
"of the natural affections of their Husbands, & seeing this divided by
the other sex,"[43] the journal accounts give no indication that Hawaiians
were disturbed in any way. Clerke noted that "they talk of this infernal
practice with all the indifference in the world, nor do I suppose they
imagine any degree of infamy in it."[44] Indeed, Samwell records that,
when the ships were finally preparing to sail north again after Cook's
death, an *ali'i* came on board the *Resolution*, "and seeing a handsome
young fellow whose appearance he liked much, offered six large hogs to
the Captain [now Clerke] if he would let him stand his Ikany for a little
while, such is the strange depravity of these Indians."[45] Such a proposal,
a complete reversal of the kind of sexual relations that the British officers assumed would take place between ship and shore, highlights the
officers' predominant response to *aikāne* relationships: not only condemnation but also, and perhaps more strongly, surprise that Hawaiians felt no shame about or need to hide these relationships.
Presumably, their own sense of reserve or embarrassment is the cause of
their rather coy descriptions. Samwell, Clerke, and King all hedge the
issue, using phrases not unlike the early twentieth century's "love that
dare not speak its name."

     John Ledyard was the only writer who actually used the word "sod-
omy"; he waxed as philosophical about *aikāne* relationships in Hawaii
as he had about cannibalism at Nootka Sound.

[I]t is a disagreeable circumstance to the historian that truth
obliges him to inform the world of a custom among [the
Hawaiians] contrary to nature, and odious to a delicate mind ...
it would be to omit the most material and useful part of
historical narration to omit it; the custom alluded to is that of
sodomy, which is very prevalent if not universal among the
chiefs, and we believe peculiar to them, as we never saw any
appearance of it among the commonalty. As this was the first
instance we had ever seen of it in our travels, we were cautious
how we credited the first indications, and waited untill
opportunity gave full proof of the circumstance. The
cohabitation is between the chiefs and the most beautiful males
they can procure about 17 years old, these they call Kikuana,
which in their language signifies a relation. These youths follow
them wherever they go, and are as narrowly looked after as the
women in those countries where jealousy is so predominant a
passion; they are extremely fond of them, and by a shocking
inversion of the laws of nature, they bestow all those affections
on them that were intended for the other sex. We did not fully
discover this circumstance until near our departure, and indeed
lamented we ever had, for though we had no right to attack or
ever to disapprove of customs in general that differed from our
own, yet this one so apparently infringed and insulted the first
and strongest dictate of nature, and we had from education and a
diffusive observation of the world, so strong a prejudice against
it, that the first instance we saw of it we condemned a man fully
reprobated. Our officers indeed did not insult the chiefs by any
means, but our soldiers and tars to vindicate their own
wonderful modesty, and at the same time oblige the insulted
women, and recommend themselves to their favours became
severe arbitrators, and the most valourous defenders and
supporters of their own tenets.[46]

Ledyard sets up his discussion with the disclaimer that it is the historian's duty to tell the truth, however unpleasant or unsavoury; he also
manages to rationalize the crew's sexual behaviour as both proof of
their manliness and their duty to comfort the women neglected by
Hawaiian men, though Clerke noted sourly that "they are profligate to
a most shameful degree in the indulgence of their lusts and passions, the
Women are much more Common than at any place we ever saw

before."[47] However, the most important function of Ledyard's account is to differentiate between Hawaiian men, particularly the *ali'i*, and Britons on the basis of what is currently called sexual orientation.

The Articles of War clearly established the criminality of *any* homosexual behaviour in the Royal Navy; Article 29 of the 1749 Articles states: "If any person in the fleet shall commit the unnatural and detestable sin of buggery of sodomy with man or beast, he shall be punished with death by the sentence of a Court Martial."[48] The Articles of War were read several times while Cook's ships were at Hawaii.[49] While the official purpose might have been to remind sailors of naval law regarding trade and sexual relations with Native peoples on the assumption that the latter would be with women, the Articles effectively police homosexual behaviour to ensure that the assumption will be truth. This constructs a moral and sexual difference between Britons and Hawaiians: the crew may engage in sexual relations with Hawaiian women, but any sexual activity with Hawaiian men is criminal. The two groups are distinguished by the constant reminder that what is a prominent feature of the highest levels of Hawaiian society is criminal in British society.

Comments regarding *aikāne*, or homosexuality, did not make their way into the official edition of the *Voyages*. However, Clerke's opinions regarding the "profligacy" and "commonness" of the Hawaiians did, thus bringing these sexual dynamics into play in the published account of the voyages and, consequently, into cultural circulation in Britain, where there was a growing discourse of homophobia in which (male) homosexuality increasingly suggested not deviant behaviour but deviant identity.[50] Such notions – like assumptions about the sexual mores and morals of peoples considered at best exotic and at worst savage – are easily exported to distant shores, where desires for sexual encounters and fears of being eaten construct a contact zone characterized by the conflation of excessive sexual and gustatory appetites.

In fact, given that the portrayal of Tahitian women's sexuality in the published text of Cook's first voyage excited more controversy than did the possibility of cannibalism in New Zealand, it might be that cannibalism provided a discourse for much that was simultaneously exciting and troubling in the New World. For cannibalism is both like and unlike other processes of incorporation, eating and sex, those elements of everyday life that construct a social contract and sense of identity for both the culture and the individual. If, "in accordance with the saying 'you are what you eat,' cultural identity is constructed by dietary taboos that define what is and what is not edible," then culinary differences construct and signify cultural differences at their most basic.[51] The New World cannibal breaks down or ignores the boundaries between what Christian Europeans define as edible and not edible; he shows a frightening lack of discernment about food sources, a kind of gustatory promiscuity that is, not surprisingly, linked to sexual promiscuity in many accounts. What transgressions might not be imagined of people who eat human flesh? British readers shocked by the unashamed sexuality of Pacific peoples, especially in women or between men, may well have found cannibalism a more socially acceptable means of discussing taboo subjects involving the human body. Indeed, cannibalism may have come to stand for these unspeakable acts, to offer a language and a discourse for talking about the scandals of the body.[52]

The publication of Cook's third voyage in 1784, especially its account of Cook's death at the hands of Hawaiians in 1779, solidified for British readers an image of Pacific societies whose savagery could be characterized equally by cannibalism and sexual promiscuity. The cannibal might be seen as the representative of the contact zone, standing for the complex mix of desire and fear European explorers felt when encountering new and different worlds. Sexual encounters between ship and shore offered one form of communication in the contact zone, a form long seen as positive.[53] The children produced by such unions offered one image of the ability of Pacific societies to incorporate European elements, including firearms, domesticated animals, and trade goods. Perhaps the cannibal suggests the process of transculturation that threatens to break down the boundaries between parties in the contact zone and that, for better or worse, more often solidified than evaporated. From the sailors' perspective, cannibalism might look like the less benevolent face of incorporation: the possibility of being consumed by the New World in an inversion of the imperial process. Voyages like Cook's were all about incorporation, aiming to bring the territories, products, and inhabitants of the non-European world into European knowledge and often under European domination. But the process by which one thing incorporates another immediately calls into question the possibility that the consumer might become the consumed.

That possibility had already been raised in Swift's *Modest Proposal* (1729), which offered a critique of British imperialism by identifying it with cannibalism. The proposal, which suggests transforming impoverished Irish from consumers to consumed, portrays the empire as a voracious mouth endlessly consuming colonial people and products. Just as their parents have been devoured by the English conquest and the corresponding appropriation of lands and the wherewithal for survival, Irish babies should be acceptable as commodities and foodstuffs for English landlords. Irony moves into social and political commentary in the speaker's description of the landlords as those who, "as they have already devoured most of the parents, seem to have the best title to the children."[54] The ironic brilliance of the proposal lies in the fact that the landlords' appetite for consuming is as renewable, as endless, a resource as are babies.[55] The proposal, which depicts the imperial relationship as cannibalistic, indicates that this appetite is for national and imperial, as well as for personal and class, consumption. The metaphor extends beyond England and Ireland to characterize the empire as a voracious appetite. The object of consumption is ultimately not an object but, rather, the process of consumption itself, the process of eating, of incorporation, where not meaning but satisfaction is endlessly deferred.[56]

This process of imperial cannibalism begins with representation, with reading. As Maggie Kilgour argues in *From Communion to Cannibalism*, the classical tradition presents scenes of great feasts made even more impressive by great speeches; the Christian tradition images knowledge as food, beginning with Genesis. The English literary tradition continues the connection: for example, Alexander Pope likened the process of acquiring knowledge to that of drinking; by contrast, Mary Shelley's Victor Frankenstein drank too deeply and became drunk with knowledge. In short, many of our metaphors for acquiring knowledge depend on some kind of incorporation though the various senses. "However, as a model for knowing, taste is not only the most basic and bodily way of making contact with the world outside of the individual but also the most intimate and intense way, resulting in a strict identity between eater and eaten."[57] Just as the products from the reaches of empire converge upon and enrich the imperial centre, cannibalism has been used historically to distinguish between civilization and savagery. For late eighteenth-century Europeans such as Douglas, cannibalism among Natives in the North or South Pacific was not a metaphor for some process of incorporation but, rather, the practice of eating human flesh, and, as such, it provided a clear boundary between those who engaged literally in such a practice and those who did not.

Cannibalism as a metaphor for the imperial process works differently. If knowledge is food, as Kilgour argues, then the belief that New World peoples are cannibals is incorporated into the European body. According to Michel de Certeau's reading of Montaigne's "Of the Cannibals," cannibalism is at the centre of the European travelogue: the

representation of the other and the place of the text are both simultaneously and causally produced, so that "discourse about the other is a
means of constructing a discourse authorized by the other."[58] It establishes the authority of colonialist texts that purport to give voice to the
hitherto silent bodies of people soon to become colonialist subjects –
and whose territories, products, crafts, and cultures are soon to be
devoured by European empires and readers. This suggests that cannibalism as a discourse is "understood," *read* (by Europeans) as if
between the lines of everyday behaviour manifested in trade relations or
religious practice; it provides a key that unlocks the mysteries of the
New World sign system. In Douglas's edition of Cook's third voyage,
the people of Nootka Sound bring human remains as trade artefacts,
which "our people plainly understood they had eaten" (III:2, 270–1);
Bayly notes that "they made signs that they were good eating & seemed
to sell them to us for that purpose, or at least all of us understood them
in that light" (Beaglehole III:1, 297). If cannibalism is predominantly a
textual and discursive rather than a gustatory practice, then perhaps the
cannibal moment really is textual in the most basic sense, occurring in
the act of *reading*. In other words, (European) readers are the true
man-eaters, metaphorically consuming the representation of non-
Europeans as literal cannibals in colonialist texts and imagining that the
true substance of the lives of savage peoples in far-off lands is being
incorporated into European knowledge.

The first British fur-trading vessel arrived at Nootka Sound one year
after Cook's official journal was published, lured by reports of the huge
profits to be made selling Nootka Sound furs in China. The motives of
later writers and publishers, particularly of traders' accounts, and the
ways their interests could be served by perpetuating the idea of Native
cannibalism, must also be considered. As in the Stockdale edition of
1784, cannibalism served as a sensational hook, a marketing technique
to increase book sales. As well, fur-traders' tales of unimaginable ferocity and savagery among Native trading partners may have been
intended to deter competitors from attempting to trade with those
Natives identified as cannibals, or to control crews for whom life on
shore (imagined as featuring food and sex in plenty) often looked more
inviting than returning to the privations of months at sea.[59]

Two facts about Nootka Sound and its inhabitants emerge from
Douglas's edition of the third voyage: the people of Nootka Sound are

cannibals and the furs traded there sell for astronomical prices in China. The first statement, attributed to Cook by Douglas, was maintained and perpetuated by later writers, passing into and *constituting* European knowledge of the Pacific coast. However, European desire for profit from the furs was evidently greater than the fear of being eaten. Spanish, Russian, and American ships met those of British traders as soon as they could be outfitted; less than fifteen years after Cook, George Vancouver arrived at Nootka Sound, in part to establish Britain's claim to it by mapping, thereby knowing and (implicitly) possessing it. In the international dispute known as the Nootka Sound Controversy (over the competing claims of Britain and Spain to the coast), the potential claim to ownership by the Nuu-chah-nulth was not considered.[60] Such dispossession is the rule of imperial and colonial expansion. But by creating an image of savagery at Nootka Sound, the discourse of cannibalism at work in Douglas's edition of Cook's third voyage offered a moral justification for claiming European possession of the land, even if only for as long as European powers were interested in trading furs there.

The image of cannibalism at Nootka Sound created by Douglas influenced later writers of exploration accounts, and not only on the Northwest Coast. In a study of two later overland explorers, Samuel Hearne and David Thompson, Marlene Goldman suggests that Douglas's decision to portray the Nuu-chah-nulth as cannibals may have affected subsequent portrayals of interior Native groups. "Douglas not only manipulate[d] the facts" in his account of Nootka Sound but "also [set] the literary parameters for future explorers."[61] The spectacular success of Douglas's edition of Cook's third voyage, due at least in part to its portrayal of savagery in the form of cannibalism at Nootka Sound and the death of Cook at Hawaii, helped to create a formula that appealed so strongly to the reading public that later writers and publishers used it to win audiences for themselves.

CHAPTER FIVE

Reconstructing Cook

Although public interest in the Northwest Coast and its trading potential had been piqued by verbal reports and anonymous publications to the extent that preparations for further voyages were already under way, the official edition of Cook's third voyage published in 1784 marks the entrance of Nootka Sound, as a territory, into the history of British imperialism. For readers of the published account, this month at Nootka Sound was only one in a series of more exciting encounters, notably the death of Cook at Hawaii a year later. However, its consequences have been far-reaching: the official account of this faraway coast and its inhabitants in words and pictures spread quickly throughout England, the rest of Europe, and the United States. Since the text itself became "the authoritative handbook for all who would navigate in the North Pacific and contact the Northwest Coast inhabitants,"[1] the information it presented became not one version of events among competing stories but, rather, marked the entry of the place that became British Columbia into history.[2] Here I must make the distinction between (1) the actual events and their consequences and (2) the written record of those events. Until relatively recently, the discourse of history has traditionally been governed by assumptions and ideals of objectivity and linguistic transparency.[3] The specific example of Cook's third voyage, however, suggests how social values, historical assumptions, and conventional paradigms inform and colour historical discourse in general.

Cook's month at Nootka Sound functions both as a historical event and as a story told about that event, part of a larger, more popular story about Cook as the representative of British imperialism and civilization. As Chris Healy argues, "European fictions of Cook have their own his-

tory: two major elements of the ruling fiction are condensed in the sub-
heading from a very popular book published during the bicentennial:
'Captain Cook discovers Australia and claims possession.'"[4] This chapter explores the history of European fictions of Cook, the constructions
that have been made of him and the uses to which he has been put both
for British imperial culture and the settler cultures that followed in his
wake. It begins by considering how moments of encounter like Cook's
at Nootka Sound have been understood in traditional settler histories
and in postcolonial reconstructions. Then, following Dening's formulation that history is the consciousness of the past used for present purposes, it looks at accounts of the death of Captain Cook at Hawaii in
February of 1779 as a case study of the uses to which the cultural icon
Captain Cook has been put. It then looks at Canadian histories of Captain Cook in order to think about the meaning of his month at Nootka
Sound for Canada in general and for British Columbia in particular.
Finally, borrowing from Healy's formulation of the fictions of Cook
(what I have called constructions of Cook), it considers the role of fic-
tion and contemporary culture in reconstructing some local versions of
Captain Cook.

Paul Carter opens *The Road to Botany Bay* by presenting a contrast:
Botany Bay then and now. "Before the name: what was the place like
before it was named? How did Cook see it? ... What we see is what the
firstcomers did not see: a place, not a historical space."[5] What we are
dealing with is a moment that has meaning only in hindsight, a moment
that is a "moment" significant and distinct from those preceding and
following it only in retrospect. Here I have fallen into the trap, jumping
from space to place in time as the marker of history, treating Cook's seeing that space as the moment announcing its entry into history. This is
also a moment created and given meaning by the expectation that history is serious business, matter to be enacted on an appropriately
imposing stage. And yet the place that Cook named and Carter discusses, Botany Bay, had a name and a meaning – a place in marked and
known human space – before Cook arrived.[6] The use of Aboriginal
words as place names further demonstrates the exercise of power
implicit in naming. It legitimates not Aboriginal claims to territory but,
rather, European claims to possession, or the claim of a particular European to discovery, as Cook, at St George's Island, restores its "native
name of Tahiti" in order to establish "his precedence there over the

island's earlier English visitor, Samuel Wallis."[7] Aboriginal spatial histories can be and were dislodged by the exercise of European power and
languages.[8]

So these different histories of space and place, as reproduced by Europeans, at least, record a European understanding of two separate
moments in time. This raises the question of historiography, of how we
understand history. Several writers have proposed ways both to
account for and critique the sense of inevitability in imperial and settler
history, according to which Europeans own not just historical discourse
but also history itself, so that the peoples they encountered enter history
only at the moment of contact. Their existence up to that moment in
time comes under the vague heading "pre-history," which really means,
in Eric Wolfe's phrase, "'without history,' supposedly isolated from the
external world and from one another."[9] This distinction is crucial: they
exist not before or prior to European history, as the prefix "pre" suggests, but *without*.[10] According to such an understanding of history,
so-called prehistoric peoples thus represent, for Europeans, a blank in
the map of human consciousness, just as their territories were imaged as
uninhabited blank spaces on (European) maps rapidly being filled in
during the eighteenth century.

Traditional imperial or settler histories present the history outside of
which these pre-historic peoples exist in different ways. Wolfe argues
that the genealogy is crucial: European history begins with Greece,
which rose, flourished, and declined, passing the torch as it were to
Rome, and then on (in turn) to Christian Europe, the Renaissance, the
Enlightenment, political revolutions resulting in political democracy,
and industrial revolution. Nations and peoples have their moment in
the spotlight, then fade into oblivion. Such a developmental scheme
misleads by turning history into a "race in time in which each runner of
the race passes on the torch of liberty to the next relay."[11] This kind of
narrative equates the rise and fall of empires, nations, or cultures with
the triumph of good over evil; defining "good" becomes the prerogative
of the conquerors, who write the histories. The genealogical model further distorts by confusing causes and effects: although the purpose of
each runner in a relay is to pass on the baton, it is not really the purpose
of any nation or empire to smooth the way for the still greater ones to
follow.[12] Since such a purpose can only be identified in hindsight, the
model is teleological (based on post-Darwinian notions of progress) as
well as genealogical. The greatest flaw in such an understanding of history is this assumption of inevitability, which flattens complex chains of

cause, effect, accident, circumstance, and response to simplify the radical uncertainty of the space of colonial encounter.[13]

Carter approaches the same problem as Wolfe: what to do with the presumption that nothing but those parts of what happened that made it into the history books could have happened, the ironing out of all other possibilities. He theorizes the replacement of a "spatial event" with a "historical stage": "According to our historians, it was always so. Australia was always simply a stage where history occurred, history a theatrical performance. It is not the historian who stages events, weaving them together to form a plot, but History itself. History is the playwright, coordinating facts into a coherent sequence: the historian narrating what happened is merely a copyist or amanuensis. He is a spectator like anybody else and, whatever he may think of the performance, he does not question the stage directions."[14] In this conception of history, the stage conventions function like Wolfe's teleological understanding, providing author and audience alike with shared assumptions governing the production of meaning. But the analogy, no less than the metaphoric relay criticized by Wolfe, is false: the imagined audience, spectator of the unfolding drama, does not exist. The only audience is the reader, following not a multitude of activities carried out and ongoing simultaneously, with various intents, purposes, and results, but a cause-and-effect series of events "unfolding in time alone." Carter calls this "imperial history," of which "the primary object is not to understand or to interpret: it is to legitimate ... Hence, imperial history's *defensive* appeal to the logic of cause and effect: by its nature, such a logic demonstrates the emergence of order from chaos."[15] And hence the need to appeal to a beginning, a founding moment, which marks, however tenuously, the passing of the torch in the race of history, bringing the New World into relation with the old. In this respect, imperial history works like Linnaean taxonomy, which classifies the New World according to its constituent elements, or like exploration, which locates a place in a map by means of latitude and longitude. That which is strange, unknown, possibly unknowable, starts to take on a shape recognizable to European eyes.

The defensive need to legitimate imperial history requires that one version be presented and treated as truth. Peter Hulme critiques this method (and indeed this sense of history) by reframing such discourse as ideology, invoking Foucault's opposition between ideology and Truth. Ideology, hiding behind the argument from nature, achieves legitimacy by being presented as truth: it is the deployment of power,

Foucault suggests, that creates notions of truth.[16] So the question becomes not what happened but, rather, who has the power to make a particular version count as truth, by what strategies, and to what end. Analyzing the imperial and colonial past from a postcolonial position requires a careful examination of the truth-claims of various statements, especially when those statements claim a transparent access to unquestioned concepts of truth and reality. By suggesting the constructedness of truth, Foucault's work points towards the importance of narration; in turn, narrative, especially in its guises as fiction or story, offers another possible opposition to truth.

I want to discuss two other critical formulations briefly before moving on to consider the making of history in relation to Cook's third voyage. One, obviously, is Mary Louise Pratt's reformulation of the colonial frontier as a contact zone. This shift from the frontier – a space that refers only back to Europe, European values and aspirations – to a contact zone characterized by "spatial and temporal copresence" suggests living, interactive processes and actors with their own understandings, histories, and agendas. The beauty of Pratt's conception is the way it presents New World peoples as historical agents occupying not a shadowy past but the very moment of contact, mutual participants whose actions are responses to present circumstances as much as they are phenomena determined by history and tradition.[17] If the genealogical or teleological model is marked by a retrospective sense of inevitability and the erasure of other possible outcomes, the notion of the contact zone assumes that no outcome of European contact with the New World was inherently inevitable. Further, it suggests that Europeans both in the New World and at home were also affected by transculturation. The period of contact can no longer be seen as a stop on the road to today, a cause leading to an effect, but is opened up, understood as full of exciting possibilities that might have led to many different todays.

The title of a collection of essays by New Zealand historian Greg Dening, *Performances,* offers another model for the making of history. The notion of performance simultaneously implies achievement, exhibition (with both positive and negative connotations), and execution or fulfillment, as of an obligation. The nature of the achievement is judged by the public exhibition. The presentation of history in essay or book, a seemingly self-contained public offering, is actually based, like a concert or painting, on much private and painstaking labour. The writing of history should then be seen as crafted, executed with "performance consciousness," an awareness of self as well as the undertaking. "We history-makers must know ourselves. We must have an ethnographic sense of our cultural persons. The past is emptied of almost all its meaning by the selective texts that survive it. We realise that the meanings in the text are mere shadows the more we experience the fullness of the meanings in our ordinary living."[18] Far from being a simple record of facts from past times, history is understood and performed through our engagement with those times and with our own present. Dening's approach suggests that this moment, today, is also a contact zone. "History is not the past: it is a consciousness of the past used for present purposes."[19] The past is also something we read – through those "selective texts that survive it" – which, as Hulme notes, will always deliver the same message, word for word.[20] The documents themselves say only what they say: changed or alternative meanings lie in the manner of reading, when historical documents are used as texts rather than as transcripts of what happened.

This is precisely my interest in exploring the texts and textual history of Cook's month at Nootka Sound. The facts are apparently simple enough: James Cook, captain of HMS *Resolution* and commander of three voyages of Pacific exploration, spent a month at Nootka Sound on the west coast of Vancouver Island. At that time he recorded his impressions and observations of the place and its inhabitants in his journal, which was edited, published, and circulated rapidly and widely through Europe. The information it offered, although in some instances altered quite radically by the editor, was taken as factual in 1784, therefore influencing later voyages to the Northwest Coast and impressions of its inhabitants. I am not a historian; I am using this happening to talk about something else, aiming essentially to suggest another consciousness of this past. A kind of Boys' Own adventure-story version of Cook as imperial culture-hero long dominated discussion of his voyages; the texts of those voyages, however, were produced under sufficiently problematic circumstances to open them up to question, interrogation, and criticism. My sources are "new" only in the sense that their juxtaposition – Beaglehole's Cook versus Douglas's Cook – reveals a gap, a discrepancy, which in turn reveals another possibility.

And yet putting new questions to the old texts reveals new answers. Douglas's edition of Cook's journal was a composite text, and a broader variety of opinions, impressions, and beliefs is actually reflected in those pages from 1784 than Douglas gives the reader to understand. The voice of a cabin-boy, or any other crewman, is still missing in an official and officer-ly text, yet more stories than Cook's are presented, even if all are blended into one by the seamless ghostwriting. Perhaps Beaglehole's and Douglas's editions together create a kind of metatext since, in Beaglehole, the footnotes provide the attributions, revealing when Douglas has borrowed from or plagiarized Bayly, Samwell, Clerke, or Anderson. There is more than one version of reality coming from the ship: the views of Britons and Europeans are not homogenous. That's before taking into account that Cook and his men met an unfamiliar culture across the beach at Nootka Sound. Dening's metaphor of islands and beaches (something like Pratt's contact zone or Webber's landing paintings) suggests the complexities of such moments of contact: islands and beaches offers "a natural metaphor for the oceanic world of the Pacific where islands are everywhere and beaches must be crossed to enter or leave them, to make them or change them. But the islands and beaches I speak of are less physical than cultural. They are the islands men and women make by the reality they attribute to their categories, their roles, their institutions, and the beaches they put around them with their definitions of 'we' and 'they.' As we shall see, the remaking of those sorts of islands and the crossing of those sorts of beaches can be cruelly painful."[21]

"The remaking of those sorts of islands and the crossing of those sorts of beaches can be cruelly painful" – and was, as Cook's death at Hawaii less than a year after the sojourn at Nootka Sound proves. The text, seemingly, is upset as a result: the Captain's hand stops moving across the page of his logbook or journal. But in fact it seems to have stopped moving some time earlier. Cook's own logbook ended on 17 January 1779 (the day the ships first arrived at Kealekekua Bay on the south coast of Hawaii); he died on 14 February, so the editor's task of splicing together the crucial moments leading up to Cook's death necessarily includes reconstructing the month or so beforehand. The same process of creating history through the scholarly apparatus of the text that I discussed in Chapter 4 is at work in the official account of Cook's death. Once again, Beaglehole's edition participates in this construction: in a footnote, Beaglehole remarks that "King rewrote his own account [of Cook's death] very carefully for publication."[22] In fact, O.H.K. Spate notes that this phrasing is suspiciously neutral since it hides the fact of "King's suppression of the explicit statement by the only commissioned officer ashore with Cook, that Cook himself ordered the Marines to

open fire." In addition, Spate argues, King's account has been constructed to present the death of Cook in the most favourable light possible through "subtle changes in wording and a discreet use of *suppressio
veri* and *suggestio falsi*."[23]

At issue is the question of whether or not Cook gave the order to fire
on the Hawaiians gathered on the beach, anxious to protect their chief –
whether Cook was the aggressor, bringing the full weight of European
weaponry against Pacific peoples armed with rocks and spears, or the
innocent victim of Native treachery, stabbed in the back by a villain.
Also at issue is the behaviour of officers and gentlemen in a conflict with
such momentous results. King's account of the death of Cook in the
official edition needed to protect the careers of the living survivors of
the third voyage as well as the posthumous reputation of Captain Cook.
King therefore, in order to support the image of Cook as a benevolent
gentleman, eliminated Phillips's claim that Cook himself ordered the
marines to fire. He tried to present the officers' behaviour in the best
possible light by finding ways to explain why they rowed back to the
ship rather than moving ashore to help Cook. William Bligh, who sailed
with Cook as master of the *Resolution* on the third voyage, offers a
much different reading, writing such comments as "The Marines fire[d]
& ran which occasioned al[l] that followed for had the[y] fixed their
bayonets & not have run, so frighte[ned] as they were, they migh[t]
have drove all before t[hem]" in the margins of his copy of Douglas's
edition.[24] At stake is the "martyrdom" of Cook and the "heroism" of
British officers.

The versions of Cook's death created by his subordinates present
largely the same image as does King: Cook is the innocent victim of
murderous savages. For example, both John Rickman's *Journal of Captain Cook's Last Voyage to the Pacific Ocean* (1781) and David
Samwell's *Narrative of the Death of Captain Cook* (1786) construct
Cook as an imperial culture-hero. Readers opening the anonymous edition by Rickman (second lieutenant on the *Discovery)* are faced with an
engraved "Representation of the Murder of Capt Cook at O-Why-Ee"
as the frontispiece. The title page promises that the text is "Faithfully
Narrated from the Original MS," although the Advertisement immediately following, which claims that "[t]he Editor of this Journal does not
make himself answerable for all the facts that are related in it," might
suggest to the sceptical reader that the truth-claim is a little suspect.
Indeed, the text, shifting between an unspecified "we" and "they,"
reads more like a novel than like a scientific voyage. The episodic plot

(reminiscent, perhaps, of Defoe's *Moll Flanders* [1722] or *Robinson Crusoe* [1719] in its description of distant shores) prepares the reader for the apostrophe on the event of Cook's death: "Reader, if thou hast any feeling for thy country in the loss of so great, so illustrious a navigator, or any tenderness for those whom he has left to lament his fate, thou wilt drop with me a tear at this melancholy relation; especially when thou reflecst, that he, who had braved dangers, and had looked death in the face in a thousand forms, should at last be cut off by the hands of a cowardly savage, who, dreading the impetuosity of his rage, came behind him, and, ruffian-like, stabbed him in the back."[25] Such fulsome prose supports Beaglehole's claim that Rickman's *Voyage* "is a fanciful and ridiculously exaggerated production, done exclusively for the market."[26] Only two years after Cook's death, and before Cook's own journal was published, the reading public was only too ready to see Cook as an imperial hero whose gifts to knowledge and civilization were brutally and tragically cut short.

Samwell's *Narrative of the Death of Captain Cook* may be less obsequious, but the sentiments it portrays are not dramatically different from Rickman's. Samwell characterizes Cook as an exemplar of "kindness and humanity," citing as evidence the Natives who "shewed the customary marks of respect, by prostrating themselves before him."[27] The stated purpose of Samwell's offering is to correct public opinion, which wrongly believes that Cook's rash behaviour at Hawaii caused his death: "He is sanguine enough to believe, that it will serve to remove a supposition, in this single instance, injurious to the memory of Captain Cook, who was no less distinguished for his caution and prudence, than for his eminent abilities and undaunted resolution."[28] Cook's behaviour in the chain of events leading up to his death exhibits his uncommon leadership abilities in Samwell's account. Far from acting impetuously, out of blind emotion, Cook demonstrates yet again his cool-headedness, his respect and concern for the people under his care. Samwell presents a Cook who evidently thinks of the Hawaiians, as well as his own crew, as children who look up to him as to a father. When the Hawaiians begin throwing rocks, he is unwilling to shoot; instead, he "expostulate[s] strongly with the most forward of the crowd, upon their turbulent behaviour ... his care was then only to act on the defensive, and to secure a safe embarkation for his small party"; finally, "in his own defense," he is forced to shoot.[29] The reader must conclude that the savagery of the Hawaiians first drove a moderate man past the limits of his tolerance, then took his life. Samwell ends this

somewhat sanitized account of Cook's death by arguing that the third
voyage did not bring venereal disease to Hawaii: "on the contrary," he
concludes, "there is every reason to believe, that they were afflicted
with it before we discovered those islands."[30] Perhaps he intends at this
point to answer another public misconception regarding the time and
circumstances of Cook's death, merely clearing the record; perhaps he
intends to imply a connection between disease, degeneracy, and savagery in Hawaii and Cook's death.

   Not just the accounts of Cook's death but also the manner of reading
them has been the focus of much scholarly debate in recent years, most
prominently between anthropologists Marshall Sahlins and Gananath
Obeyesekere over how Cook was viewed by Hawaiians. The debate is
instructive in many ways, revealing a variety of interpretations of the
same texts recounting incidents long treated as historical fact. The
debate is characterized by a certain amount of ad hominem argument.
Obeyesekere called Sahlins an agent of cultural imperialism; Sahlins
returned fire with a book ridiculing Obeyesekere and "native" irratio-
nality; Obeyeskere's response to Sahlins's response was called "On
De-Sahlinization."[31] Essentially, each man attacks the premises of the
other's argument. Sahlins, a Pacific historian and ethnographer of international prominence, considered how the arrival of Europeans could be
understood by and incorporated into Hawaiian culture; he discussed
Cook's death as a case study of the workings of cultural processes and
structuralist theory. Obeyesekere saw Sahlins's reading of Cook as a
Lono-figure as an example of another kind of cultural process at work,
that of the European assumption of superiority over Native peoples. To
consider the meaning of Cook's death, and the uses to which it has been
put, it is necessary to look more closely at Sahlins's and Obeyesekere's
arguments.

   Sahlins suggested that "the incidents of Cook's life and death at
Hawaii were in many respects historical metaphors of a mythical reality." Hawaiians, he argued, could see Cook's time at Kealekekua Bay
according to one of their culture's central mythic structures,

> the annual ritual alternation of the gods Lono and Ku. The
> transition from mackeral to bonito fishing marks the definitive
> end of ceremonies celebrating the sojourn in the Islands of the
> peaceable and productive god Lono. Come with the winter rains
> to renew the fertility of nature and the gardens of the people,
> Lono's advent is the occasion of an elaborate and prolonged rite

of four lunar months called the Makahiki (Year). During this time the normal Ku ceremonies, including human sacrifice, are suspended. At the end of the Makahiki, however, Lono returns to the invisible land (Kahiki – or to the sky, which is the same) whence he had come. Ku, together with his earthly representative, the ruling chief, now regains the ascendancy. The historic significance of all this is that Captain Cook was by Hawaiian conceptions a form of Lono; whereas the chief with whom he dealt and who would ritually claim his death, Kalaniopuu – he was Ku.[32]

The arrival and departure of Cook's ships coincided with that of Lono; the ships' voyage around the Island took a little longer but followed the same direction as the progression of Lono taking possession of the land; surely the ships' sails must have resembled the image of Lono, a "crosspiece ensign, with white tapa cloth hanging from the horizontal bar."[33] Cook was greeted, honoured, and fêted in ceremonies celebrating Lono; he was called Lono (Erono or Orono) throughout the ships' stay at Kealekekua.[34] A further coincidence highlights the similarity between Cook's visit and Lono's time. As the Makahiki ended (probably 1 February 1779), the return of Ku and, with him, human sacrifice was played out with the death of a seaman on the *Resolution*, who was buried in a Hawaiian temple at the chiefs' request.[35] The *Resolution* and *Discovery* left on 4 February 1779.

As even this brief summary indicates, Sahlins develops "the [remarkable] correlation between the ritual movements of the Makahiki image Lono and the historical movements of Captain Cook in 1778–79" in considerable and convincing detail to suggest a way of reading the death of Captain Cook as it might have looked to Hawaiians in 1779.[36] Cook arrived when Lono was scheduled to arrive; he sailed around the island near the same time and in the same direction as Lono travelled to mark his possession of the land; at the time of Ku's return, the time of human sacrifice, a seaman died and his body was buried in a Hawaiian temple with Hawaiian as well as Christian rites; and Cook left when Lono was scheduled to leave, promising to come back the following year. From this account, it seems clear that Cook's arrival could have been seen by Hawaiians as conforming to this cultural and ritual system; they could have read Cook according to the narrative of Lono.

But then Cook broke with the mythic structure. A week later the ships returned to Kealekekua Bay, where they had previously been shown such hospitality, to make repairs to the *Resolution*'s damaged foremast. But this return on 11 February 1779 was well in advance of Lono's return. It was an event "out of season."[37] The very warmth and extent of that earlier hospitality was in a sense a historical accident; Cook was, to put it simply, in the right place at the right time. The Makahiki was a time of renewal and plenty; the violence characteristic of Ku was prohibited, and Cook had benefitted by corresponding to the Lono narrative. But he returned in the time of Ku, a god of violence and human sacrifice. The Hawaiians' attitude seemed inexplicably changed to the men on the *Resolution* and *Discovery*: no longer friendly and eager to please, they were truculent, surly, and thieving. When one of the ship's cutters was stolen, Cook responded in his regular fashion to such an event, attempting to take Kalaniopuu hostage against its return. When a crowd of Hawaiians tried to rescue their chief, he ordered the marines to open fire; the Hawaiians attacked, and he was killed. Cook was no longer a peaceful god in a peaceful season but, rather, a violent man in a violent season. He lost his life as a result.

Obeyesekere attacked Sahlins's portrayal of Cook as a personification of the god Lono to the Hawaiians as yet another example of the European assumption of superiority over Native cultures, manifested in the tendency to see Europeans as gods in the New World. Obeyesekere suggests instead that Cook was invested with the power and title of a chief and, hence, was called Lono for reasons related to the islands' political situation and Kalaniopuu's desire to exploit Cook's power for his own political ends. The return of Cook's ships, by the same token, was not perceived as an event out of season by the Hawaiians but, rather, as an economic and nutritional threat: the British had already depleted Hawaiian food sources. Cook's violent behaviour escalated this tension. When he tried to kidnap Kalaniopuu, the Hawaiians' fear for their chief – and the sailors' fears for their Captain and their own lives – led to Cook's death. It was *after*, not before, his death that Cook was deified, on the grounds that, as Obeyeskere argues, the post-mortem deification of a high chief was a Hawaiian custom. Accordingly, he uses "the term *deification* for the Hawaiian custom of converting dead chiefs into gods and *apotheosis* for the European myth of the redoubtable white man as a god to natives."[38]

Obeyesekere accounts for the European belief that Cook appeared as the god Lono to the Hawaiians by analyzing the language of Douglas's 1784 edition of the third voyage, in which King's word for the attitude of Hawaiians towards Cook (and his remains) is "adoration."[39] He sees in this language of adoration and religious veneration a projection onto the Hawaiians of the officers' own feelings towards Cook. The ordinary seamen commonly assumed that Natives thought of Europeans in general and Cook in particular as gods or immortals. This belief conformed to popular shipboard as well as exploration literature traditions. At the same time, a European hagiography of Cook proceeded according to European mores and values: "the intellectual mythologization of Cook as the humane embodiment of the Enlightenment."[40] In effect, Cook was mythologized as a hero for the New World order because of this notion of his humanity.[41] Against the evidence of Cook's frequent and irrational violence on the third voyage (more severe and frequent disciplining of his own crew[42] as well as increasingly violent behaviour towards Native peoples, like that which led to his own death) stands the myth of the humane explorer.

Whether seen as a god by Hawaiians or Europeans, Cook can be read according to pre-existing narratives signalled by the phrase "Cook appeared to the Hawaiians as a version of their god Lono." Although this phrase seems to signal a similar concern in each work, in fact the concerns it signals are entirely different. Sahlins's and Obeyesekere's arguments, although set in opposition around the meaning of the phrase, explore entirely different subjects: the use to which the arrival of Europeans could be put for Hawaiian culture in Sahlins's case, and the use to which the apotheosis of Cook could be put for European imperial culture in Obeyesekere's case. Each writer deals with what Dening calls "a consciousness of the past used for present purposes," but with a different purpose in the present. At stake is the meaning of the word "god," which seems to me insufficiently distinguished by the debate: Obeyesekere treats the word as if it means one thing in Sahlins's account when in fact it does not. "Of course the Hawaiians did not call the Euro-American strangers 'gods'. They called them *akua*," writes Dening. "That is the problem of cross-cultural history. Both sides experience one another in translation."[43] And *akua* in Hawaiian does not mean the same thing as do "god" or "God" in English. Sahlins's discussion of Cook-as-Lono in fact has nothing whatsoever to do with European assumptions about Native peoples; he explores the meaning of Cook's arrival for Hawaiian society. But even though Obeyesekere has essentially missed Sahlins's point about the structures used by Hawaiian society to incorporate the arrival of strangers, he raises another point which is also significant: for centuries Europeans did in fact read their differences from non-European societies as superiority. The assumption by Europeans that they appeared as gods to Native peoples is an undoubtable feature of the European encounter with the New World.[44] Readers of Douglas's edition of Cook's third voyage[45] would not have wondered whether the "adoration" paid to Cook was different in purpose from the veneration they themselves saw as due the Christian God; indeed, it was in the presumed Native inability to distinguish between mortal men and one immortal deity that Europeans found the difference between civilization and savagery, between religion and paganism. Obeyesekere's argument about the apotheosis of Captain Cook – the use to which myths of Cook were put for British imperialism – and the structures used by European society to incorporate understandings of Native peoples is a useful addition to Cook studies. Leaving aside the ad hominem attacks, both Sahlins and Obeyesekere have something to tell us about the ways that versions of the past are used to construct the present.[46]

In the mid–1950s "J.C. Beaglehole said he was going to write the life of Cook: the preliminary step – and how lightly that was once viewed – would be a new and scholarly edition of the Journals. Preliminary, perhaps; in the event this called for twenty years' work."[47] The meticulous research and dedication to the subject demonstrated by *The Life of Captain James Cook* formally mirrors the man presented within the text. Beaglehole scrupulously foregrounds his evidence and sources, even the absence of sources, in his portrayal of Cook as a complex man in a complex era. Beaglehole's Cook is both attentive to detail, a careful surveyor, and passionately caught up in the grand project of exploration; both humane and despotic in his treatment of his crews as well as Native peoples; both ordinary, following the common but illegal practice of listing his young sons on the *Endeavour*'s crew, and extraordinary, rising from obscurity to international prominence through industry, merit, and incredible luck. In its ambition to achieve completeness and in the clear sense of the writer's admiration for its subject – an admiration readers are expected to share – Beaglehole's *Life of Cook* reminds the reader of another famous eighteenth-century life, Boswell's of Johnson.

This is the Cook to whom memorials are constructed. At Nootka Sound, for example, there is a cairn marking Cook's visit; in New Zealand, the use of Cook imagery in the currency constitutes a kind of ancestor worship. One side of the fifty-cent piece depicts the *Endeavour*, and

Nathaniel Dance's 1776 portrait of Cook provides the watermark on the bills. The contrast between memorial cairns in isolated, hard-to-reach places and the coins and bills people handle every day suggests a distinction between versions of Cook in the North and South Pacific, or perhaps between the British Commonwealth in general and Canada in particular. This distinction is borne out by two biographies that aim to summarize the man and his life succinctly: the entry in the *Dictionary of National Biography* (1917) and the entry by Glyndwr Williams in the *Dictionary of Canadian Biography* (1979). Taken together, they reveal some of the constructions that have been made of Cook for purposes having little or nothing to do with the man himself.

These two portrayals agree about the details of his early life, but when Cook arrives in North America they diverge markedly: the *Dictionary of National Biography* briefly sketches this time in his life, moving on fairly quickly to the first South Pacific voyage for which his early career apparently prepared him (the teleological model at work), while the *Dictionary of Canadian Biography* devotes rather more attention to these years. Unlike the *Dictionary of National Biography*, Williams's account does not portray Cook's years charting Gaspé bay and harbour, the St Lawrence, and the coast of Newfoundland merely as preliminary training for his more significant South Pacific ventures; rather, they mark crucial episodes in maritime and imperial history and indicate Cook's character: "the sight of unknown shores, crudely represented on existing maps and yet playing vital parts in the strategy and diplomacy of the war, seem to have stimulated Cook in a way which service in home waters might not have."[48] Williams presents a Cook, painstaking and methodical in his survey work, who nonetheless is mindful of "the political direction behind his work."[49]

Although it may well be partly due to the sixty-year gap between the *Dictionary of National Biography* and the *Dictionary of Canadian Biography*, the difference in prose style reveals different constructions of Cook in the two accounts. Williams tends to use an active voice, while much of the *Dictionary of National Biography* entry is couched in the passive: for example, "six months were spent on the coast of New Zealand, which was for the first time sailed round, examined, and charted with some approach to accuracy."[50] The sentence structures beg the question: by whom? Cook's absence as the agent in his own life history in the *Dictionary of National Biography* culminates in the representation of his death at Hawaii: "As his back was turned a native stunned him by a blow on the head; he sank on his knees, and another stabbed him with a dagger. He fell into the water, where he was held down by the seething crowd; but having struggled to land, was again beaten over the head with clubs and stabbed repeatedly, the islanders 'snatching the daggers out of each other's hands to have the horrid satisfaction of piercing the fallen victim of their barbarous rage.'"[51] Like Julius Caesar, Cook as victim – whose "truest and best memorial is the map of the Pacific"[52] – symbolizes "man's inhumanity to man," with a twist: Cook stands for man and the Hawaiians stand for inhumanity. The imperial mission to civilize the savages is thus constructed by this strangely ahistoric version of Cook not as the exercise of self-interest but as self-sacrifice.

The *Dictionary of Canadian Biography* presents a Cook who is a little less high-minded, a little more implicated in the world around him. It suggests that he "was tempted to undertake [the third voyage] because of recent discoveries, which had renewed optimism that a navigable [northwest] passage might be found and the £20,000 award offered by an act of parliament in 1775."[53] During his time at Nootka Sound (which the *Dictionary of National Biography* does not mention), Cook speculates about previous contact between Europeans and Natives and the practicability of a fur trade between England and Nootka Sound. Essentially, this construction of Cook is shaped by different national and cultural considerations from the construction in the *Dictionary of National Biography* and, accordingly, locates him in a local and specific historical framework that explores his role as an active agent "in the shaping of modern Canada."[54]

But Canadians are not so far removed from this version of Cook as culture-hero as two intervening centuries and two different hemispheres might suggest: history textbooks of the twentieth century demonstrate that Cook has a place as a Canadian cultural icon.

Spanish explorers were the first to tell of a visit to British Columbia, but its history really begins with the coming, in 1778, of James Cook to Nootka Sound, on the west coast of Vancouver Island. This great navigator came to discover, if possible, a north-west passage between the Pacific and Atlantic Oceans. Not succeeding in his first attempt, he went to spend the winter in the Sandwich Islands, and there he was murdered by the natives. His ships, however, returned to England and brought glowing accounts of the rich furs to be found on the north-west coast of America. Soon many fur-trading ships, chiefly British and

American, sought the coast, and named some of its islands and many of its bays and straights. (1906)[55]

In 1776 an expedition left England under the command of Captain James Cook, one of the most illustrious of British seamen, for the discovery of a passage from the northern Pacific to the Atlantic. Cook reached Nootka Sound in March, 1778, and opened a very valuable trade in furs and skins with the natives. He then continued northward past Prince of Wales Island to the strait separating the two continents, which he named Bering Strait, but, because of the ice, he was unable to make his way through the Arctic. Cook's expedition gave Britain a claim to the north-west coast of America by right of discovery and likewise revealed the possibility of developing a very lucrative fur trade. (1927)[56]

On the return journey, the English ships stopped at Canton, China. Here the overjoyed sailors found that the sea-otter skins purchased from the Indians at Nootka brought a very high price from the Chinese ... The news spread, and a rich fur trade began which lasted for about forty years. Sailors visited every Indian village they could find, looking for furs. As a result, the northwest coast was thoroughly explored. Once more the fur trade has led the way! (1949)[57]

Although Captain Cook failed to discover the North-West Passage, he made it possible for England to keep the Canadian West from falling into the hands of other countries. Not long after Cook's visit to our shores, some of his sailors returned to start a rich trade in furs. By coming to British Columbia to live and trade, these men helped to hold this part of Canada for England. (1954)[58]

The man who is given credit for being the first European to visit these waters is not Juan de Fuca but Captain James Cook ... He was the first European that the natives of the Northwest Coast saw. He was also the first European known to have landed on the west coast of what is now Canada. (1980)[59]

These quotations generally indicate the importance of the adjective "British" in the province named "British Columbia": the early ones in particular indicate the significance of Cook's voyages to British imperialism and a sense of pride in Canada's place in the empire, or Commonwealth, including the shared history of "discovery" by Cook.[60] These passages also hint at a larger theme in Canadian history, of which this episode at Nootka Sound is but a brief moment: the fur trade, understood as the organizing principle of Canadian history,[61] and its record in textbooks produced for use in public schools. In hindsight, it seems that nothing could more clearly represent a colonial legacy – a legacy of economic, political, cultural, and intellectual domination – than these accounts stating that the sole importance of land and people lay in producing resources for the imperial centre. Such an understanding of Canadian history also makes sense only in hindsight; the importance of the lives of sailors on Cook's ships, if not of Cook himself, amounts only to their having "helped to hold this part of Canada [before there was a Canada] for England," according to the retrospective teleology. The language of the most recent of these accounts (1980) seems to have changed: Cook is described as "the man who is given credit for being *the first European to visit* these waters" rather than the man who *discovered* them, but this shift in terminology does not really change the nature of the presentation. Cook was still "first" to visit Nootka Sound, and his importance to the Growth of the Nation is duly noted.

These examples construct Cook as a cultural icon officially sanctioned by Canadian boards of education and instilled into young Canadian minds. Chosen from Canadian history textbooks more or less at random, they suggest how histories of British Columbia have used Cook and the "founding moment" to imagine this place "hung precariously at the edge of Britain's literal and symbolic empire."[62] This phenomenon is not exclusive to schoolbook histories of British Columbia. Alexander Begg's 1894 *History of British Columbia* devotes the first chapter to Cook, relying heavily on Douglas's edition (and quoting Douglas's supposition that the human hands offered as trade articles indicated cannibalism at Nootka Sound). In his 1928 history, *British Columbia: The Making of a Province*, F.W. Howay opens a discussion of the maritime fur trade with an overview of Cook's third voyage and its role in stimulating further exploration of the coast throughout the last half of the 1780s. Both of these accounts connect Cook's visit to Nootka Sound and the Northwest Coast to the larger context of his Pacific voyages, especially his death in Hawaii, to connect British Columbia to imperial centres of power. They assume that "British Columbia's history began in 1778 when Captain Cook and his crew became the first white men to set foot upon her territory."[63] Margaret Ormsby's *British Columbia: A History* (1958, rev. 1971), by contrast, locates British Columbia's beginnings in the complex interplay of British and Spanish competition over rights to trade on the Northwest Coast and to the coast itself.

The 1990s saw the publication of several histories that changed the colonialist perspective on the province's origins and Cook's month at Nootka Sound as a founding moment. These works can be grouped into two basic categories: histories of British Columbia and histories of Canada from First Nations perspectives. In the first category are Jean Barman's *The West beyond the West: A History of British Columbia* (1991, rev. 1996), George Woodcock's *British Columbia: A History of the Province* (1990), and George Bowering's *Bowering's BC: A Swashbuckling History* (1996). The second category also produced three books in the 1990s, histories that treat First Nations as central rather than as peripheral to narratives of the Canadian nation: Arthur Ray's *I Have Lived Here since the World Began* (1996), Olive Dickason's *Canada's First Nations: A History of Founding Peoples from Earliest Times* (1997), and J.R. Miller's *Skyscrapers Hide the Heavens: A History of Indian-White Relations in Canada* (1991, rev. 2000). This is a change in Canadian historiography that seems to me at least as significant as the shift from a national history organized around Confederation, the fur trade, and the building of the Canadian Pacific Railway to a social history organized around the experience of workers, women, and ethnic groups.

Compare, for example, the way that earlier histories present Cook's arrival at Nootka Sound as the beginning of British Columbia's history with George Woodcock's depiction, in which Cook does not appear until the third chapter. Woodcock begins with a discussion of the geographical and political forces that created a place called British Columbia and made it a province of Canada and only then goes on to consider the human experiences that predate the written record. His first chapter considers the archaeological evidence of early Aboriginal cultures; his second looks at Native societies at the time of first contact with Europeans. Although Woodcock also calls attention to the Native canoes coming to greet Cook's ships as they arrived at Nootka Sound on the third voyage, his version has a sense of ceremony that emphasizes the meeting of cultures: "there is still a special drama about the moment of first contact, the day when a Haida or a Nootka chief danced before a Spanish or English captain, scattering the eagle down of welcome over the water and taking his place – the first of his kind – in the actual historical record."[64] As creator and editor of the academic journal *Canadian Literature* (also the first of its kind), Woodcock was long involved in mapping the contours of Canada's cultural terrain. In his history of British Columbia he offers a founding moment envisioned not as a static tableau (the *Resolution* and *Discovery* sail up to a coast whose inhabitants are waiting to be "discovered") but as a process of mutual discovery for Europeans and Natives who meet and read each other through their respective cultural narratives. Here the BC coast and its inhabitants enter not history but the "historical record."

Like Woodcock's, Jean Barman's history connects Cook's arrival to the forces pushing European nations progressively further from home: "The need for contact with Europeans did not emanate from British Columbia's indigenous population, but came rather from the seemingly insatiable demands of the whites. Since the late fifteenth century the nations of Europe have been moving ever further afield in search of lands to exploit economically."[65] Cook is not the first European to appear on its shores but, rather, is located within a complex matrix of Spanish, Portuguese, French, English, and Russian attempts to acquire control of the non-European world's resources. Barman dispenses with the image of the moment of encounter entirely; instead, her account emphasizes that European activity in the maritime fur trade was always part of a larger goal determined in imperial centres far from the coast. Barman's title, marking British Columbia as "the west beyond the west," suggests the ways in which this province has been inscribed within historical discourse as distant in imaginative as well as geographic terms. From the perspective of the imperial centre, British Columbia is a kind of "nowhereland"[66] that can be understood only in relation to other geographies. Those maps of Cook's Pacific voyages thus connect British Columbia, through the dotted line tracing the round-trip from Britain through the South Pacific to the Northwest Coast, to the rest of the known world.

Indicative of the changed perspective of the 1990s histories of British Columbia, *Bowering's BC* does not treat Cook's arrival as the moment when the province's history begins. What my many quotations from earlier histories of British Columbia present as a founding moment, the encounter of Cook's ships and Native canoes, does not really even appear in *Bowering's BC*. The closest Bowering gets to such a description is this:

Cook's ships, beaten around by the Pacific Ocean, sailed right on by the Strait of Juan de Fuca, and fetched up at Nootka, near the end of March, 1778. Actually, no one there called the place Nootka. Pérez had not called it Nootka. But Captain Cook, who had been the first European commander to spend months talking to Polynesians, liked to use native names for places. He asked the people what they called their place. Unfortunately, they thought he was asking for directions and so told him to sail *around* the island, using the word *notka*.

The first people he saw were in three canoes. In one of the canoes stood a man covered in feathers and paint. This creature was shouting something and throwing white downy feathers toward the English ships. His companions were throwing some kind of red powder. The important-looking man was shaking something, which, when they got close enough to hear, turned out to be a rattle. Nowadays we think that this personnage was Maquinna, which is a name worn by the most important man in the most important clan of the Nootka people. James Cook, in his elegant journals, does not mention the names of any Native people.[67]

Clearly, this does not have at all the status of a founding moment: Cook's ships, "beaten around by the Pacific Ocean," missing Juan de Fuca Strait, and "fetch[ing] up at Nootka," arrive not by destiny but by chance.[68] Like the histories by Barman and Woodcock, *Bowering's BC* locates Cook's arrival within the context of eighteenth-century European exploration on the Northwest Coast and a network of national and local agendas.[69] Nothing less like the teleological model of history criticized by Wolfe than *Bowering's BC* could be imagined. Bowering writes a postmodern history of the province, one that relies on juxtaposition, irony, and narrative. But Bowering's use of historical narrative is idiosyncratic (as his title implies); using archaeology as the organizing principle, he reminds readers constantly that what we call history is full of holes and that these holes are not simply gaps in knowledge to be filled in but, rather, are meaningful in their own right, something essential to the reading of history. The example of Bowering's own education demonstrates that one such gap lies in the province's school system, where he was taught to write essays about the causes of the First World War but not that Discovery Street in Vancouver is named for the ship in which the explorer of that name first arrived in this part of the world.

Cook is relatively unimportant in the histories by Woodcock, Barman, and Bowering; the same is true of Olive Dickason's *Canada's First*

Nations, where he appears as a minor figure in the fur trade, mentioned briefly twice in a chapter on westward and northward expansion and once in a footnote referring to his experience in the South Pacific.[70] In Miller's *Skyscrapers Hide the Heavens*, Cook is not mentioned in the index or in the chapter on "Contact, Commerce, and Christianity on the Pacific," except in the caption to a reproduction of Webber's painting of the *Resolution* and *Discovery* at Nootka Sound.[71] In Arthur Ray's *I Have Lived Here since the World Began*, Cook is a symbol of historic processes, part of the beginnings of a European presence on the Northwest Coast. Perhaps this quotation from a Native fisher at Yuquot, Ray Williams, will indicate the shift in perspective this kind of history demonstrates:

> Captain Cook, he was out there lost in the fog when Maquinna's great-grandfather took a bunch of warriors and guided his ship in. The people then helped nurse the crew back to health. They were in poor shape. They stayed across in Resolution Cove for over a month, repairing their ship. During that time, Captain Cook and his crew used to go to Yuquot [Friendly Cove], treat the ladies in a real mean way, and raid whatever they could get their hands on: smokehouses and sun-dried fish. Then they left for Hawaii or somewhere.[72]

The arrival of Cook's ships can no longer to be viewed according to the old imperial perspectives as a founding moment.

Clearly, fictions of Cook have a history in Canada, an official history in the service of nation-building that changes over time, as the shifts in representations of Cook over the twentieth century demonstrate. His influence extends beyond colonialist versions of Canadian history into popular culture. In Vancouver, the city bearing the name of a man who first came to this part of the world as a young officer under Cook and who later returned as Captain of the *Discovery* and a voyage of exploration in his own right, there are signs and traces of the hero of British imperialism. These range from the obvious – Cook Street, Captain Cook Travel – to the more postmodern. There used to be a restaurant called the Captain Cook on East Broadway: the theme was carried out in the neon street sign displaying the *Endeavour* in full sail as well as in bad reproductions of Dance's portrait and numerous tableaux of events from Cook's voyages, almost exclusively in the South Pacific. The restaurant, then open twenty-four hours with patrol cars in the parking lot, changed hands in the early 1990s and became a sushi bar. It took the new owners a few years to take down the neon sign illuminating Cook's name. Perhaps the global movement of capital, products, and culture implied in this change is no less emblematic of Cook's legacy than is the more obvious referent in the street.

Strangely enough, the more obvious markers of Cook's presence are hard to find, not only in BC but throughout the world. A cairn was erected at Nootka Sound in 1924, and although it was unveiled with considerable ceremony, the area's isolation and inaccessibility by road mean that few British Columbians or visitors will ever see it, or even know it exists.[73] In similar fashion, the important sites of Cook's life – his childhood home, the house on Mile End Road in London where Cook (or at least his wife and children) lived, the ships in which he sailed, the spot on the Hawaiian beach where he was killed – are either difficult to locate or exist only as replicas. It is possible for the would-be Cook pilgrim to visit a "Cook's Cottage," but it is to be found in Melbourne, Australia, and not in the Yorkshire village of Great Ayton.[74] Martin Dugard's biography is organized around such a pilgrimage: he begins in Newport, Rhode Island, where the *Endeavour* and *Resolution* are supposed to be – at the bottom of the harbour. In London, he finds that "What's left of Cook's home stands next to a unisex fashion store, whose block-lettered, red-and-white neon sign stands in stark contrast to the polished marble plaque adorning the single remaining brick wall of Cook's home, approximately where the front door once stood." He ends his pilgrimage in Hawaii, where he tours a replica of the *Endeavour* and tries to find the spot on the beach where Cook died. "I spy a plaque buried beneath the waterline and climb over a fallen tree for a closer look, for I haven't seen mention of this in any guidebooks. 'Near this spot,' it reads simply, 'Captain James Cook Met His Death February 14th, 1779.' The incoming tides and slick algae have pushed the plaque from its mount. I heave it square, preserving it from the sea a few days more."[75]

The pilgrimage implies a rather worshipful approach that is disappointed by the uneasy impermanence of the plaques or even campy replicas marking Cook's passage through history. Such worshipful approaches are no longer the only possibilities when discussing the man and his influence on European and New World histories. Cultural epistemologies are actively constructed as choices, not passively received as inevitable, as Chris Healy argues in an article on Aboriginal history; public culture is decided by those traditions that are eliminated as well as by those that are maintained. Healy questions "what happens to the European history of Captain Cook if we read Aboriginal histories of Captain Cook."[76] The point is not to compare different versions in order to assess their accuracy or consistency but, rather, to change and expand the notion of history. In one Aboriginal version, "Cook is an archetype, he is the embodiment of structural principles that provide the Yarralin with a means of elaborating the long-term relations of force and constituting this historical process as the problem."[77] With similar intent, Stephen Nothling's *Lets Have a Drink and Celebrate* (1986) (see Figure 7) transforms the Cook who is presented in European texts as a bringer of civilization and such gifts as pigs, cattle, sheep, and goats to the South Pacific into a taker, a man who says mostly, imperiously, "I want," and whose dubious gifts are represented in the ambiguous, plastic-coated New World Chicken.

Nothling's highly ironic image works at several levels to set up and deflate the heroic stereotype of Cook. The visual background framing the explorer's face (a visual quotation from Nathaniel Dance's portrait) features supermarket labels advertising price specials; the phrase "New World" informs the viewer of the geographic and ideological context reiterated by the phrase at the bottom of the image, "Lets have a drink and celebrate." Celebrate what, and with what? These questions are unavoidable given the phrase in extra-large lettering above Cook's face: "I want your food." Here my end punctuation is misleading, for the Cook constructed in this image continues "and your trees and your soil." The list goes on: food is evidently the first item, on an all-inclusive list, that this Cook wants. Perhaps naturally ("What's wrong with that") he longs for the erasure of cultural difference, but his agenda is constructed in sinister and menacing tones: "Of course I know we're equal. But I'm better." The drink of celebration thus carries the taint of genocide – the destruction of Aboriginal cultures through trade with Europeans, particularly of trade goods (like alcohol) that undermined cultural underpinnings – and a threat about the potential use of European military power. "Lets have a drink and celebrate" is ultimately not an invitation but an imperative.

In Canada, Cook as Commonwealth culture-hero has been reconstructed through fiction in George Bowering's *Burning Water*. Although Bowering's novel primarily presents a meditation on questions of discovery, knowledge, and perfection in George Vancouver, it simultaneously presents a somewhat less heroic version of Cook than has been customary. After all, Vancouver, whose charts of the Pacific coastline were used long after he made them, must continually grapple with a somewhat embarrassing mistake made by his predecessor and former captain: "Here is the lad become captain himself, and one of the things he will do is to resume Cook's voyage and rename Cook's River. He will have the people in the boats measure the entire thing carefully, and then will dub it Cook's Inlet."[78] Like the continued nuisance of the question of Juan de Fuca Strait (which Cook missed, passing it by in a fog) separating the southern tip of Vancouver Island from what is now the mainland of Washington State, much of Vancouver's work as a navigator, by virtue of his diligence and attention to detail, necessarily calls into question Cook's attentiveness to the Pacific coastline. "How much more galling that would make it when the British made Cook a living saint and let Vancouver know that they could have done without his return."[79]

Vancouver learned the practice and methodology of exploration and command from Cook: painstaking attention to detail, treatment of Native peoples, the importance of diet (hence, in the novel, Vancouver's never-ending bowls of sauerkraut). Cook provides for this fictional Vancouver a father-figure far more significant than his biological father: "with Cook assuming the responsibility, he had dared to try his edge, to see if he could *ne plus ultra*."[80] However, *Burning Water* creates something like a Freudian drama in which the son (Vancouver) must not only surpass and symbolically kill his father (Cook) but also, perhaps because there is no mother in the all-male environment of the ship, desires in some way to incorporate the father's power by eating or consuming him. "When he had collected as much as he could of his father's body and caused it to be retired with proper respect and a requisite expenditure of gunpowder, he had fought down an urging to touch his tongue to the insulted flesh, to taste his continuance. For the next week he had vomited all his meals into the ocean."[81] In part this homoerotic drama is played out between Vancouver and the Spanish commander, Don Juan Francisco de la Bodega y Quadra, a man closer in age and experience to Cook than to Vancouver, and whose role in *Burning Water* as Vancouver's father-figure and lover challenges the image of Cook. The Cook traditionally commended for his sexual abstinence amongst scantily clad Pacific women is, in the somewhat fevered imagination of the fictional character named Vancouver, abstinent possibly not only for reasons of morality.[82]

Lionel Kearns's long poem *Convergences* offers a similarly postmodern take on Cook, juxtaposing excerpts from the published accounts of the third voyage, biographical data about its officers, Webber's illustrations of Nootka Sound, Native oral traditions, and the poet's own meditations on history, ethnography, philosophy, and language: "You think these are the actual thoughts of the men who were at Nootka in 1778? Well, you may be right, though I will give you absolutely no assurance as to the absolute accuracy and authenticity of the quotations. It does not matter much to me as long as it all fits into my poem."[83] Kearns uses this pastiche to consider the ways in which Cook's month at Nootka Sound has been made to mean something that comes from other contexts, other purposes. By foregrounding his own arrangement of the material on the page, he questions the construction of history through the official voice of the Great Man, Douglas's univocal gentleman-explorer-hero. In Kearns's account, Ledyard, Samwell, Clerke, Bayly, Burney, and King speak as frequently as does Cook; the moment of encounter begins not with a sailor shouting "land!" but with the image of "Sticks sticking out of the sea, a disturbing sight for Tsaxawasip and Nanaimis, two Mooachaht aristocrats, strolling along the beach south of Yuquot village." Even the neutral description appropriate to a voyage of scientific exploration starts to reverberate here, suggesting an eerie distance from the events described while Kearns's meditation connects them to the here and now.

In *Constructing Colonial Discourse* I examine several European discourses – exploration, aesthetics, science, the panoply of myths and assumptions clustered around cannibalism, and history – at work in the various texts documenting, describing, or commenting on Cook's month at Nootka Sound. I attempt to demonstrate how these different constructions of reality shaped both Cook's responses and also, more important, the textual creation of the place and its inhabitants.

The presentation of Nootka Sound by means of European discourses such as aesthetics and the science of natural history legitimates Cook's claim to having been there. They function as proof, the verbal equivalent of the maps and charts demonstrating quantitative knowledge of latitude, longitude, depth of water, and the physical appearance of the shoreline. Ultimately these discourses document his claim, as the King's proxy, to possession of what Cook initially named, after all, "King Georges Sound." Indeed, the consequences of such discourses were

explicitly material, resulting in economic exploitation. Of greater interest than the land as real estate were the sea otter pelts that commanded
such astronomical prices in China. For such profits European nations
(England, Spain, Russia) and "Yankee traders" were willing to go to
considerable effort to claim exclusive trading rights to the territory that
produced them, at least until the Nootka Sound controversy, war in
Europe, and declining sea otter resources made committing resources to
the area less attractive to decision makers far away.[84]

If Bruce Greenfield's argument – that the central conflict of American
history has been not slavery but the appropriation of territory from
Native peoples – can be applied to Canadian history, then the centrality
of fear and hostility between Europeans and their Canadian descendants and First Nations lies in European knowledge of wrongdoing and
guilt, the understanding that we live in stolen territories.[85] The continuing history of British Columbia illustrates this kind of hostility. Jean
Barman has identified racial conflict as one of the forces shaping and
creating a British Columbia identity:

> The importance of class in shaping British Columbia identity has
> been paralleled or surpassed by that of race and ethnicity. British
> Columbia was long the most overtly racist province in Canada
> by virtue of possessing the overwhelming majority of individuals
> against whom all Canadians of the dominant society would just
> as easily have discriminated. Any individuals, not just Asians,
> who did not conform to a stereotype formed in Canadians' own
> image were unacceptable. But the force of race in shaping the
> British Columbia identity went beyond the particular groups
> doing the discriminating or being discriminated against. To a
> significant extent it was race that helped create and maintain the
> province as a place apart. British Columbians of the dominant
> society were long convinced that they possessed a unique
> problem not understood by the federal government or by other
> Canadians. The most racist of actions taken in the west coast
> province – the head tax on Chinese arrivals, rejection of the
> Komagata Maru, Japanese evacuation – each contributed to a
> sense of autonomy.[86]

Such attitudes and ideas find their expression in the title of Patricia
Roy's history of British Columbia, A White Man's Province. The name
of the province where people of colour could not vote until nearly the

1950s (South Asians in 1947; First Nations, Chinese, and Japanese in 1949) "still suggests more aptly than any other name could do, the sentiments and the outlook of the Canadian people who live in the further west," Margaret Ormsby concludes.[87] Although some attitudes have changed since the revised edition of her *British Columbia: A History* was published in 1971, the language of the 1991 *Delgamuukw* decision in the Supreme Court[88] and the 2002 provincial referendum on treaty principles[89] suggest that, to some politically and culturally dominant groups, the "British" in "British Columbia" is still important.

While I try to demonstrate the connection between the political and material conditions and certain European discourses in the texts of Cook's voyage, these discourses are of course most significant at the level of what Chris Healy calls "documentation," methods of "possessing the indigenous people [and in this instance, the place Nootka Sound] by 'knowing' them."[90] The function of this process is not only domination or possession of Aboriginal knowledge but also, as Healy points out, the reproduction of European knowledge, what Edward Said has called Orientalism in another geographical context. Documentation by such discourses – regardless of how Pacific peoples were portrayed, or according to which stereotypes – "was a component of the decision-making of those Europeans who would enter the Pacific in their thousands and eventually dominate it."[91] That world is connected to the one we live in today, a world that is part of the legacy of Cook's voyages (both expeditions and books) and the culture that produced them. Edward Said has argued for the necessity of these kinds of connections between the past, its present, and our own time: "To lose sight of or ignore the national and international context of, say, Dickens's representations of Victorian businessmen, and to focus only on the internal coherence of their roles in his works is to miss an essential connection between his fiction and its historical world. And understanding that connection does not reduce or diminish the novels' values as works of art: on the contrary, because of their *worldliness*, because of their complex affiliations with their real setting, they are *more* interesting and *more* valuable as works of art."[92]

Cook's *Voyages* have long been treated not as works of art but as supreme non-fictions; if his ships were imagined as floating laboratories, the published texts were similarly viewed as an assemblage of facts. Although they look like the opposite of Said's project, his point holds true. Hawkesworth and Douglas edited Cook's *Voyages* using the cultural discourses familiar to eighteenth-century Britons: discourses governing the presentation of the non-European world, aesthetic impressions, scientific knowledge about the natural world, cannibalism, and history. I have located the account of Nootka Sound – a relatively brief, uncharacteristic, and often-overlooked episode from a vast body of material – within those European discourses to see what happened when they were transported to the Pacific. Examining the discourses shaping the accounts of Nootka Sound in Cook's third voyage reveals the cultural values at work in eighteenth-century Britain. When applied to New World contexts in Douglas's edition of the third voyage, the eighteenth-century discourses of exploration, aesthetics, science, cannibalism, and history became colonial discourses.

Notes

1 The full title of the first official edition of Cook's third voyage is *A Voyage to the Pacific Ocean Undertaken by the Command of His Majesty, for making Discoveries in the Northern Hemisphere. To Determine the Position and Extent of the West Side of North America; its Distance from Asia; and the Practicability of a Northern Passage to Europe. Performed Under the Direction of Captains Cook, Clerke, and Gore, in His Majesty's Ships the Resolution and Discovery. In the Years 1776, 1777, 1778, 1779, and 1780.* 3 Vols. (London: Printed by W. & A. Strahan for G. Nicol and T. Cadell, 1784). Because this study makes much of Douglas's and others' editorial changes to Cook's journals, I cite different editions of the voyages using the editor's name; the numbers I, II, and III correspond to Cook's first, second, and third voyages. Hence "Douglas III:2" refers to Volume 2 of Douglas's three-volume edition of Cook's third voyage, while "Beaglehole II" refers to Beaglehole's scholarly edition of the second voyage and "Beaglehole III:1" refers to Volume 1 of Beaglehole's two-volume edition of the third voyage. This citation would thus appear as Douglas III:2, 265–6. For clarity's sake, I occasionally provide parenthetical citations for textual material from the various editions rather than providing the information in footnotes.

2 Tobias Furneaux had trouble with scurvy on the *Adventure* during the second voyage, however, because he did not follow Cook's instructions.

3 Quoted in Abbott, *John Hawkesworth,* 139.

4 These are generalizations about exploration discourse; however, Cook's situation at Nootka Sound is much more complex. Contrary to the idea of the discovery of an empty land that can be named and thereby possessed, Cook's first words about Nootka Sound indicate a recognition that the

land is not, in fact, empty, just as they seem to indicate that its inhabitants have a culture he does not understand. The terra nullius, or "empty land," argument was not important in his account of Nootka Sound or, indeed, in most of the Pacific (the eastern coast of Australia being the notable exception). However, Britain's actions in the Nootka Sound controversy of 1790 corresponded to those indicating a European nation's territorial claim by right of discovery as described by Frost in *Botany Bay Mirages*. See his Chapter 9, "Our Original Aggression?" for a detailed discussion of the terra nullius concept.

5 In *Maps and Dreams*, Brody identifies the need for newcomers to deny the existence of Aboriginal inhabitants of New World territories in order to justify imprinting their law on an "empty" land.

6 MacLaren discusses the effect of the four-stages theory on Douglas's edition of Cook's third voyage in "Exploration/Travel Literature and the Evolution of the Author."

7 Warkentin, ed., *Canadian Exploration Literature*, ix. See her Introduction for an overview of these issues.

8 Warkentin, *Canadian Exploration Literature*, xi.

9 Beaglehole, ed., *The Voyage of the Resolution and Discovery, 1776–1780*, vol. III:1 of *The Journals of James Cook on His Voyages of Discovery*, 4 vols., Hakluyt Society Extra Series 36 (Cambridge: Hakluyt Society at the University Press, 1967).

10 These official editions, like many of the later ones that follow them, are available on microfilm through the Canadian Institute for Historical Microreproductions (CIHM). MacLaren outlines the importance of the CIHM holdings, which make several different editions of Cook's *Voyages*, as well as the texts of other explorers, readily accessible to Canadian researchers, in "Explorers' and Travellers' Narratives: A Peregrination through Different Editions."

11 In addition to the official texts published by Nicol and Cadell, Beddie's *Bibliography of Captain James Cook* lists a 1783 London edition published by Fielding and a 1784 edition (later abridged) by Kearsley (CIHM 17672) ; another 1784 edition (discussed in the chapter on cannibalism) was published by Stockdale, Scatcherd & Whitaker, John Fielding, and John Hardy (CIHM 17638–17642). A Dublin edition also appeared in 1784 (CIHM 42432–42436). By 1790, editions of Cook's circumnavigations containing two, or even all three, voyages began appearing: the Newcastle edition (CIHM 17753) was supplemented with a section by Phillips on Botany Bay, while a 1790 "omnibus" (CIHM 17752) was supplemented with the journal of Tobias Furneaux (commander of the *Discovery* on Cook's sec-

ond voyage). Dutch, French, Italian, and American versions continued to appear throughout the late eighteenth century and into the nineteenth century, when Cook's *Voyages* began also to appear in what I would call "imperial libraries": "Routledge's Excelsior Series" (1880; CIHM 14801), "Routledge's World Library" (1886; CIHM 29559), Everyman's Library (1906). However, these editions essentially derive from Douglas's first official edition, abridging or editing it to serve their purposes, or from derivations of that edition.

12 The following section draws heavily on Beaglehole's textual history of the third voyage, published as part of the introductory material of his edition.

13 Beaglehole III:1, clxxi.

14 Ibid., ccii.

15 Ibid.

16 Beaglehole III:1, lxxvii.

17 Ibid., lxxvi.

18 Beaglehole, ed., *The Voyage of the Resolution and Discovery, 1776–1780*, vol. III:2 of *The Journals of Captain James Cook on His Voyages of Discovery*, 4 vols., Hakluyt Society Extra Series 36 (Cambridge: Hakluyt Society at the University Press, 1967).

19 Beaglehole III:1, ccvi.

20 MacLaren, "Exploration/Travel Literature and the Evolution of the Author," 56.

21 Greenfield claims that "it is the published narrative produced with the travel-reading market in mind that influences subsequent travel writers" (*Narrating Discovery*, 19). Or, as Todorov puts it, "the reception of statements is more revealing for the history of ideologies than their production: and when an author is mistaken, or lying, his text is no less significant than when he is speaking the truth" (*Conquest of America*, 54).

22 Dennis Porter, *Haunted Journeys*, 7. Porter uses psychoanalytic concepts to examine travellers' motivations and often ambivalent reactions to a foreign country (transference and projection of negative and positive desires). Like Warkentin's model of reading between the lines, Porter's psychoanalytic model suggests the ability of the reader/analyst to hear the kind of fantasies of which the text/patient may be unconscious. While his discussion of contemporary critical and cultural theory opens up the genre of travel literature, his use of psychoanalysis depends on the choice of *travel* (as opposed to *exploration*) as the operative term. Psychoanalysis, exploring the inner landscapes of the individual and family, offers a useful critical approach to travel, which can be characterized as personal and private. The explorer, by contrast, travels with a national or corporate rather than

a personal agenda; exploration belongs in the public realm, shaped by both history and politics. Consequently, any unconscious fantasies in the texts of Cook's *Voyages* reveal not only an individual but also a cultural self-fashioning through the scholarly apparatus of the edition.

23 Pratt, *Imperial Eyes*, 6.

24 Or more: Volume II of Beaglehole's edition of the third voyage indicates considerable differences between kinds of encounter between ship and shore at Nootka Sound, governed by variables such as class, rank, and gender.

25 Cook called them the "Nootka" or "Nootkans" and they were generally known by this name until the nations of Vancouver Island's west coast decided to call themselves, collectively, the Nuu-chah-nulth.

26 Clayton, *Islands of Truth*, 28. See Chapter 2, especially pages 22–7, for a discussion of Native histories, and Chapter 7 for a discussion of the geographies of Native power in the Nootka Sound fur trade.

27 Clayton, *Islands of Truth*, 49.

28 Wittig, *The Straight Mind*, 68–9.

29 Two recent biographies, *Captain James Cook* by Richard Hough (first published in 1994) and *Farther Than Any Man: The Rise and Fall of Captain James Cook* by Martin Dugard (2001), emphasize this version of Cook.

30 Dening, "Sharks That Walk on the Land," *Performances*, 75.

31 Fisher, *Contact and Conflict*, 2.

32 Barman, *The West beyond the West*, 13. Barman's comment refers to British Columbia generally, but it clearly applies to Nootka Sound in the aftermath of Cook's voyage.

33 See Clayton's *Islands of Truth* for a discussion of this process, especially the Nootka Crisis of the 1790s.

CHAPTER ONE

1 Dewald, "Introduction," Herodotus, *The Histories*, xvi.

2 Dewald, "Introduction," xvii.

3 *Tacitus on Britain and Germany: A New Translation of the "Agricola" and the "Germania,"* 140.

4 See, for example, the description of the land past Caffilos: "Thence one goes to another land, where the people are of evil customs. They train great dogs to worry men. And when their friends are getting near death and they believe they can live no longer, they make their dogs to worry them; for they will not let them die naturally in their beds lest they suffer too much pain in dying. When they are dead, they eat their flesh instead of

venison" (134). Although the word "cannibal" is not used in this edition
of Mandeville's *Travels* (raising the issue of translation as it relates to textual construction), the running page-heading reads 'Cannibals, Troglodytes
and Cynocephali." Only two pages earlier, the phrase "truly I saw with
my own eyes" was used, but everything that follows is a description of
another place couched exclusively in the third person: "From this island
men go by sea to another"; "thence men go across the Great Sea Ocean to
another island called Caffilos"; and from "thence one goes to another
land," where humans eat human flesh "instead of venison." *The Travels of
Sir John Mandeville*, 132–4.

5 As in Charles Clerke's parodic account published in the *Philosophical
Transactions* of the Royal Society in 1767 (Salmond, *Between Worlds*,
94). Clerke sailed with Cook on all three voyages: first as master's mate
and then 3rd lieutenant on the *Endeavour*, as 2nd lieutenant on the *Resolution* on the second voyage, and as commander of the *Discovery* and,
after Cook's death, of the expedition, until Clerke's own death on August
22, 1779.

6 The Arctic coast of North America is the obvious exception.

7 Throughout much of the eighteenth century, the Grand Tour was the gentleman's finishing school. At the beginning of the century, it followed a
more or less standardized itinerary designed to acquaint young men of the
ruling class with the geography and military fortifications of nations with
which they might one day be at war. As the century progressed, the Tour
assumed cultural and aesthetic dimensions; travellers began visiting museums and galleries, often returning home with the beginnings of an art collection. (Banks's collection of "curios" brought home from Cook's first
voyage is the exploration equivalent.) Presumably the interest in landscape
painting led to scenic tourism in search of landscapes resembling the paintings. By the century's end, such scenic tourism – at home in the British
Isles as well as on the Continent – had trickled down from the aristocracy
to the middle classes. For a lively first-hand account, see the two volumes
of James Boswell's Grand Tour: *Boswell on the Grand Tour: Germany
and Switzerland* and *Boswell on the Grand Tour: Italy, Corsica, and
France, 1765–6*. See also Withey, *Grand Tours and Cook's Tours* for an
accessible history of the Grand Tour.

8 "The eighteenth century … saw the writing of a travel account as an
important undertaking for the well-educated man or woman who, having
made a trip, wished to convey in an artistically pleasing fashion the information he had gleaned." Batten, *Pleasurable Instruction*, 3.

9 Pratt, *Imperial Eyes*, 9.

10 Ibid., 25.

11 Colley, *Britons: Forging the Nation*. It is also worth noting that a sense of British *imperial* identity was forged largely in opposition to Spain, via the contrast between popular images of British rationality and compassion in the New World – an idea for which Cook was the model – in contrast to cruel Spanish conquistadors. Dening's description of Spaniards at Marquesas in 1595 provides a sense of the image of Spanish cruelty: "They had killed easily and massively. Some of them said that they killed because they liked to kill. Others said that they killed because of what their colleagues would say. Mostly they killed because the otherness of the islanders relieved any qualm of conscience that suggested they be treated as themselves." *Islands and Beaches*, 11. Note that Dening does not attempt to paint an image of Spanish cruelty; his description, however, conveys an image that would have been viewed as such by eighteenth-century Britons.

12 Hough, *Captain James Cook*, 67.

13 According to Abbott, "all belligerents were under orders to treat him, if they should encounter him, as a commander of a neutral and allied power." *John Hawkesworth*, 139.

14 Clayton, *Islands of Truth*, 8.

15 Batten, *Pleasurable Instruction*, 6.

16 See Batten's *Pleasurable Instruction* for a full discussion of observations and reflections in eighteenth-century travel literature.

17 See Chapter 2 of Percy Adams's *Travel Literature and the Evolution of the Novel* for an overview.

18 Greenfield, *Narrating Discovery* 19–20.

19 Ibid., 18.

20 By way of comparison, Frances Burney's *Evelina*, published in three volumes in January 1778, was priced at seven shillings and sixpence in sewed bindings and at nine shillings bound, according to the advertisement published in the *London Evening Post*, 27–29 January 1778 (Burney, *Evelina*, 1). While I have not been able to discover how much Douglas earned as editor of Cook's *Voyages*, Hawkesworth earned the "astonishing sum of £6000" for editing the volume containing Cook's first voyage. In a footnote discussing the division of profits from the third *Voyage*, Beaglehole writes that "Mrs Cook got £2000 and upwards [the Cook family's share of the profits was half]. It seems hardly possible that Douglas gave his services gratis" (III:1, cc).

  Regarding the price of books relative to necessities, Roy Porter notes that, broadly speaking, approximately thirty to forty pounds would be necessary to support a family throughout most of the eighteenth century:

"a careful artisan family could hope to keep itself from hunger and out of debt on a pound a week" when "for much of the century a full loaf of bread cost about 4d and a pot of ale 1d; a meal could be bought in a London tavern for about 6d" (*English Society in the Eighteenth Century*, xv). Jacqueline Pearson cites James Raven's estimation that "an annual income of £50 might have been the minimum which allowed the buying of books, and that in 1780 about 150,000 households came into this category" (*Women's Reading in Britain, 1750–1835*, 12).

21 Beaglehole III:1, ccii.

22 Beaglehole, *The Life of Captain James Cook*, 692.

23 Quoted in Beaglehole III:1, cciv.

24 See Wilson's *The Sense of the People* for a discussion of political culture in urban centres in Hanoverian England. Although she does not discuss Cook's *Voyages* specifically, Wilson indicates the degree to which material of national interest was widely disseminated.

25 MacLaren, "Exploration/Travel Literature and the Evolution of the Author."

26 As MacLaren notes in another context, "such a version of events played out an ideology if it did not quite represent matters as accurately as was thought by credulous readers of travel and exploration literature, who nearly always find the putative testimony of the eyewitness irresistible." "Inscribing the Empire," 4.

27 Cook used this phrase in the *Endeavour* journal (17 August 1770; Beaglehole I, 380). Here it suggests a sense of self somewhat at odds with the gentlemanly image carefully constructed by Douglas. See also Megaw, ed., *Employ'd as a Discoverer*.

28 I am indebted to MacLaren's discussion of rhetorical devices in "Exploration/Travel Literature and the Evolution of the Author"; it should be noted that I reach similar, though not identical, conclusions in this chapter.

29 As subsequent examples in this chapter demonstrate, Douglas made such changes quite regularly. Partly this tendency to elevation reflects the trends of the period. McIntosh has analyzed changes in English prose styles over the eighteenth century and argues that, as the century progressed, prose was increasingly gentrified. "It is no accident that 'propriety' was a key term in prescriptive grammars of the time; like other key terms ... ('decorum,' 'correctness,' 'ease,' 'wit,' 'refinement'), it applies both to language and deportment; the presumption of a system of social rank is deeply implicated in the language itself" (*The Evolution of English Prose*, 23). The effect was to eliminate the oral qualities of prose in favour of more writerly styles. "For better or worse, it was not possible in 1790 to write

as Defoe and Swift had written in 1710 – the age demanded greater formality and precision; the age applauded a more flowery style" (*The Evolution of English Prose*, 1).

30 Glickman, *The Picturesque and the Sublime*, 33.

31 Quoted in Abbott, *John Hawkesworth*, 159. See also Beaglehole II, 661, as well as *Boswell: The Ominous Years, 1774–1776*, 308–9.

32 MacLaren, "Creating Travel Literature," 81.

33 Ibid., 93.

34 Beaglehole III:1, cxcix.

35 Ibid., cxcviii.

36 Ibid., clxxii-clxxiii. See also Beaglehole's analysis of Cook's progression in *Cook the Writer*.

37 Quoted in Beaglehole III:1, cxcix.

38 Beaglehole, *Cook the Writer*, 19.

39 Beaglehole III:1, cci.

40 Clayton, *Islands of Truth*, 27.

41 I refer here to the expectations of the majority of armchair explorers reading Cook's *Voyages*; for others, more knowledgeable about maritime matters, details of everyday life on board Cook's ships would be worth reading about in and of themselves.

42 MacLaren, "Exploration/Travel Literature and the Evolution of the Author," 46.

43 Beaglehole argues that the officers of Cook's third voyage – who included "a dozen future captains, and an admiral" – essentially form a bridge between Cook and Nelson as two high-water marks of British naval history (III:1, cci).

44 Each had asserted exclusive rights to trade and settle on the Northwest Coast; the Nootka Convention gave them shared rights. Clayton discusses the Nootka Crisis and its connection to "the material and ideological importance of overseas trade to Britons" (174) in considerable detail in *Islands of Truth*.

45 In scholarly accounts of Vancouver's accomplishment, words like "meticulous," "accuracy," "systematic and painstaking," and "exactness" were repeated throughout the nineteenth and twentieth centuries, echoing Vancouver's own rather prosaic statement of his project: to make "an accurate survey." Even his self-portrayal as a plodding, somewhat self-satisfied measurer demonstrated the end of the romance that had previously been attached to the possible unknown. See, for example, Glyndwyr Williams, "Myth and Reality: The Theoretical Geography of Northwest America from Cook to Vancouver"; Beaglehole; and W. Kaye Lamb's edition of

The Voyage of George Vancouver IV:1, 390 (cited in Clayton, *Islands of Truth*, 191); see also George Vancouver, *A Voyage of Discovery*, 243. Even Clayton, who disagrees with "the idea that Vancouver's team charted in a more or less truthful way a geography that was waiting to be discovered" (the assumption underpinning traditional assessments of Vancouver's voyage), argues for a larger importance: "Vancouver created a geography, [one with] imperial connotations. His cartography facilitated geopolitical processes of appropriation that worked at a distance from Native peoples" (*Islands of Truth*, 191, 192).

46 Quoted in Edwards, *The Story of the Voyage*. Edwards adds "It is hard not to agree; Vancouver's style is stilted, pompous, periphrastic, ponderous, and above all humourless" (129).

47 So important was control of what was written about the mutiny to Bligh that he "kept writing materials strictly to himself"; apparently he even "appropriated" a notebook belonging to one of the midshipmen (Edwards, *The Story of the Voyage*, 131–2). This suggests that Bligh wanted to control either the paper resources necessary to continuing the log or the representation of events, knowing how eagerly the reading public would snap up an account of a mutiny.

48 Edwards, *The Story of the Voyage*, 133.

49 Ibid., 131.

50 Quoted from a letter to James Burney (dated 26 July 1791) in Mackaness, *The Life of Vice-Admiral William Bligh*, 24. See pages 22–35 for a discussion of Bligh's objections to the published edition of Cook's third voyage.

51 Edwards, *The Story of the Voyage*, 132.

CHAPTER TWO

1 As one journal writer, George Gilbert, put it, "indeed we had need for we experienc[e]d very little [Comfort] from our own provisions, which were only just Sufficient to keep us alive." George Gilbert, *Journal, 1776–1780*, 66.

2 Frost, "Become a Name: Beaglehole's *Life of Cook*," 97.

3 Beaglehole, *Life of Captain James Cook*, 583–4.

4 Sprat, *History of the Royal Society*, 113.

5 MacLaren, "Samuel Hearne and the Landscape of Discovery," 28.

6 Jasen notes that Burke's use of the term was "the single most important influence in establishing the link between landscape, emotion, and pleasure" (*Wild Things*, 5). Stafford notes that "the issue of the individual consciousness locating itself outside itself bears on the varieties of the Sublime (rhetorical, natural, religious) enumerated in antiquity and compellingly

recast by Edmund Burke. In Longinus's definition of *hypsos*, or height, the reader is 'uplifted' as though he physically undergoes what he merely hears. That is, the encounter with artistic excellence (the 'rhetorical Sublime') is structurally cognate with the lived transcendence excited in the observer during the meeting with landscape (the 'natural Sublime')" (*Voyage into Substance*, 353).

7 I have drawn heavily on the work of Elizabeth A. Bohls in this chapter. See her *Women Travel Writers and the Language of Aesthetics* for a discussion of the implications of Burke's theory of the Sublime.

8 Joppien and Smith, *The Voyage of the* Resolution *and* Discovery, *1776–1780*, 5.

9 Hunt and Willis, eds., *Genius of Place*, 12.

10 See MacLaren, "The Aesthetic Mapping of Nature in the Second Franklin Expedition," 40; and Roy Porter, *English Society in the Eighteenth Century*, 57, 60.

11 See, for example, MacLaren's "The Aesthetic Mapping of Nature in the Second Franklin Expedition"; "Aesthetic Mappings of the West by the Palliser and Hind Survey Expeditions, 1857–1859"; "The Grandest Tour"; and "Samuel Hearne and the Landscape of Discovery."

12 Barrell, *The Idea of Landscape and the Sense of Place, 1730–1840*, 6. Hunt and Willis note that "Pope's dictum, recorded by Spence in his *Anecdotes*, that 'all gardening is landscape-painting,' applied throughout the eighteenth century" (*Genius of Place*, 13).

13 MacLaren, "Aesthetic Mappings of the West by the Palliser and Hind Survey Expeditions, 1857–1859." Although the Palliser survey expedition occurred nearly a century after Cook was at Nootka Sound, the aesthetic responses to the Canadian West it recorded are articulated according to notions developed well before Cook's time (Burke's *Philosophical Enquiry* was published in 1757 or contemporaneous with the publication of his journals (notably William Gilpin's *Observations on the River Wye*, published in 1783). As Hunt and Willis note, by mid-century "those who sought wilder scenery than the [picturesque] English country estate usually provided were following Gilpin's picturesque tours into Scotland and the Lake District" in the 1760s and 1780s (*Genius of Place*, 33). As a national pastime, such picturesque tours were still popular, or at least culturally relevant, by 1813, as Elizabeth Bennett's tour of Darcy's picturesque estate in *Pride and Prejudice* suggests.

14 Stafford, *Voyage into Substance*, 353.

15 It may be that as 'Picturesque travel' became more and more accessible to middle-class tourists, the Picturesque lost some of its exclusive cachet and

the less accessible Sublime – available only to those who could afford to travel further than the Lake District with one of Gilpin's package tours – gained in prestige in consequence.

16 Catharine Parr Traill writes "I was disappointed in the forest trees, having pictured to myself hoary giants almost primeval with the country itself, as greatly exceeding in majesty of form the trees of my native isles, as the vast lakes and mighty rivers of Canada exceed the locks and streams of Britain" (*The Backwoods of Canada*, 96). Visiting Niagara Falls in the winter of 1836, having come to Canada to attempt a reconciliation with her husband, Anna Brownell Jameson wrote: "All the associations which in imagination I had gathered round the scene, its appalling terrors, its soul-subduing beauty, power and height, and velocity and immensity, were all diminished in effect, or wholly lost" (*Winter Studies and Summer Rambles*, 59).

17 Bohls, *Women Travel Writers and the Language of Aesthetics*, 7.

18 In his *Spectator* piece of 21 June 1712, for example, Addison claimed that the "Man of Polite Imagination" is capable of feeling aesthetic pleasure in a way that both distinguishes him from "the Vulgar" and gives him "a Kind of Property in every thing he sees" (Bohls, *Women Travel Writers and the Language of Aesthetics*, 8). See Bohls's third chapter on the connections between gardening and painting, and the real and imaginative possession of landscape and women.

19 Bann, "From Captain Cook to Neil Armstrong," 216.

20 Guest, "Curiously Marked," 105.

21 Smith, *European Vision and the South Pacific*, 5.

22 Stafford, *Voyage into Substance*, 25.

23 Beaglehole III:1, ccxxiii.

24 Smith, *Imagining the Pacific*, 74.

25 Joppien and Smith, *The Voyage of the* Resolution *and* Discovery, *1776–1780*, 28. This analysis of Webber's general strategies and accomplishments in the encounter paintings accompanies *The Harbour of Annamooka* (not reproduced here).

26 Solkin, "Portraiture in Motion," 3.

27 Joppien and Smith, *The Voyage of the* Resolution *and* Discovery, *1776–1780*, 80.

28 Ricou, "Never Cry Wolfe," 174–5. Ricou's analysis suggests the ways West's self-promotion mirrors the economic motivations governing imperial expansion: British aristocrats "could see their dying generals as martyrs in a cause that was both British and Christian, and envisage their empire as carrying on some abstract values that they attributed to the

empires of the ancient past ... The martyr may be dying, but Britannia has prevailed" ("Never Cry Wolfe," 184).

29 The process by which Webber's drawings were turned into engravings was entirely independent from Douglas's editing.

30 Tippett and Cole, *From Desolation to Splendour*, 15–7.

31 King, *Journal*, 1402.

32 MacLaren, "The McGregor Syndrome," 124.

33 Ledyard, *A Journal of Captain Cook's Last Voyage*, 70.

34 Clerke, *Journal*, 1323.

35 MacLaren, "The Aesthetic Mapping of Nature," 40, 41.

36 Tippett and Cole, *From Desolation to Splendour*, 21.

37 Joppien and Smith, *The Voyage of the* Resolution *and* Discovery, *1776–1780*, 81.

38 Smith, *Imagining the Pacific*, 76.

39 Kearns's description of the incident records Webber as having traded first the contents of his pockets, then his buttons, then his shoes, and finally all his clothing, so that he finished the drawing naked. "You remember the story; he had to buy time by giving away everything in his pockets, then his buttons one by one, then his shoes, and finally his clothes. He sketched as fast as he could, trying to include all the details. When he was completely naked his hosts stopped pestering him, allowing him all the time he needed to finish." *Convergences*, n.p.

40 Douglas III:2, 280.

41 Bohls, *Women Travel Writers and the Language of Aesthetics*, 96.

42 Ibid., 97.

43 Ibid.

44 On the first voyage, Cook's official rank was first lieutenant of the *Endeavour*: as Beaglehole puts it, "Cook was to command, and in nautical parlance he would be the captain, but the captain of a ship might not necessarily be a captain in the navy list" (*Life of Cook*, 134). The title page of the second *Voyage* lists Cook as "Commander of the *Resolution*," while his second-in-command is listed as "Captain Furneaux" (Douglas II:1). Not until the third voyage is Cook both captain and commander.

45 Clayton, *Islands of Truth*, 174.

46 It remains a lighthouse station operated by the Coast Guard.

CHAPTER THREE

1 Regis, *Describing Early America*, 5–6.

2 Pratt, *Imperial Eyes*, 27–8.

3 "A Linnaean specimen entry begins with the generic name, then offers the 'specific differential character,' the elements of the plant which distinguish it from others in the genus. A third part is the trivial name, which, with the generic name, makes up the two Latin names that are entered in the lists. A fourth part is the plant's habitat, and last is a brief description or annotation, or synonyms, often with reference to earlier systems or illustrations of the plant in question." Regis, *Describing Early America*, 20.

4 For a considerably different approach, see Alfred W. Crosby's *Ecological Imperialism*. Crosby argues that Old World weeds, animals, and bacteria accompanying and sometimes preceding Europeans achieved the conquest of what he calls the "Neo-Europes," those countries whose populations now consist primarily of the descendants of Europeans instead of those of the original inhabitants. On the unknowability of the New World to Europeans, he notes that "Joseph Banks, the naturalist who came to New Zealand with Captain Cook in 1769, recognized only fourteen of the first four hundred plants he examined" (220). However, by 1773 canary grass, "a Mediterranean plant whose seeds have tiny wings for riding the wind, made its way ashore" to be observed by Georg Forster on Cook's second voyage (228). Such unintentional imports, Crosby contends, were ultimately as vital to European conquest – remaking the New World in the image of the Old World – as were more obvious ones such as Bibles or smallpox blankets.

5 Regis, *Describing Early America*, 12.

6 Lovejoy, *The Great Chain of Being*, 232.

7 Regis, *Describing Early America*, 14.

8 Ibid., 22.

9 Regis, *Describing Early America*, 22. "Nature," already a complex and possibly overdetermined concept in the eighteenth century, is starting to take on a life of its own in these pages; here I think it carries a sense of inevitability as well as a sense of "found in nature" or "naturally occurring."

10 Merchant, *The Death of Nature*, 7.

11 Ibid., 189, 132.

12 See Stepan's *The Idea of Race in Science* for an analysis of the role of English scientific discourses in the development of modern racism.

13 Sprat, *History of the Royal Society*, 113.

14 Lefevre, *Invention as a Social Act*, 99.

15 What Sprat calls the "digressions, amplifications, and swellings of style" are relegated to the realm of the female, increasingly represented in eighteenth-century literature by the novel of sentiment and sensibility, in con-

trast to such male literary forms as the epic or mock-epic (think of the order, precision, exactness of Pope's couplets or the highly controlled structure of Fielding's novels) or the leisurely, dispassionate, and above all gentlemanly periodical essays of Steele and Addison or Samuel Johnson.

16 In marked contrast to other kinds of written language, which highlight the agency and choices of the writer, "to write science is commonly thought not to write at all, just simply to record the natural facts" in a transparent, purely denotative language, unaffected by nuance or connotation, not to mention the conscious or unconscious choices of the writer. See Bazerman, *Shaping Written Knowledge*, 14.

17 Merchant, *The Death of Nature*, xix.

18 Regis, *Describing Early America*, 21–2.

19 Stearn, "Linnaeus's Sexual System," 29.

20 Ibid., 32.

21 Pratt, *Imperial Eyes*, 27.

22 Many European collectors owed their place in the scientific community to the work of plant hunters who sent them specimens. For an example, see Regis's discussion of the relationship between John Bartram, an American farmer and collector of plants who taught himself enough Latin to use the Linnaean system, and his British patron, Peter Collinson, to whom Bartram sent specimens. When Bartram requested payment in the form of a book that would help develop his knowledge of the Linnaean system, Collinson patronizingly refused to send it. "In botany, as in all the sciences, the work of collection – whether of specimens or of 'observations that could not be duplicated at some other time and place' – was what Europe most wanted from America" (*Describing Early America*, 10).

23 See the prefatory material to Jonathan Swift, *A Tale of a Tub* (1704), where the Grub Street hack lists such other publications as "A general history of Ears" and "A Modest Defense of the Proceedings of the Rabble in all Ages" – not to mention "A Voyage into England, by a Person of Quality in Terra Australis incognita, translated from the Original"!

24 Stepan, *The Idea of Race in Science*, xviii.

25 See Miner's "Body Ritual Among the Nacirema" for an example and critique.

26 Beaglehole III:1, 312.

27 Douglas III:2, 303.

28 Beaglehole III:1, 311.

29 Who were, as Fisher, "Cook and the Nootka," 94–5, argues, most probably slaves.

30 Abbott, *John Hawkesworth*, 155.

31 As Cook put it in a letter to Douglas, he wanted the official edition of the second voyage to be "unexceptionable to the nicest readers." Withey notes that Cook was willing to accept changes of substance to avoid offending readers: "Cook's statement that 'the [Malekulan] men are naked .. but the Penis is wraped round with a piece of cloth or a leaf' became 'the men go quite naked, except a piece of cloth or a leaf used as a wrapper'" (*Voyages of Discovery*, 311). The ambiguity of that wrapper is characteristic of Douglas's editorial changes.

32 Hulme, *Colonial Encounters*, xii-xiii.

33 Ibid., 158–9.

34 Encountering Maori again at Queen Charlotte Sound on the second voyage, Cook noted that, on the first voyage, "whatever favours a few [women] might have granted to the crew of the Endeavour it was generally done in a private manner and without the men seeming to intrest themselves in it, but now we find the men are the chief promoters of this Vice, and for a spike nail or any other thing they value will oblige their Wives and Daughters whether they will or no and that not with the privacy decency seems to require, such are the concequences of a commerce with Europeans and what is still more to our Shame civilized Christians, we debauch their Morals already too prone to vice and we interduce among them wants and perhaps diseases which they never before knew." (Beaglehole II, 174–5). In his account of Hawaii in January 1778, Cook wrote of the difficulties preventing the sailors and officers, even those with "the venereal," from seeking sexual encounters with Native women (Beaglehole III:1, 266). Beaglehole's footnotes for this page, however, highlight the seriousness with which Cook treated such men: a man named Will Bradley received two dozen lashes "for disobeying orders [...] and having connections with women knowing himself to be injured, with the Veneral disorder."

35 Pratt, "Scratches on the Face of the Country," 139. Pratt traces this trope as far back as Mandeville's *Travels*.

36 Kearns, *Convergences*, n.p.

37 Joppien and Smith, *The Voyage of the* Resolution *and* Discovery, *1776–1780*, 90.

38 Ibid., 91–2.

39 Ibid., 92.

40 Ibid.

41 Ibid.

42 Pratt, "Scratches on the Face of the Country," 139.

43 See Fabian, *Time and the Other*; and Stephen Jay Gould, *The Mismeasure of Man*.

44 Kupperman, *Settling with the Indians*, 106.

45 Fisher, "Cook and the Nootka," 84.

46 King in Beaglehole III:2, 1407.

47 MacLaren, "Exploration/Travel Literature and the Evolution of the Author," 48–9.

48 Ledyard, *A Journal of Captain Cook's Last Voyage*, 72.

49 See, for example, Robin Ridington's discussion of the assumptions under-lining Chief Justice Allan McEachern's decision in *Delgamuukw v. BC* (1991). These include the assumption that "societies can be ranked on a 'scale of progress' from 'primitive' to 'civilized.' Civilized societies are inherently superior to primitive ones and have a natural evolutionary right to dominate and replace them. They are more complex and more 'devel-oped' in every way. The idea of development is accepted uncritically as an absolute measure of superiority" ("Fieldwork in Courtroom 53: A Witness to *Delgamuukw v. BC*," 17–18). Such assumptions, expressed in exactly those words (without the ironic distance implied by Ridington's inverted commas), would have been heartily endorsed by editor Douglas.

50 Beaglehole III:1, 308.

CHAPTER FOUR

1 Hulme offers an overview of this debate in his "Introduction" to *Cannibal-ism and the Colonial World*. Arens's point in his influential book is quite clear, however. He has no interest in debating whether cannibalism has ever existed or not; rather, he considers cannibalism, understood as a con-cept or discourse, as one of the means by which "anthropology makes it object," to borrow the subtitle of Fabian's *Time and the Other*. See Arens, *The Man-Eating Myth*.

2 In *Divine Hunger*, in order to challenge Arens's attempt to debunk the myth of cannibalism as a prevalent cultural feature, Sanday treats canni-balism as a physical act that has cultural and symbolic meanings. How-ever, Sanday does not discuss the symbolism of the Christian communion; instead, she develops her analysis of cannibalism through looking at exam-ples from non-European cultures only, arguably proving Arens's point by default.

3 Hulme, "Introduction: The Cannibal Scene," 4.

4 For a discussion of ritual and ceremonial cannibalism, see McDowell, *Hamatsa*.

5 I am thinking here of Norris's discussion of "flesh, blood, divinity": "Over the centuries, Christians have grown adept at finding ways to disincarnate the religion, resisting the scandalous notion that what is holy can have

much to do with the muck and smell of a stable, the painful agony of death on a cross. The Incarnation remains a scandal to anyone who wants religion to be a purely spiritual matter, an etherized, bloodless bliss" (*Amazing Grace*, 114). See also Marcus J. Borg's (*The God We Never Knew*) discussion of the effect of Enlightenment changes in worldview on images of God's transcendence.

6 Salmond's *Two Worlds: First Meetings between Maori and Europeans, 1642–1772* (1991) briefly discusses Maori cannibalism and European responses to it in this early period; her *Between Worlds: Early Exchanges between Maori and Europeans, 1773–1815* (1997) provides a detailed discussion of the accounts of Maori cannibalism from Cook's second voyage. The following section relies considerably on Salmond's work, particularly *Between Worlds*. See also Beaglehole's edition of the second voyage, particularly his "Introduction," lxxvi-lxxxi; Cook's own account of 23 November 1773, Beaglehole ii, 292–5; "Burney's Log," 749–52; "Furneaux's Narrative," 743–4; and "The Journal of William Wales," 818–9.

7 This account of 23 November covers pages 292 to 195 in Beaglehole's scholarly edition of the second voyage; the running heads at the top of the page read "The Happy Cannibal" (293) and "Cannibal Philosophy" (295).

8 Beaglehole footnotes Clerke's description of the "circumstantial details" at Cook's phrase "a peice of flesh had been broiled in the presince of most of the officers"; Clerke's account makes it clear that he conducted this first experiment (Beaglehole ii, 293). See also Salmond, *Between Worlds*, 94.

9 Wales, "Journal of William Wales" in Beaglehole ii, 776–869, 818–9; also quoted in Salmond, *Between Worlds*, 96.

10 Furneaux, "Furneaux's Narrative," 744.

11 Burney, "Burney's Log," 751.

12 Salmond, *Between Worlds*, 104.

13 Burney in Beaglehole ii, 751.

14 *A Voyage towards the South Pole, and Round the World. Performed by His Majesty's Ships the* Resolution *and* Adventure, *In the Years 1772, 1773, 1774, and 1775. Written by James Cook, Commander of the* Resolution. *In Which is included, Captain Furneaux's Narrative of his Proceedings in the* Adventure *during the Separation of the Ships.* 2 vols. (London: Printed for W. Strahan and T. Cadell in the Strand, 1777) (hereafter Douglas ii).

15 Furneaux in Douglas ii:2, 255.

16 Burney in Douglas ii:2, 256.

17 It seems significant that Douglas followed so closely the original journals recording Maori cannibalism, given his transformation of Cook's account

of Nootka Sound. Of course, Cook never saw the published version of the second voyage, which came out a year after he had left England for his third Pacific voyage; however, as MacLaren has noted, Cook's death during the course of the third voyage no doubt freed up Douglas's editorial hands somewhat.

18 For example, they are described as "appearing very friendly" when they first come to the *Adventure* to trade. See Furneaux's account in Douglas II:2, 243.

19 The same is true of the *Resolution*'s account: Douglas's Cook uses the term "natives" throughout, and only after finding proof of "these cannibals" does he use the word "savage" (Douglas II:1, 243–5).

20 Cook's dietary measures, including the consumption of fresh greens whenever possible and of intended antiscorbutics from the ships' stores when fresh greens were unavailable, were part of the scientific discovery of his voyages. In 1776 the Royal Society of London awarded Cook the Copley Gold Medal for his paper on the measures taken to prevent scurvy on his circumnavigations. See James Cook, "The Method Taken for preserving the Health and Crew of His Majesty's ship the *Resolution* during her Late Voyage around the World," 405. For a crewman's rather acerbic comments on Cook's dietary measures, see Alexander Home, "Home on Cook as a Dietician" in Beaglehole III:2, 1455–6.

21 Salmond, *Between Worlds*, 94.

22 Ibid., 95–6.

23 Quoted in Salmond, *Between Worlds*, 93. See also Beaglehole, who notes that the incident "led the Forsters to conclude that the English were to blame, because if they had not wanted to buy so many curios the New Zealanders would not have had to send out a war party to replenish their stocks, and if they had not done so no one would have been killed, and consequently no one would have been eaten" (II, lxxvii).

24 Salmond, *Between Worlds*, 160.

25 Ibid., 67. In similar fashion, notwithstanding the sensational news that ten men had been "murdered and eaten" at Queen Charlotte Sound, newspapers ran stories recommending the Bay of Plenty as a fertile spot suitable for British settlement (Salmond, *Between Worlds*, 105). Location may be significant here: the Bay of Plenty, on the east coast of the North Island, is a few hundred kilometres away from Queen Charlotte Sound, located at the north end of the South Island. For eighteenth-century Britons, this distance might well have seemed both huge and insignificant – huge given contemporary means of transportation, and insignificant given the way people tend to make generalizations about entire countries or continents

from a distance (a tendency Canadians travelling outside of Canada often hear in comments like: "I have a friend in Canada. Maybe you know him? His name's Mike and he lives in Toronto.") However, this discrepancy is also characteristic of the exploration genre and, indeed, of imperial culture: the land inhabited by apparently ferocious savages is nonetheless advertised as a desirable possession and sometimes colony.

26 Salmond, *Between Worlds,* 159–60. Other possible causes for Cook's increasing violence on the third voyage have been identified as frustration over his failure to find the Northwest Passage, exhaustion, and Vitamin B deficiency. See Dening, "Sharks That Walk on the Land," 67.

27 B, f 150 is Add. MSS 27888 in the Manuscript department of the British Museum, one of the second voyage's two holograph MSS. See also Salmond, *Between Worlds,* 94.

28 In "Cook and the Nootka," Fisher notes that Lieutenant John Williamson conducted an experiment similar to that of Edgar and reached the same conclusion. "When he was unable to persuade an Indian to eat human flesh by offering him large quantities of iron and brass, he was satisfied that he had found conclusive evidence" that the Natives were not cannibals (85).

29 Ledyard, *A Journal of Captain Cook's Last Voyage to the Pacific Ocean,* 73.

30 Ibid., 74.

31 Archer, "Cannibalism in the Early History of the Northwest Coast," 463.

32 King in Beaglehole III:2, 1406.

33 Samwell, "Samwell's Journal," in Beaglehole III:2, 1092.

34 *A Voyage to the Pacific Ocean; Undertaken by Command of His Majesty, for making Discoveries in the Northern Hemisphere: Performed under the Direction of Captains Cook, Clerke, and Gore, In the Years 1776, 1777, 1778, 1779, and 1780. Being a copious, comprehensive, and satisfactory Abridgement of the Voyage written by Captain James Cook, F.R.S. and Captain James King, LL.D and F.R.S.* 4 vols. (London: Printed for John Stockdale, Scatcherd & Whitaker, John Fielding, and John Hardy, 1784), CIHM 17640.

35 Archer, "Cannibalism in the Early History of the Northwest Coast," 461, 462.

36 In this chapter, of course, I am arguing that cannibalism serves this purpose. I'm sure it is significant that there is no specific mention of cannibalism among women, although this may be hidden behind the generic "he."

37 "Men and boys with homosexual orientations obviously found the sexual aspect of maritime employment cordial and others adopted homosexual

practices if not homosexuality as they found themselves deprived of female partners and in a milieu where sodomy was accepted practice" (Burg, *Sodomy and the Pirate Tradition*, 3). Burg argues that some crew members chose long ocean voyages, instead of similar employment closer to home (such as the merchant marine), precisely because of the possibility of homosexual relations. See also Arthur Gilbert, "Buggery and the British Navy, 1700–1861," for a different perspective. While Gilbert demonstrates the seriousness with which the navy treated sodomy, his account also demonstrates how impossible it was to prevent, let alone stamp out, the practice. Indeed, the seriousness of the prohibtion, no less than the number of recorded cases, suggests a certain prevalence: why prohibit behaviour that does not exist? Gilbert quotes a British officer's comments (in 1910): "to my knowledge, sodomy is a regular thing on ships that go on long cruises. In the warships I would say that sailors preferred it" (73). Such a perception is a likely source for the famous phrase credited to Winston Churchill. According to the *Oxford Dictionary of Quotations* (151), the source of this phrase is Sir Peter Gretton's *Former Naval Person: Winston Churchill and the Royal Navy.* Apparently, one of Churchill's proposals as First Lord of the Admiralty drew criticism from a senior officer on the grounds that it went against accepted naval tradition. Churchill's response: "Don't talk to me about naval tradition. It's nothing but rum, sodomy, and the lash" (Gretton, *Former Naval Person*, 2).

38 Morris, "*Aikāne*: Accounts of Hawaiian Same-Sex Relationships in the Journals of Captain Cook's Third Voyage."

39 Samwell in Beaglehole III:2, 1171–2.

40 Ibid., 1190.

41 Beaglehole III:1, 596.

42 Ibid., 502. However, Palea is also a figure around whom an understanding of the social place of *aikāne* and the events of Cook's voyage revolve. When Cook's ships first arrived at Hawaii, Palea as *aikāne* was Kalaniopuu's representative; when they return to repair the mast, Kamehameha has become the *aliʻi's* favourite. As a result, "Palea's personality has changed; he is now a rogue and provocateur. It is he, the journalists agree, who sets up the incident of theft and the chain of events that lead ultimately to Cook's death. Thus, it may be that two or three of the leading *aikāne* as *aikāne* were crucial in one of the greatest dramas of history" (Morris, "*Aikāne*," 33–4).

43 King in Beaglehole III:2, 624.

44 Clerke in Beaglehole III:2, 596.

45 Samwell in Beaglehole III:2, 1226.

46 Ledyard, *John Ledyard's Journal of Captain Cook's Last Voyage*, 132–3.

47 Clerke in Beaglehole III:2, 596.

48 Gilbert, "Buggery and the British Navy, 1700–1861," 79. Gilbert notes that "buggery remained a capital offense in England until 1861" and that the army and navy treated the offence far more harshly than did the civil courts (72). However, Gilbert also notes that there were a variety of unofficial responses to buggery: "it is certain that the rank and file ..., knowing that conviction might mean death for the offenders, never reported known cases." Captains, for their part, might quietly discharge a man after lashing him for an unspecified charge such as "uncleanliness" (72) or find him guilty of a lesser offence (80). In the eighteenth-century navy, a man was more likely to be hanged for buggery than for murder, provided that the murder was not that of an officer by a sailor (80). From 1755 to 1797 a man might receive almost twice as many lashes for a homosexual offence (527) as for mutiny (282). See Gilbert, "Buggery and the British Navy," 84.

49 Morris, "*Aikāne*," 27.

50 Straub, *Sexual Suspects,* 47. See also Randolph Trumbach, "The Birth of the Queen" and "Sodomitical Assaults, Gender Role, and Sexual Development in Eighteenth-Century London."

51 Kilgour, "Cannibals and Critics," 20.

52 In his study of homosexuality and cannibalism in the novels of American writer Herman Melville, Crain suggests that homosexuality – an intensely taboo subject for Melville's readers – is made available for discussion in the guise of survival cannibalism. Crain opens his discussion with an analysis of Théodore Géricault's *La reseau de la Méduse*, in which unspeakable "cannibalism was symbolized by physical intimacy between statuesque nude men" (Crain, "Lovers of Human Flesh," 26).

53 Though not without dangers of its own: sailors going ashore hoping for sexual encounters carried diseases to which Native peoples had no immunity whatsoever, often leaving epidemics of syphilis and gonorrhea behind them.

54 Swift, *A Modest Proposal,* 441.

55 This whole notion of transforming the Irish from a nation of consumers to consumed depends for some of its irony on a traditional English representation of the Irish as a wild, savage, cannibal people, beginning in the sixteenth century with *The Chronicles of Froissart* (1522–5), translated in 1903 by Sir John Bourchier, Lord Berners. This edition was reduced to a one-volume text by G.C. Macauley in 1913. Cannibalism seems to work as a political red herring: within ten years, two editions of a medieval

French text, which seemingly documented Irish cannibalism, were published in London at the very time that the question of Irish sovereignty was a matter of heated public debate in England as well as in Ireland.

56 Livant, "The Imperial Cannibal."

57 Kilgour, *From Communion to Cannibalism*, 8–9.

58 de Certeau, *Heterologies*, 68. Slemon elaborates on the meaning of cannibalism as a discourse: it "enables mobility for the imperial subject and permits the political production of *meaning*. De Certeau thus calls cannibalism 'an *economy of speech*, in which the body is the price'" ("Bones of Contention," 66).

59 Archer notes that "fear of being eaten on Northwest Coast duty was a preoccupation of many seamen" ("Cannibalism on the Northwest Coast," 465).

60 In its later forms (through, for example, the ban on the potlatch), the discourse of cannibalism worked to dispossess the original inhabitants of their culture if not the actual territory. See Bracken, *The Potlatch Papers*.

61 Goldman, "A Taste of the Wild," 44. Her analysis draws on MacLaren's "Exploration/Travel Literature and the Evolution of the Author."

CHAPTER FIVE

1 Archer, "Cannibalism in the Early History of the Northwest Coast," 462.

2 While Spanish explorers had visited Nootka Sound in 1774, Spain kept such records secret. In consequence, Britain's claim to the territory, based on Cook's "discovery," enjoyed widespread circulation throughout Europe before the Spanish contact became public knowledge.

3 I am thinking here of Clifford Geertz's description of what happened to ethnography when ethnographers started to see it as something to "look *at* as well as through" (*Works and Lives*, 132).

4 Healy, "We Know Your Mob Now," 521.

5 Carter, *The Road to Botany Bay*, xiii–xiv.

6 See P.K. Page's poem "Cook's Mountains" for its consideration of names and naming in the context of European exploration in general and Cook's voyages in particular.

7 Carter, *The Road to Botany Bay*, 67. Mindful that he was making a claim to the Northwest Coast, Cook initially called Nootka Sound King George's Sound, but later changed the name to Nootka Sound, believing that "Nootka" was the inhabitants' name for the place. His third voyage is commemorated in the names he gave the features of the Sound: Cook Channel, Resolution Cove, Bligh Island, and Clerke Peninsula, named

respectively for himself, his ship, its master William Bligh, and the *Discovery*'s captain Charles Clerke.

8 For a discussion of Aboriginal spatial histories, see Chatwin's *The Songlines*. For an extended treatment of conflicting sign systems in the New World, see Todorov's *Conquest of America*, in which Todorov argues that the Aztecs were defeated by the Spaniards primarily because of the latter's greater control of sign systems.

9 Wolfe, *Europe and the People without History*, 4.

10 Wittig's use of the term "ahistoric" suggests its potential usefulness to express what "prehistoric" theoretically ought to mean – before contact with Europeans and the resulting entry into European history. The paradox of the reversal of terms (since the prefix "a" means "not, without") is entirely appropriate to the field: although we "know" that the European discovery of the New World is a figure of speech, that figure has long been treated literally (*The Straight Mind*, 22).

11 Wolfe, *Europe and the People without History*, 5.

12 Ibid.

13 Wolfe offers the example of "schoolbook histories of the United States," informed by a "*teleological understanding* that thirteen colonies clinging to the eastern rim of the continent would, in less than a century, plant the American flag on the shores of the Pacific." His point is instructive: the many other possibilities for political and social organization can be unthinkable or meaningless "only if we assume a God-given drive toward geopolitical unity on the North American continent." Perhaps his method can be applied to the blind spot revealed here: Canadians, although schoolbook versions of *our* history tend also to be formulated with the "teleological understanding" of the birth of the nation, a colonial history, know that "geopolitical unity" is not yet a fact on the North American continent (*Europe and the People without History*, 6).

14 Carter, *The Road to Botany Bay*, xiv.

15 Ibid., xvi.

16 Hulme, *Colonial Encounters*, 6.

17 Pratt, *Imperial Eyes*, 7.

18 Dening, *Performances*, 30.

19 Dening, "Sharks That Walk on the Land: The Death of Captain Cook," *Performances*, 72. In the brief discussion preceding the section of *Performances* called "Making a Present Out of the Past: History's Anthropology," Dening offers another version of the same thought: "History is not the past. It is the past transformed into something else, story. Metonymy: history is metonymy of the present. These stories in their telling are *our* present" (34).

20 Hulme, *Colonial Encounters*, 11. Of course, documents are fragile things; they can disappear, or be changed, as in Russian histories of the Communist era; but Hulme's point refers to the more prosaic cases, in which new perspectives on the past reread archival documents often left untouched for years. My thanks to Michael Khmelnitsky for this point.

21 Dening, *Islands and Beaches*, 3.

22 Beaglehole III:1, 556. See also page 351. In his account of the night before Cook's death, Beaglehole notes at King's comment that a "peice [gun] missed fire": "these words are written over a very thorough deletion, and in the margin, very faint, are the others, 'droped his peice'; so possibly King thought to modify the truth a little." This example illustrates Beaglehole's practice of noting deletions and revisions in the account of Cook's death and the events leading up to it.

23 Spate, "Splicing the Log at Kealakekua Bay," 117.

24 Mackaness, *The Life of Vice-Admiral William Bligh*, 30. Although Bligh's marginal comments suggest he kept a journal of the third voyage, this volume is lost. His record survives only in these marginal comments, many of which were written in pencil and have faded to illegibility, and many of which were cut off by rebinding. Bligh's account disagrees with those of King, Samwell, and the other officers (published and unpublished) and is strongly marked by his sense that his contributions were inadequately recognized in the official *Voyage*.

25 Rickman, *Journal of Captain Cook's Last Voyage to the Pacific Ocean*, 320.

26 Beaglehole III:1, ccv.

27 Samwell, *Narrative of the Death of Captain Cook*, 4, 13.

28 Ibid., 2.

29 Ibid., 17–8.

30 Ibid., 40–1.

31 See Sahlins, *Historical Metaphors and Mythical Realities: Structure in the Early History of the Sandwich Islands Kingdom* and *Islands of History*; Obeyesekere, *The Apotheosis of Captain Cook*; Sahlins, *How "Natives" Think*; and Obeyesekere's Afterword, "On De-Sahlinization," in the revised edition of *The Apotheosis of Captain Cook*. Dening's analysis in "Sharks that Walk on the Land: The Death of Captain Cook" (in the original version published in *Meanjin* as well as in *Performances*) supports Sahlins's analysis of Cook as a Lono-figure.

32 Sahlins, *Historical Metaphors and Mythical Realities*, 11.

33 Ibid., 21.

34 Dening, "Sharks that Walk on the Land," *Performances*, 68.

35 Sahlins, *Historical Metaphors and Mythical Realities*, 20, 22.

36 Ibid., 20.

37 Dening, "Sharks that Walk on the Land," *Performances*, 70.

38 Obeyesekere, *The Apotheosis of Captain Cook*, 91.

39 Ibid., 120.

40 Ibid., 127.

41 See also Smith's *Imagining the Pacific* for one version of this myth: describing the effect of Cook's voyages in economic terms, Smith identifies Cook as Adam "Smith's global agent, [developing] markets and [spreading] the notion of enlightened self-interest, bringing to prehistoric cultures the disguised checks and balances of a market economy" (236).

42 Obeyesekere quotes Dening's statistics from *The Bounty: An Ethnographic History*: "Cook flogged 20, 26 and 37 percent respectively on his three voyages." By the third voyage, Cook used flogging almost twice as much as he had on his first voyage (Obeyesekere, *The Apotheosis of Captain Cook*, 203).

43 Dening, "Sharks that Walk on the Land," *Performances*, 76.

44 For example, Burkhardt, Angus, and Kochanek suggest an explanation for Cook's death that demonstrates Obeyesekere's point: "since Cook's deification, it was no longer important whether he was alive or dead; as a god he was equally powerful in either state. In practical terms the natives may have reasoned that dead gods eat less" (*Sailors and Sauerkraut*, 189).

45 Obeyesekere's analysis is based on Douglas's edition of 1784; Sahlins does not cite Douglas but, rather, uses a Dublin edition of 1784 as well as Beaglehole's scholarly edition of 1967 (both parts).

46 Hynes's satire ("99" in *Publish and Perish*) of the debate between Sahlins and Obeyesekere suggests that it may also reveal the workings of academic capital or the marking of territorial authority.

47 So wrote the historian's son, T.H. Beaglehole, in the "Preface" to his father's *Life of Captain James Cook* (xi). J.C. Beaglehole wrote this biography at the end of his career after editing scholarly editions of the texts of the three voyages as well as one of Banks's *Endeavour* journals. He died before the finishing the revisions, which were completed by his son.

48 Williams, "James Cook," *Dictionary of Canadian Biography*, 163.

49 Ibid., 164.

50 "Cook, James," *The Dictionary of National Biography*, 992.

51 Ibid., 994

52 Ibid.

53 Williams, "James Cook," 165.

54 Ibid., 167.

55 Lawson, *History of Canada for Use in Public Schools*, 227–8.
56 McArthur, *History of Canada for High Schools*, 283–4.
57 Brown, Harman, and Jeanneret, *The Story of Canada*, 198–9.
58 Cameron, Innis, and Boggs, *Living in Canada*, 307.
59 Garrod, McFadden, and Neering, *Canada: Growth of a Nation*, 184.
60 The general context of imperialism is signified here by the feminized version of Columbus's name, the counterpart of "America" as the feminized name of Amerigo Vespucci given to the continent. It may also mark England's claim to possession of the territory over that of the United States: *British* Columbia against the *American* District of Columbia in Washington, DC.
61 This is the "staples theory" first articulated by Innis in *The Fur Trade in Canada*.
62 Perry, *On the Edge of Empire*, 3.
63 G.P.V. and Helen B. Akrigg, *British Columbia Chronicle, 1778–1846*, 4. I should note that I have taken this statement from the Akriggs' book out of context in order to indicate the understanding of BC history presented by writers like Begg and Howay. The full sentence reads "*For the purposes of this chronicle*, British Columbia's history began in 1778 when Captain Cook and his crew became the first white men to set foot upon her territory" (emphasis mine).
64 Woodcock, *British Columbia*, 15.
65 Barman, *The West beyond the West*, 17.
66 Justine Brown discusses the tension in Sir Thomas More's *Utopia* between "*eutopos* (a good place) and *outopos* (no place)" in "Nowherelands: Utopian Communities in BC Fiction," 6.
67 Bowering, *Bowering's BC*, 47–8.
68 It should be said that the only founding moment Bowering presents is that which occurs when Old Man, with the help of Coyote (or Raven on the coast) makes the world. Everything that happens after that is the result of social and cultural forces at work in response to environments and attitudes and the place now called British Columbia and elsewhere (e.g., Europe, the rest of Canada, and the United States).
69 The same is true for national histories produced in the 1990s, such as Bumstead's *The Peoples of Canada* and Conrad, Finkel, and Jaenen's *History of the Canadian Peoples*.
70 Dickason, *Canada's First Nations*, 176, 180, 432n13.
71 Miller, *Skyscrapers Hide the Heavens*, 181.
72 Ray, *I Have Lived Here since the World Began*, 112. Clayton also discusses the ethnographic record of Native perceptions of Cook and other explorers in *Islands of Truth*, 22–7.

73 See Clayton's discussion of the ceremony in *Islands of Truth*, 3–5.

74 The cottage was purchased in 1933 by an Australian businessman, then it was taken apart and transported to Melbourne, where it was re-erected to commemorate Cook's charting of the Victoria coastline. Although the cottage was built by Cook's father, it is by no means certain that James Cook himself ever lived in it. As a museum, it tries to replicate what the cottage that Cook or his parents lived in was probably like. The postmodern irony is presumably unintentional.

75 Dugard, *Farther Than Any Man*, 44, 286.

76 Healy, "'We Know Your Mob Now,'" 512.

77 Ibid., 518.

78 Bowering, *Burning Water*, 21–2.

79 Ibid., 22.

80 Ibid., 136.

81 Ibid., 126.

82 It should perhaps be noted that *Burning Water*'s take on history was not universally appreciated: MacLaren described it as a "droll if superficial entertainment fashioned out of this particular explorer and his modest literary remains" ("Inscribing the Empire," 4); Marcia Crosby argues that its dependence on derogatory stereotypes of Native women undermines the novel's parodic claims ("The Construction of the Imaginary Indian"). Bowering ends the Bibliography of his *Bowering's BC* with the comments by historian W. Kaye Lamb on the novel: "taking only scant account of historical facts and good taste ... he has bespattered his pages with numerous errors of fact that are both pointless and needless ... without a shred of supporting evidence ... the facts speak for themselves" (*Bowering's BC*, 406).

83 Kearns, *Convergences*, n.p.

84 See Akrigg and Akrigg, *British Columbia Chronicle, 1778–1846*, for their chronicle of seasonal trading between English and Nuu-chah-nulth, particularly at Nootka Sound, after Cook. For a more recent historical perspective, see Woodcock, *British Columbia: A History of the Province*. As Barman argues, "No European power considered the Pacific Northwest sufficiently important to make the effort necessary to secure exclusive sovereignty. The more important goal was to ensure that no other nation did so" (*The West beyond the West*, 30).

85 Greenfield, *Narrating Discovery*, 3.

86 Barman, *The West beyond the West*, 352.

87 Ormsby, *British Columbia: A History*, 495.

88 In 1991 Chief Justice Allan McEachern's 394-page judgment in *Delgamuukw v. BC* echoed the colonialist language of previous centuries in

its reliance on attitudes remarkably similar to the four-stages theory so important to Dr Douglas. (See the BC *Studies* special issue entitled *Anthropology and History in the Courts* 95 [1992]) for responses to Chief Justice McEachern's comments.) In the 1997 *Delgamuukw* decision, now considered the legal foundation for Aboriginal title in Canada, the Supreme Court of Canada overturned the BC court's ruling.

89 The 2002 BC referendum asked British Columbians to provide yes or no answers to such questions as "Do you agree that the Provincial Government should adopt the principle that private property should not be expropriated for treaty settlements?" (question 1) and "Do you agree that the Provincial Government should adopt the principle that the terms and conditions of leases and licenses should be respected; and fair compensation for unavoidable disruption of commercial interests should be insured?" (question 2). Notwithstanding considerable outcry from First Nations, church, and social groups that the referendum itself and particularly the manner in which the questions were posed was (1) intended to manipulate voters into answering "yes" and (2) derailed the negotiating process established in the wake of the 1997 *Delgamuukw* decision, the government maintained that its position on all eight questions was "yes." It did, however, acknowledge that it would not consider the results binding – especially, one presumes, in the event that the majority of British Columbians voted "no." Although the referendum was preceded by considerable public debate on both sides of the issue, almost nothing has been publicised about its results.

90 Healy, "'We Know Your Mob Now,'" 22.

91 Smith, *Imagining the Pacific*, 191.

92 Said, *Culture and Imperialism*, 13.

Bibliography

In this study I have, primarily, used two sets of Cook's journals. The first of these is the official edition published in three volumes in 1784. Because the account of the month at Nootka Sound appears in the second volume, the 1784 edition is cited mostly as Douglas III:2. The second set of Cook's journals used extensively is Beaglehole's scholarly edition for the Hakluyt Society, one volume per voyage. They are similarly cited as Beaglehole I, II, or III. The text of the last comes in two parts: Beaglehole III:1 refers to Part 1, which consists of the official journal written by Cook, then Clerke, and finally King; Beaglehole III:2 refers to Part 2, which consists of the journals of William Anderson and David Samwell and extracts from the other officers' journals, to supplement the official account. In Chapter 4's discussion of the textual construction of cannibalism, I cite one other edition of Cook's journals, an abridgment of the third voyage published by John Stockdale, Scatcherd and Whitaker, John Fielding, and John Hardy in 1784, cited as Stockdale. The complete listings for all these editions are to be found under the editors' names in the following Bibliography, although partial references to these editions are also made under James Cook.

The discussion of the textual history of the third voyage (located in Chapter 1) lists a number of other editions of the text. I have listed only those editions that I mention specifically, deeming it unnecessary to duplicate Beddie's excellent *Bibliography* (cited below). Readers who want the complete textual history of Cook's *Voyages* should consult it.

Abbott, John Lawrence. *John Hawkesworth: Eighteenth-Century Man of Letters*. Madison, WI: University of Wisconsin Press, 1982.
Adam, Ian and Helen Tiffin, eds. *Past the Last Post: Theorising Post-Colonialism and Post-Modernism*. Calgary: University of Calgary Press, 1990.

Adams, Carol J. *The Sexual Politics of Meat: A Feminist Vegetarian Critical Theory.* New York: Continuum, 1991.

Adams, Percy. *Travel Literature and the Evolution of the Novel.* Lexington: University Press of Kentucky, 1983.

– ed. *Travel Literature through the Ages: An Anthology.* New York and London: Garland, 1988.

Akrigg, G.P.V., and Helen B. Akrigg. *British Columbia Chronicle, 1778–1846: Adventures by Sea and Land.* Victoria, BC: Discovery, 1975.

Allen, Paula Gunn. *The Sacred Hoop: Recovering the Feminine in American Indian Traditions.* Boston: Beacon, 1986.

Anderson, William. *A Journal of a Voyage made in his Majestys Sloop Resolution May 16 1776.* Wm Anderson, 30 May 1776–2 September 1777.

Anthropology and History in the Courts. BC *Studies* (special issue) 95 (1992).

Archer, Christon I. "Cannibalism in the Early History of the Northwest Coast: Enduring Myths and Neglected Realities." *Canadian Historical Review* 61, 4 (1980): 253–79.

– "The Spanish Reaction to Cook's Third Voyage." In *Captain James Cook and His Times*, ed. Robin Fisher and Hugh Johnston, *Captain James Cook and His Times*, 99–119. Seattle, WA: University of Washington Press, 1979.

Arens, W. *The Man-Eating Myth: Anthropology and Anthropophagy.* New York: Oxford University Press, 1979.

– "Rethinking Anthropophagy." In *Cannibalism and the Colonial World*, ed. Francis Barker, Peter Hulme, and Margaret Iverson, 39–62. Cambridge: Cambridge University Press, 1998.

Ashcroft, Bill, Gareth Griffiths, and Helen Tiffin. *The Empire Writes Back: Theory and Practice in Post-Colonial Literatures.* New Accents Series. London and New York: Routledge, 1989.

Auerbach, Erich. *Mimesis: The Representation of Reality in Western Literature.* Trans. Willard Trask. New York: Anchor-Doubleday, 1957 [1946].

Austen, Jane. *Pride and Prejudice.* Markham, ON: Penguin, 1972 [1813].

Bann, Stephen. "From Captain Cook to Neil Armstrong: Colonial Expansion and the Structure of Landscape." In *Reading Landscape: Country – City – Capital*, ed. Simon Pugh, 214–30. Manchester and New York: Manchester University Press, 1990.

Barker, Francis, Peter Hulme, and Margaret Iverson, eds. *Cannibalism and the Colonial World.* Cambridge: Cambridge University Press, 1998.

– eds. *Colonial Discourse/Postcolonial Theory.* Manchester and New York: Manchester University Press, 1994.

Barman, Jean. *The West beyond the West: A History of British Columbia.* Rev. ed. Toronto: University of Toronto Press, 1996.

Barrell, John. *The Idea of Landscape and the Sense of Place, 1730–1840: An Approach to the Poetry of John Clare.* Cambridge: Cambridge University Press, 1972.

Bartroli, Tomás. *Brief Presence: Spain's Activity on America's Northwest Coast, 1774–1796.* Vancouver, BC: Electric Print, 1991. (UBC Rare Book and Special Collections pamphlet files spam 21814.)

Batten, Charles L., Jr. *Pleasurable Instruction: Form and Convention in Eighteenth-Century Travel Literature.* Berkeley, Los Angeles, London: University of California Press, 1978.

Bayly, William. *Astronomical Observations.* London, 1782 (CIHM 17414).

Bazerman, Charles. *Shaping Written Knowledge: The Genre and Activity of the Experimental Article in Science.* Madison, WI.: University of Wisconsin Press, 1988.

Beaglehole, J.C. *Cook the Writer.* Sydney: Sydney University Press, 1970.

– ed. *The Endeavour Journal of Joseph Banks, 1768–1771.* Sydney Trustees of the Public Library of New South Wales in association with Angus and Robertson, 1962.

– ed. *The Life of Captain James Cook.* Vol. IV of *The Journals of Captain James Cook on His Voyages of Discovery.* 4 vols. Hakluyt Society Extra Series 37. London: The Hakluyt Society, 1974.

– ed. *The Voyage of the* Endeavour, *1768–1771.* Vol. I of *The Journals of Captain James Cook on His Voyages of Discovery.* 4 vols. Hakluyt Society Extra Series 34. Cambridge: Hakluyt Society at the University Press, 1955.

– ed. *The Voyage of the* Resolution *and* Adventure, *1772–1775.* Vol. II of *The Journals of Captain James Cook on His Voyages of Discovery.* 4 vols. Hakluyt Society Extra Series 35. Cambridge: Hakluyt Society at the University Press, 1961.

– ed. *The Voyage of the* Resolution *and* Discovery, *1776–1780.* 2 parts. Vol. III of *The Journals of Captain James Cook on His Voyages of Discovery.* 4 vols. Hakluyt Society Extra Series 36. Cambridge: Hakluyt Society at the University Press, 1967.

Beaglehole, T.H. "Preface." In *The Life of Captain James Cook.* By J.C. Beaglehole. London: Adam and Charles Black, 1974.

Beddie, M.K. *Bibliography of Captain James Cook, R.N., F.R.S., Circumnavigator.* 2nd ed. Sydney: Mitchell Library, 1970.

Begg, Alexander. *History of British Columbia: From Its Earliest Discovery to the Present Time.* The Ryerson Archive Series. Toronto, Montreal, New York, London, Sydney, Mexico, Panama, Johannesburg, Dusseldorf, Rio de Janeiro, New Delhi, Kuala Lumpur, Singapore: McGraw-Hill Ryerson, 1972 [1894].

Behn, Aphra. *Oroonoko: Or, the Royal Slave*. Ed. and intro. Lore Metzger. New York: Norton, 1973 [1688].

Berger, John, Sven Blomberg, Chris Fox, Michael Dibb, and Richard Hollis. *Ways of Seeing*. London: BBC and Penguin Books, 1972.

Bernal, Martin. *The Fabrication of Ancient Greece, 1785–1985*. Vol. 1 of *Black Athena: The Afroasiatic Roots of Classical Civilization*. 3 vols. London: Free Association, 1987.

Blaise, Clark, and Bharati Mukherjee. *Days and Nights in Calcutta*. Rev. ed. Markham, ON: Penguin, 1986.

Bohls, Elizabeth A. *Women Travel Writers and the Language of Aesthetics, 1716–1818*. Cambridge Studies in Romanticism. Cambridge: Cambridge University Press, 1995.

Borg, Marcus J. *The God We Never Knew: Beyond Dogmatic Religion to a More Authentic Contemporary Faith*. San Francisco: Harper, 1997.

Boswell, James. *Boswell: The Ominous Years, 1774–1776*. Ed. Charles Ryskamp and Frederick A. Pottle. New York: McGraw-Hill, 1963.

– *Boswell on the Grand Tour: Germany and Switzerland, 1764*. Ed. Frederick A. Pottle. Toronto: McGraw-Hill, 1953.

– *Boswell on the Grand Tour: Italy, Corsica, and France, 1765–6*. Ed. Frank Brady and Frederick A. Pottle. Toronto: William Heinemann, 1955.

– *Boswell's London Journal*. Ed. Frederick A. Pottle. Toronto: McGraw-Hill, 1950.

Bowering, George. *Bowering's BC: A Swashbuckling History*. Toronto: Viking, 1996.

– *Burning Water*. Don Mills, ON: Musson, 1980.

Bracken, Christopher. *The Potlatch Papers: A Colonial Case History*. Chicago: University of Chicago Press, 1997.

Brody, Hugh. *Maps and Dreams: Indians and the British Columbia Frontier*. Vancouver and Toronto: Douglas and McIntrye, 1988.

Brown, George W., Eleanor Harman, and Marsh Jeanneret. *The Story of Canada*. Toronto: Copp Clark, 1949.

Brown, Justine. "Nowherelands: Utopian Communities in BC Fiction." *BC Studies* 109 (1996): 4–28.

Brown, Laura. "The Romance of Empire: *Oroonoko* and the Trade in Slaves." In *The New Eighteenth Century: Theory, Politics, English Literature*, ed. Felicity Nussbaum and Laura Brown, 41–61. New York: Methuen, 1987.

Brydon, Diana. "New Approaches to the New Literatures in English: Are We in Danger of Incorporating Disparity?" In *A Shaping of Connections: Commonwealth Literature Studies – Then and Now*, ed. Hena Maes-Jelinek, Kirsten Holst Petersen, and Anna Rutherford, 89–99. Sydney: Dangeroo, 1989.

Bryson, Norman. *Tradition and Desire: From David to Delacroix.* Cambridge Studies in French. New York: Cambridge University Press, 1984.

Bumstead, J.M. *The Peoples of Canada: A Pre-Confederation History.* Toronto: Oxford University Press, 1992.

Burg, B.R. *Sodomy and the Pirate Tradition: English Sea-Rovers in the Seventeenth-Century Caribbean.* New York: New York University Press, 1984.

Burke, Edmund. *Philosophical Enquiry into Our Ideas of the Sublime and Beautiful.* Ed. and intro. Adam Phillips. Oxford and New York: Oxford University Press, 1990 [1757].

Burkhardt, Barbara, Barrie Angus, and Doris Kochanek. *Sailors and Sauerkraut.* Sidney, BC: Gray's Publishing, 1978.

Burney, Frances. *Evelina.* Ed. Stewart J. Cooke. Norton Critical Edition. New York and London: W.W. Norton, 1998 [1778].

Burney, James. "Burney's Log." Beaglehole II, 746–52.

– *Journal of the Proceedings of His Majys. Sloop, the Discovery, Chas. Clerke, Commander, in company with the Resolution, Captn. Jas. Cook, Jas. Burney, Latona.* Ts. of 4 vol. ms. in Mitchell Library, Sydney, Australia. University of British Columbia Special Collections.

Cameron, Alex A., Mary Quayle Innis, and Arnold Boggs. *Living in Canada.* Toronto: Clarke, Irwin, 1954.

Campbell, Mary B. *Witness and the Other World: Exotic European Travel Writing, 400–1600.* Ithaca and London: Cornell University Press, 1988.

Carter, Paul. *The Road to Botany Bay: Essays in Spatial History.* London and Boston: Faber and Faber, 1987.

Cartier, Jacques. "Cartier's First Voyage, 1534." In *The Voyages of Jacques Cartier,* trans. H.P. Biggar, ed. and intro. Ramsay Cook, 3–34. Toronto: University of Toronto Press, 1993.

– *Navigations to Newe Fraunce.* Trans. John Florio. Ann Arbor, MI: University Microforms 1966 [1580].

Carver, Jonathan. *Travels through the Interior Part of North America, in the Years 1776, 1777, and 1778.* London, 1778.

Chatwin, Bruce. *The Songlines.* Markham, ON: Penguin, 1987.

The Chronicles of Froissart, 1522–5. Trans. Sir John Bourchier, Lord Berners. London: David Nutt, 1903. (Abridged ed. G.C. Macauley, London: MacMillan, 1913.)

Clayton, Daniel Wright. *Islands of Truth: The Imperial Fashioning of Vancouver Island.* Vancouver and Toronto: UBC Press, 2000.

Cleland, John. *Memoirs of a Woman of Pleasure.* Intro. Peter Quennell. New York: Putnam, 1963 [1749].

Clerke, Charles. *Journal*. Beaglehole III:2, 1301–39.

Clifford, James. "Introduction: Partial Truths." In *Writing Culture: The Poetics and Politics of Ethnography*, ed. James Clifford and George E. Marcus, 1–26. Berkeley, Los Angeles, and London: University of California Press, 1986.

– *The Predicament of Culture: Twentieth-Century Ethnography, Literature, and Art*. Cambridge, MA: Harvard University Press, 1988.

Cobbe, Hugh, ed. *Cook's Voyages and Peoples of the Pacific*. London: British Museum Publications, 1979.

Colley, Linda. *Britons: Forging the Nation, 1707–1837*. London: Pimlico, 1992.

Columbus, Christopher. *Letter of Columbus. Select Documents Illustrating the Four Voyages of Columbus, including those contained in R.H. Major's Select Letters of Christopher Columbus*. Vol. 1 of 2. Trans. and ed. Cecil Jane. London: Hakluyt Society, 1930.

Conrad, Joseph. *Heart of Darkness*. In *The Portable Conrad*. Rev. ed. Morton Dauwen Zabel, 490–603. Markham, ON: Penguin Viking, 1975 [1899].

Conrad, Margaret, Alvin Finkel, and Cornelius Jaenen. *History of the Canadian Peoples: Beginnings to 1867*. Vol. 1 of 2. Rev. ed. Toronto: Copp Clark Pitman, 1998 [1993].

[Cook, James.] *The British Navigator; Containing Captain Cook's Three Voyages Round the World ...* London: John Fielding, 1783.

– *Captain Cook's Three Voyages Round the World: with a Sketch of His Life*. Ed. Charles R. Low. Routledge's Excelsior Series No. 57. London: Routledge, 1880 (CIHM 14801).

– *Captain Cook's Voyages of Discovery*. Ed. Sir John Barrow. Everyman's Library: Travel and Topography Series. London: JM Dent; New York: EP Dutton, 1906.

– *A Compendious History of Captain Cook's [Last] Voyage ...* London: G. Kearsley, 1784 CIHM 17627.

"Cook, James." In *The Dictionary of National Biography*. Vol. 4, ed. Sir Leslie Stephen and Sir Sidney Lee, 991–5. Oxford: Oxford University Press; London: Humphrey Milford, 1917 – .

Cook, James. "The Method Taken for preserving the Health of the Crew of His Majesty's Ship the *Resolution* during her Late Voyage around the World." In *The Philosophical Transactions of the Royal Society of London*. Vol. 66, 402–6. London: The Royal Society, 1776.

– *The Third and Last Voyage of Captain Cook*. Intro. Hugh Reginald Haweis. Routledge's World Library. London and New York: Routledge 1886 (CIHM 29559).

- *The Voyage of the* Resolution *and* Adventure *1772–1775*. ed. J.C. Beaglehole.
- *The Voyage of the* Resolution *and* Discovery *1776–1780*. Ed. J.C. Beaglehole.
- *A Voyage to the Pacific Ocean* ... Ed. Bishop Douglas. London, 1784.
- *A Voyage to the Pacific Ocean* ... [Abridged ed.] Printed for John Stockdale, Scatcherd and Whitaker, John Fielding, and John Hardy. London, 1784.
- *A Voyage to the Pacific Ocean* ... Dublin, 1784 (CIHM 42432–42436).

Cook, James and Tobias Furneaux. *Captain Cook's Voyages Round the World ... including Captain Furneaux's Journal of his Proceedings during the Separation of the Ships* ... Newcastle, 1790 (CIHM 17752).

Cook, James, Arthur Phillip, and Constantin John Phipps. *A Voyage to the Pacific Ocean ... with The Voyage of Governor Phillip to Botany Bay*. Newcastle, 1790 (CIHM 17753).

Cook, Ramsay. "Donnacona Discovers Europe: Rereading Jacques Cartier's Voyages." In *The Voyages of Jacques Cartier*, trans. H.P. Biggar, ed. and intro. Ramsay Cook, ix-xli. Toronto: University of Toronto Press, 1993.

Cowell, Andrew. "The Apocalypse of Paradise and the Salvation of the West: Nightmare Visions of the Future in the Pacific Eden." *Cultural Studies* 13, 1 (1999): 138–60.

Crain, Caleb. "Lovers of Human Flesh: Homosexuality and Cannibalism in Melville's Novels." *American Literature* 66, 1 (1994): 25–53.

Crosby, Alfred W. *Ecological Imperialism: The Biological Expansion of Europe, 900–1900*. Cambridge: Cambridge University Press, 1986.

Crosby, Marcia. "The Construction of the Imaginary Indian." In *Vancouver Anthology: The Institutional Politics of Art*, ed. Stan Douglas, 267–91. A Project of the Or Gallery. Vancouver: Talonbooks, 1991.

Culpepper, Nicholas. *The English Physician Englarged* ... London, 1770 [1653].

Darwin, Charles. *Journal of Researches into the Geology and Natural History of the Various Countries Visited by H.M.S. Beagle*. Facs. rpt. New York and London: Hafher, 1952 [1839].

Dathorne, O.R. *Imagining the World: Mythical Belief versus Reality in Global Encounters*. Westport, CT and London: Bergin and Garvey, 1994.

Dawson, Christopher, ed. *The Mongol Mission: Narratives and Letters of the Franciscan Missionaries in Mongolia and China in the Thirteenth and Fourteenth Centuries*. New York: Sheed and Ward, 1955.

De Certeau, Michel. *Heterologies: Discourse on the Other*. Trans. Brian Massumi. Minneapolis: University of Minnesota Press, 1986.

Defoe, Daniel. *Moll Flanders*. Ed. Edward Kelly. New York: Norton, 1973 [1722].

– *Robinson Crusoe*. Ed. Angus Ross. Markham, ON: Penguin, 1965 [1719].

Denham, Sir John. *Cooper's Hill*. Ed. Brendan O'Hehir, *Expans'd Hieroglyphicks: A Critical Edition of Sir John Denham's* Coopers Hill. Berkeley: University of California Press, 1969 [1665].

Dening, Greg. *The Bounty: An Ethnographic History*. Monograph Series No. 1. Melbourne: University of Melbourne History Department, 1988.

– *Islands and Beaches: Discourse on a Silent Land, Marquesas, 1774–1880*. Carlton, Vic.: Melbourne University Press, 1980.

– "Sharks that Walk on the Land: The Death of Captain Cook." *Meanjin* 41, 4 (1982): 427–37.

– "Sharks that Walk on the Land: The Death of Captain Cook." In *Performances*, 64–78. Chicago: University of Chicago Press, 1996.

Dewald, Carolyn. "Introduction." In Herodotus. *The Histories*, trans. Robin Waterfield, ix-xli. Oxford: Oxford University Press, 1998.

Dickason, Olive Patricia. *Canada's First Nations: A History of Founding Peoples from Earliest Times*. 2nd ed. Toronto: Oxford University Press, 1997.

– *The Myth of the Savage and the Beginning of French Colonialism in the Americas*. Edmonton: University of Alberta Press, 1984.

Diderot, Denis et d'Alembert. *L'Encyclopédie, ou Dictionnaire Raisonné des Sciences, des Arts et des Lettres ...* 1751–65. Facs. ed. Elmsford, NY and Paris: Pergamon, 1969.

Discovery 1778: Captain James Cook and the Peoples of the Pacific / Découvertes 1778: le Capitaine James Cook et le Peuplades du Pacifique. Vancouver: Vancouver Museums and Planetarium Association, 1982.

Douglas, Bishop John, ed. *A Voyage to the Pacific Ocean Undertaken by the Command of His Majesty, for making Discoveries in the Northern Hemisphere. To Determine the Position and Extent of the West Side of North America; its Distance from Asia; and the Practicability of a Northern Passage to Europe. Performed Under the Direction of Captains Cook, Clerke, and Gore, in His Majesty's Ships the* Resolution *and* Discovery. *In the Years 1776, 1777, 1778, 1779, and 1780*. 3 Vols. London: Printed by W. and A. Strahan for G. Nicol and T. Cadell, 1784.

– *A Voyage towards the South Pole, and Round the World. Performed by His Majesty's Ships the* Resolution *and* Adventure, *In the Years 1772, 1773, 1774, and 1775. Written by James Cook, Commander of the* Resolution. *In Which is included, Captain Furneaux's Narrative of his Proceedings in the* Adventure *during the Separation of the Ships*. 2 vols. London: Printed for W. Strahan and T. Cadell in the Strand, 1777.

Dugard, Martin. *Farther Than Any Man: The Rise and Fall of Captain James Cook*. New York, London, Toronto, Sydney, and Singapore: Pocket, 2001.

Duncan, James. "Sites of Representation: Place, Time and the Discourse of the Other." In *Place/Culture/Representation*, ed. James Duncan and David Ley, 39–56. London and New York: Routledge, 1993.

Edgar, Thomas. *Portion of an Incomplete Journal*. Dublin, 1784 (CIHM 18145).

Edwards, Philip. *The Story of the Voyage: Sea-Narratives in Eighteenth-century England*. Cambridge: Cambridge University Press, 1994.

Ellis, William. *An Authentic Narrative of a Voyage Performed by Captain Cook ...* London, 1782 (CIHM 37249).

Encyclopédie Larousse Méthodique. Dir. Paul Angé. 2 tomes. Paris: Larousse, 1955.

Fabian, Johannes. *Time and the Other: How Anthropology Makes Its Object*. New York: Columbia University Press, 1983.

Fielding, Henry. *Tom Jones*. Ed. Sheridan Baker. New York: Norton, 1973 [1749].

Fisher, Robin. *Contact and Conflict: Indian-European Relations in British Columbia, 1774–1890*. Vancouver: UBC Press, 1977.

– "Contact and Trade, 1774–1849." In *The Pacific Province: A History of British Columbia*, ed. Hugh J.M. Johnston, 48–67. Vancouver and Toronto: Douglas and McIntyre, 1996.

– "Cook and the Nootka." In *Captain James Cook and His Times*, ed. Robin Fisher and Hugh Johnston, 81–98. Seattle, WA: University of Washington Press, 1979.

Fisher, Robin, and Hugh Johnston, eds. *Captain James Cook and His Times*. Seattle, WA: University of Washington Press, 1979.

– *From Maps to Metaphors: The Pacific World of George Vancouver*. Vancouver: UBC Press, 1993.

Foucault, Michel. *Discipline and Punish: The Birth of the Prison*. Trans. Alan Sheridan. New York: Vintage, 1977.

– *The History of Sexuality: An Introduction*. Vol. 1 of 3. Trans. Robert Hurley. New York: Vintage, 1978.

Frost, Alan. "Become a Name: Beaglehole's Life of Cook." *Meanjin* (1975): 96–8.

– *Botany Bay Mirages: Illusions of Australia's Convict Beginnings*. Carlton, Vic.: Melbourne University Press, 1994.

Furneaux, Tobias. "Furneaux's Narrative." Beaglehole II, 729–45.

Garrod, Stan, Fred McFadden, and Rosemary Neering. *Canada: Growth of a Nation*. Toronto: Fitzhenry and Whiteside, 1980.

Geertz, Clifford. *Works and Lives: The Anthropologist as Author*. Stanford: Stanford University Press, 1988.

Gilbert, Arthur. "Buggery and the British Navy, 1700–1861." *Journal of Social History* 10, 1 (1976): 72–98.

Gilbert, George. *Journal, 1776–1780*. Typescript. British Museum MSS (Additional 38530) University of British Columbia Special Collections.

Gilpin, William. *Observations on the River Wye and Several Parts of South Wales, &c. relative chiefly to Picturesque Beauty; made in the Summer of the Year 1770*. 5th ed. London, 1800.

Glickman, Susan. *The Picturesque and the Sublime: A Poetics of the Canadian Landscape*. Montreal: McGill-Queen's University Press, 1998.

Goldman, Marlene. "A Taste of the Wild: A Critique of Representations of Natives as Cannibals in Late Eighteenth- and Nineteenth-Century Canadian Exploration Literature." In *Literary Studies East and West*. Vol. 10: *Multiculturalism and Representation: Selected Essays*, ed. John Rieder and Larry E. Smith, 43–64. Honolulu: University of Hawaii and the East-West Centre, 1996.

Gough, Barry M. *Distant Dominion: Britain and the Northwest Coast of North America, 1579–1809*. Vancouver: UBC Press, 1980.

– *The Northwest Coast: British Navigation, Trade, and Discoveries to 1812*. Vancouver: UBC Press, 1992.

Gould, Stephen Jay. *The Mismeasure of Man*. New York: Norton, 1981.

Greenblatt, Stephen. *Marvelous Possessions: The Wonder of the New World*. Chicago: University of Chicago Press, 1971.

Greenfield, Bruce. *Narrating Discovery: The Romantic Exploration in American Literature, 1790–1855*. New York: Columbia University Press, 1992.

Gretton, Sir Peter. *Former Naval Person: Winston Churchill and the Royal Navy*. London: Cassell, 1968.

Guest, Harriet. "Curiously Marked: Tattooing, Masculinity, and Nationality in Eighteenth-Century British Perceptions of the South Pacific." In *Painting and the Politics of Culture: New Essays on British Art, 1700–1850*, ed. John Barrell, 101–34. Oxford and New York: Oxford University Press, 1992.

Hakluyt, Richard, ed. *The Principall Navigations, Voiages and Discoveries of the English Nation*. Facs. ed. Intro. David Beers Quinn and Raleigh Ashlin Skelton. 2 vols. Cambridge: Hakluyt Society and the Peabody Museum of Salem, 1965 [1589].

Healy, Chris. "'We Know Your Mob Now': Histories and Their Cultures." *Meanjin* 49, 3 (1990): 512–23.

Hearne, Samuel. *A Journey from Prince of Wales's Fort in Hudson's Bay to the Northern Ocean undertaken by order of the Hudson's Bay Company for the Discovery of Copper Mines, A North West Passage &c. In the Years 1769, 1770, 1771, and 1772.* Edmonton: Hurtig, 1971 [1795].

Henige, David. *In Search of Columbus: The Sources for the First Voyage.* Tucson: University of Arizona Press, 1991.

Herodotus. *The Histories.* Trans. Robin Waterfield. Oxford: Oxford University Press, 1998.

Home, Alexander. "Home on Cook as a Dietician." Beaglehole III:2, 1455–6.

Hough, Richard. *Captain James Cook.* New York and London: Norton, 1997.

Howay, F.W. *British Columbia: The Making of a Province.* Toronto: Ryerson, 1928.

Howse, Derek, ed. *Background to Discovery: Pacific Exploration from Dampier to Cook.* Berkeley, Los Angeles, and Oxford: University of California Press, 1990.

Hulme, Peter. *Colonial Encounters: Europe and the Native Caribbean, 1492–1797.* New York: Methuen, 1986.

– "Introduction: The Cannibal Scene." In *Cannibalism and the Colonial World*, ed. Francis Barker, Peter Hulme, and Margaret Iverson, 1–38. Cambridge: Cambridge University Press, 1998.

Hume, Kathryn. *Fantasy and Mimesis: Responses to Reality in Western Literature.* New York and London: Methuen, 1984.

Hunt, John Dixon, and Peter Willis, eds. *The Genius of Place: The English Landscape Garden, 1620–1820.* San Francisco: Harper and Row, 1975.

Hynes, James. *Publish and Perish: Three Tales of Tenure and Terror.* New York: Picador USA, 1997.

Innis, Harold A. *The Fur Trade in Canada: An Introduction to Canadian Economic History.* Rev. ed. Toronto: University of Toronto Press, 1956 [1930].

Jameson, Anna Brownell. *Winter Studies and Summer Rambles.* Toronto: McClelland and Stewart, 1990 [1838].

Jasen, Patricia. *Wild Things: Nature, Culture, and Tourism in Ontario, 1790–1914.* Toronto: University of Toronto Press, 1995.

Johnson, Samuel. *A Dictionary of the English Language.* Facs. ed. 2 vols. New York: AMS, 1967 [1755].

Joppien, Rüdiger, and Bernard Smith. *The Voyage of the* Resolution *and* Discovery, *1776–1780.* Vol. 3, Part 1 of *The Art of Captain Cook's Voyages.* Melbourne: Oxford University Press in association with the Australian Academy of the Humanities, 1987.

Kearns, Lionel. *Convergences.* Toronto: Coach House, 1984.

Kilgour, Maggie. "Cannibals and Critics: An Exploration of James de Mille's *Strange Manuscript.*" *Mosaic* 30, 1 (1997): 19–37.

– *From Communion to Cannibalism: An Anatomy of Metaphors of Incorporation.* Princeton, NJ: Princeton University Press, 1990.

– "The Function of Cannibalism at the Present Time." In *Cannibalism and the Colonial World,* ed. Francis Barker, Peter Hulme, and Margaret Iverson, 238–59, Cambridge: Cambridge University Press, 1998.

King, James. *Journal.* Beaglehole III:2, 1361–1454.

Kingsley, Mary. *Travels in West Africa: Congo Français, Coriso and Cameroons.* London: Frank Cass, 1965 [1897].

Kupperman, Karen Ordahl. *Settling with the Indians: The Meeting of English and Indian Cultures in America, 1580–1640.* Totowa, NJ: Rowman and Littlefield, 1980.

Lawson, Maria. *History of Canada for Use in Public Schools.* Ed. A.H. Reynar. Gage's Twentieth-Century Series, Authorized for use in the Schools of British Columbia. Toronto: Gage, 1906.

Ledyard, John. *John Ledyard's Journal of Captain Cook's Last Voyage.* Ed. James Kenneth Munford et al. Oregon State Monographs: Studies in History #3. Corvallis, OR: Oregon State University Press, 1963.

– *A Journal of Captain Cook's Last Voyage to the Pacific Ocean, and in Quest of a North-West Passage, between Asia and America; Performed in the Years 1776, 1777, 1778, and 1779.* Hartford, CT, 1783.

Lefevre, Karen Burke. *Invention as a Social Act.* Carbondale and Edwardsville: Southern Illinois University Press and the Conference on College Composition and Communication, 1987.

Lévi-Strauss, Claude. *The Elementary Structures of Kinship.* Boston: Beacon, 1969.

– *Tristes Tropiques.* Trans. John Russell. New York: Criterion, 1961 [1955].

Livant, Bill. "The Imperial Cannibal." In *Cultural Politics in Contemporary America,* ed. Ian Angus and Sut Jhally, 26–36. New York and London: Routledge, 1989.

Locke, John. *An Essay Concerning Human Understanding.* Ed. Peter H. Nidditch. Oxford: Clarendon, 1975 [1690].

Lovejoy, Arthur. *The Great Chain of Being: A Study of the History of an Idea.* New York: Harper Torchbooks, 1960 [1936].

Lyons, Paul. "From Man-Eaters to Spam-Eaters: Literary Tourism and the Discourse of Cannibalism from Melville to Paul Theroux." *Arizona Quarterly* 52, 2 (1995): 33–62.

MacCannell, Dean. *The Tourist: A New Theory of the Leisure Class.* New York: Schocken, 1976.

Mackaness, George. *The Life of Vice-Admiral William Bligh*. 2 vols. in 1. New York and Toronto: Farrar and Rinehart, 1936.

Mackay, David. *In the Wake of Cook: Exploration, Science and Empire, 1780–1801*. London: Croom Helm, 1985.

Mackenzie, Alexander. *Voyages from Montreal on the River St Laurence through the Continent of North America to the Frozen and Pacific Oceans in the Years 1789 and 1793 with a Preliminary Account of the Rise, Progress, and Present State of the Fur Trade of that Country*. Ed. Roy Daniells. Edmonton: Hurtig, 1971 [1801].

MacLaren, I.S. "The Aesthetic Mapping of Nature in the Second Franklin Expedition." *Journal of Canadian Studies* 20, 1 (1985): 39–57.

– "Aesthetic Mappings of the West by the Palliser and Hind Survey Expeditions, 1857–1859." *Studies in Canadian Literature* 10, 1–2 (1985): 24–52.

– "Creating Travel Literature: The Case of Paul Kane." *Papers of the Bibliographical Society of Canada* 27 (1988): 80–95.

– "David Thompson's Imaginative Mapping of the Canadian Northwest, 1784–1812." *Ariel* 15, 2 (1984): 89–106.

– "Exploration/Travel Literature and the Evolution of the Author." *International Journal of Canadian Studies/Revue internationale d'Ètudes canadiennes* 5 (1992): 39–68.

– "Explorers' and Travellers' Narratives: A Peregrination through Different Editions." *Facsimile* 12 (1994): 8–16.

– "The Grandest Tour: the Aesthetics of Landscape in Sir George Back's Exploration of the Eastern Arctic, 1833–1837." *English Studies in Canada* 10, 4 (1984): 436–56.

– "Inscribing the Empire: the Role of the Editor and Publisher in the Literature and Art of Nineteenth-Century Arctic Exploration." Transcript of a paper for the *Vancouver Conference on Exploration and Discovery*. Simon Fraser University, Vancouver, BC, 26 April 1992. University of British Columbia Special Collections SPAM 22887.

– "The McGregor Syndrome; or, The Survival of Patterns of Isolated Butterflies on Rocks in the Haunted Wilderness of the Unnamed Bush Garden beyond the Land Itself." (Review of *The Wacousta Syndrome: Explorations in the Canadian Landscape* by Gaile McGregor.) *Canadian Poetry* 18 (1986): 118–30.

– "Notes Towards a Reconsideration of Paul Kane's Art and Prose." *Canadian Literature* 113, 4 (1987): 179–205.

– "Retaining Captaincy of the Soul: Response to Nature in the First Franklin Expedition." *Essays on Canadian Writing* 28 (1984): 57–92.

– "Samuel Hearne and the Landscape of Discovery." *Canadian Literature*
  103 (1984): 27–41.

Malinowski, Bronislaw. *Argonauts of the Western Pacific: An Account of
Native Enterprise and Adventure in the Archipelagoes of Melanesian New
Guinea*. London: Routledge; New York: Dutton, 1922.

– *A Diary in the Strict Sense of the Term*. Trans. Norbert Guterman. New
  York: Harcourt, Brace, and World, 1967.

Mandeville, John. *The Travels of Sir John Mandeville*. Trans. C.W.R.D.
Mosely. Markham, ON: Penguin, 1983.

Mark, Carl. *Captain Cook at Nootka: Two Sides of the Coin; Two Sides of
the Story*. Victoria, BC: Captain Cook Bicentennial Committee, 1978.
University of British Columbia Special Collections SPAM 13809.

Mason, Peter. *Deconstructing America: Representations of the Other*. London
and New York: Routledge, 1990.

McArthur, Duncan. *History of Canada for High Schools*. Authorized for use
in the Schools of Nova Scotia and British Columbia. Toronto: Gage,
1927.

McCormick, E.H. *Omai: Pacific Envoy*. Auckland: Auckland University Press
and Oxford University Press, 1977.

McDonnell, Porter W., Jr. *Introduction to Map Projections*. New York and
Basel: Marcel Dekker, 1979.

McDowell, Jim. *Hamatsa: The Enigma of Cannibalism on the Northwest
Coast*. Vancouver: Ronsdale, 1997.

McIntosh, Carey. *The Evolution of English Prose, 1700–1800: Style,
Politeness, and Print Culture*. Cambridge, New York, and Melbourne:
Cambridge University Press, 1998.

Megaw, J.V.S., ed. *Employ'd as a Discoverer: Papers Presented at the Captain
Cook Bi-Centenary Historical Symposium, Sydney*. Sydney: A.H. and A.W.
Reed for the Sutherland Shire Council, 1971.

Merchant, Carolyn. *The Death of Nature: Women, Ecology, and the Scientific
Revolution*. London: Wildwood House, 1982.

Miller, J.R. *Skyscrapers Hide the Heavens: A History of Indian-White Relations
in Canada*. 3rd ed. Toronto: University of Toronto Press, 2000 [1991].

Miner, Horace. "Body Ritual Among the Nacirema." *American
Anthropologist* 58, 3 (1956): 503–7.

Montaigne. "Of Cannibals." 1:31 of *The Complete Essays of Montaigne*,
trans. Donald M. Frame, 150–9. Stanford: Stanford University Press,
1958.

Moorehead, Alan. *The Fatal Impact: The Invasion of the South Pacific,
1767–1840*. London: Hamish Hamilton, 1966.

Morris, Robert J. "*Aikāne*: Accounts of Hawaiian Same-Sex Relationships in the Journals of Captain Cook's Third Voyage, 1776–80." *Journal of Homosexuality* 19, 4 (1990): 21–54.

Morrison, Toni. *Playing in the Dark: Whiteness and the Literary Imagination.* Cambridge, MA and London: Harvard University Press, 1992.

Neatby, Leslie H. *In Quest of the North West Passage.* London: Constable; Toronto: Longman, Green, 1958.

Norris, Kathleen. *Amazing Grace: A Vocabulary of Faith.* New York: Riverhead, 1998.

Obeyesekere, Gananath. *The Apotheosis of Captain Cook: European Myth-making in the Pacific.* Rev. ed. Princeton, NJ: Princeton University Press, 1997.

– "'British Cannibals': Contemplation of an Event in the Death and Resurrection of James Cook, Explorer." *Critical Inquiry* 18, 4 (1992): 630–54.

– "Cannibal Feasts in Nineteenth-Century Fiji: Seamen's Yarns and the Ethnographic Imagination." In *Cannibalism and the Colonial World*, ed. Francis Barker, Peter Hulme, and Margaret Iverson, 63–86.

Ormsby, Margaret. *British Columbia: A History.* Vancouver: MacMillan, 1971 [1958].

Osborne, Lawrence. "Does Man Eat Man? Inside the Great Cannibalism Controversy." *Lingua Franca* (April/May 1997): 28–38.

The Oxford Dictionary of Quotations. 3rd. ed. Toronto: Oxford University Press, 1979.

The Oxford English Dictionary. 2nd ed. Prep. by J.A. Simpson and E.S.C. Weiner. 20 vols. Oxford: Clarendon, 1989.

Page, P.K. "Cook's Mountains." In *The Glass Air: Selected Poems*, 71. Toronto: Oxford University Press, 1985.

Pearson, Jacqueline. *Women's Reading in Britain, 1750–1835: A Dangerous Recreation.* Cambridge, New York, Melbourne: Cambridge University Press, 1999.

Perry, Adele. *On the Edge of Empire: Gender, Race, and the Making of British Columbia, 1849–1871.* Toronto: University of Toronto Press, 2001.

Pethick, Derek. *First Approaches to the Northwest Coast.* Vancouver: J.J. Douglas, 1976.

Pope, Alexander. *An Essay on Man.* In *The Twickenham Edition of Pope's Poems*, vol. 3, part 1, ed. Maynard Mack. London: Methuen; New Haven, Conn.: Yale University Press, 1950 [1733–4].

– *Imitations of Horace.* In *The Twickenham Edition of Pope's Poems*, vol. 4, ed. John Butt. London: Methuen; New Haven, Conn.: Yale University Press, 1969 [1733 and 1734].

- "Windsor-Forest." In *Windsor Forest, 1712: A Study of the Washington University Holograph*, ed. Robert M. Schmitz. Washington University Studies: Language and Literature no. 21. St. Louis: n.p., 1952 [1713].

Popkin, Richard. "The Philosophical Basis of Eighteenth-Century Racism." In *Studies in Eighteenth-Century Culture*. Vol. 3, ed. Howard Pagliaro, 245–62. Cleveland: The Press of Case Western Reserve University, 1973.

Porter, Dennis. *Haunted Journeys: Desire and Transgression in European Travel Writing*. Princeton, NJ: Princeton University Press, 1991.

Porter, Roy. *English Society in the Eighteenth Century*. Rev. ed. Markham, ON: Penguin, 1990.

Pratt, Mary Louise. *Imperial Eyes: Travel Writing and Transculturation*. New York: Routledge, 1992.

- "Scratches on the Face of the Country; or, What Mr. Barrow Saw in the Land of the Bushmen." In *"Race," Writing, and Difference*, ed. Henry Louis Gates Jr., 138–62. Chicago and London: Chicago University Press, 1985.

Radcliffe, Ann. *The Mysteries of Udolpho*. Ed. Bonamy Dobreé. Oxford and New York: Oxford University Press, 1970 [1794].

Ranford, Barry. "Bones of Contention." *Equinox* 74 (1994): 69–87.

Ray, Arthur. *I Have Lived Here Since the World Began: An Illustrated History of Canada's Native People*. Toronto: Lester and Key Porter, 1996.

Reed, Joel. "Restoration and Repression: The Language Projects of the Royal Society." *Studies in Eighteenth-Century Culture*, vol. 19, ed. Leslie Ellen Brown and Patricia Craddock, 399–412. n.p.: American Society for Eighteenth-Century Studies, 1989.

Regis, Pamela. *Describing Early America: Bartram, Jefferson, Crèvecoeur, and the Rhetoric of Natural History*. DeKalb, IL: Northern Illinois University Press, 1992.

Rennie, Neil. *Far-Fetched Facts: The Literature of Travel and the Idea of the South Seas*. Oxford: Clarendon, 1995.

Richardson, Samuel. *Pamela*. Ed. T.C. Duncan Eaves and Ben D. Kimpel. Riverside. Boston: Houghton Mifflin, 1971 [1740–2].

Rickman, John. *Journal of Captain Cook's Last Voyage to the Pacific Ocean on Discovery: performed in the years 1776, 1777, 1778, 1779 ...* London, 1781.

Ricou, Laurie. "Never Cry Wolfe: Benjamin West's *The Death of Wolfe* in *Prochain Episode* and *The Diviners*." *Essays on Canadian Writing* 20 (1980–81): 171–85.

Ridington, Robin. "Fieldwork in Courtroom 53: A Witness to *Delgamuukw v. BC*." BC *Studies* 95 (1992): 12–24.

Rigby, Nigel. "Sober Cannibals and Drunken Christians: Colonial Encounters of the Cannibal Kind." *Journal of Commonwealth Literature* 27, 1 (1992): 171–82.

Robertson, William. *History of America*. London, 1777.

Rosenthal, Elizabeth. "Myth of the Man-Eaters: An Interview with Dr. William Arens." *Science Digest* (April 1983): 25–9.

Rousseau, J.J. *On the Social Contract*. Trans. Judith R. Masters, ed. Roger D. Masters. New York: St-Martin's, 1978.

Roy, Patricia E. *A White Man's Province: British Columbia Politicians and Chinese and Japanese Immigrants, 1858–1914*. Vancouver: UBC Press, 1989.

Ryan, Simon. *How Explorers Saw Australia*. Cambridge, New York, Melbourne: Cambridge University Press, 1996.

Sahlins, Marshall. *Historical Metaphors and Mythical Realities: Structure in the Early History of the Sandwich Islands Kingdom*. Ann Arbor: University of Michigan Press, 1981.

– *How "Natives" Think: About Captain Cook, For Example*. Chicago and London: University of Chicago Press, 1995.

– *Islands of History*. Chicago: University of Chicago Press, 1985.

Said, Edward W. *Culture and Imperialism*. New York: Knopf, 1993.

– *Orientalism*. New York: Vintage, 1979.

Salmond, Anne. *Between Worlds: Early Exchanges Between Maori and Europeans, 1773–1815*. Honolulu: University of Hawaii Press, 1997.

– *Two Worlds: First Meetings between Maori and Europeans, 1642–1772*. Harmondsworth, Middlesex and Auckland, NZ: Penguin Viking, 1991.

Samwell, David. *Narrative of the Death of Captain Cook*. Rpt. as *Captain Cook and Hawaii*. Intro. Sir Maurice Holmes. San Francisco: David McGee; London: Francis Edwards, 1957 [1786].

– *Samwell's Journal*. Beaglehole III:2, 987–1300.

Sanday, Peggy Reeves. *Divine Hunger: Cannibalism as a Cultural System*. New York: Cambridge University Press, 1986.

"Sauvage." In *Le Grand Robert de la Langue Française*. 2me éd. Tome 8, 606–7. Paris: Le Robert, 1985.

Seaton, Dorothy. "Colonising Discourses: The Land in Australian and Western Canadian Exploration Narratives." *Australian-Canadian Studies* 6, 2 (1989): 3–14.

Sedgwick, Eve Kosofsky. *Between Men: English Literature and Male Homosocial Desire*. New York: Columbia University Press, 1985.

Shakespeare, William. *Othello*. Ed. M.R. Ridley. Arden. London and New York: Methuen, 1958 [1604?].

Shelley, Mary. *Frankenstein, or the Modern Prometheus*. Ed. M.K. Joseph. Oxford and New York: Oxford World's Classics, 1969 [1818; 1831].

Slemon, Stephen. "Bones of Contention: Post-Colonial Writing and the 'Cannibal' Question." In *Literature and the Body*, ed. Anthony Purdy, 163–77. Amsterdam and Atlanta, GA: Rodolpi, 1992.

Smith, Bernard. *European Vision and the South Pacific*. 2nd ed. New Haven, CT: Yale University Press, 1985.

– *Imagining the Pacific: In the Wake of the Cook Voyages*. New Haven and London: Yale University Press, 1992.

Smollett, Tobias. *The Expedition of Humphrey Clinker*. Intro. and notes Thomas R. Preston, ed. O.M. Brack Jr. Athens, GA.: University of Georgia Press, 1990 [1771].

– *Travels through France and Italy*. Ed. Frank Felsenstein. Toronto: Oxford University Press, 1979 [1766].

Soft Gold: The Fur Trade and Cultural Exchange on the Northwest Coast of America. Intro. and anno. Thomas Vaughan; ethnographic anno. Bill Holm. Portland: Oregon Historical Society, 1982.

Solkin, David H. "Portraiture in Motion: Edward Penny's *Marquis of Granby* and the Creation of a Public for English Art." *Huntington Library Quarterly* 49, 1 (1986): 1–24.

Spate, O.H.K. *Monopolists and Freebooters*. Vol. 2 of *The Pacific Since Magellan*. 4 vols. London and Canberra: Croom Helm, 1983.

– "Splicing the Log at Kealakekua Bay: James King's Sleight-of Hand." *Journal of Pacific History* 19, 1–2 (1984): 117–20.

Sprat, Thomas. *The History of the Royal Society*. London, 1667.

Sproat, Gilbert Malcolm. *The Nootka: Scenes and Studies of Savage Life*. Ed. and anno. Charles Lillard. West Coast Heritage Series. Victoria, BC: Sono Nis, 1987 [1868].

Spurr, David. *The Rhetoric of Empire: Colonial Discourse in Journalism, Travel Writing, and Imperial Administration*. Post Contemporary Interventions Series. Durham and London: Duke University Press, 1993.

Stafford, Barbara Maria. *Voyage into Substance: Art, Science, Nature, and the Illustrated Travel Account, 1760–1840*. Cambridge, Mass.: MIT Press, 1984.

Stearn, William Thomas. "Linnaeus' Sexual System of Classification." In *Species Planatarum*. Vol. 1. 24–35.

– "Four Supplementary Linnaean Publications: *Methodus*, 1736." *Species Planatarum*. Vol. 2. 73–84.

– ed. *Species Planatarum: A Facsimile of the First Edition*, 1753. 2 vols. London: Ray Society, 1957.

Stepan, Nancy. *The Idea of Race in Science: Great Britain, 1800–1960.*
London: MacMillan, 1982.

Sterne, Laurence. *The Life and Opinions of Tristram Shandy, Gentleman.* Ed.
Ian Watt. Riverside. Boston: Houghton Mifflin, 1965 [1759–67].

– *A Sentimental Journey through France and Italy by Mr Yorick.* London:
Cassell, 1905 [1768].

Stockdale, John, et al. *A Voyage to the Pacific Ocean; Undertaken by
Command of His Majesty, for making Discoveries in the Northern
Hemisphere: Performed under the Direction of Captains Cook, Clerke, and
Gore, In the Years 1776, 1777, 1778, 1779, and 1780. Being a copious,
comprehensive, and satisfactory Abridgement of the Voyage written by
Captain James Cook, F.R.S. and Captain James King, LL.D and F.R.S.* 4
Vols. London: Printed for John Stockdale, Scatcherd and Whitaker, John
Fielding, and John Hardy, 1784 (CIHM 17640–17642).

Stone, Lawrence. *The Family, Sex and Marriage in England, 1500–1800.*
London: Weidenfeld and Nicholson, 1977.

Story, Norah. *The Oxford Companion to Canadian History and Literature.*
Toronto: Oxford University Press, 1967.

Straub, Kristina. *Sexual Suspects: Eighteenth-Century Players and Sexual
Ideology.* Princeton, NJ: Princeton University Press, 1992.

Swift, Jonathan. *The Battle of the Books.* 1704. *Gulliver's Travels and Other
Writings.* 355–80.

– *Gulliver's Travels.* In *Gulliver's Travels and Other Writings.* Ed. Louis A.
Landa, 1–239. Boston: Houghton Mifflin, 1960 [1726].

– *Gulliver's Travels and Other Writings.* Ed. Louis A. Landa. Riverside.
Boston: Houghton Mifflin, 1960.

– "A Modest Proposal." In *Gulliver's Travels and Other Writings,* ed. Louis
A. Landa, 439–46. Boston: Houghton Mifflin, 1960 [1729].

– *A Tale of a Tub.* In *Gulliver's Travels and Other Writings,* ed. Louis A.
Landa, 241–353. Boston: Houghton Mifflin, 1960 [1704].

*Tacitus on Britain and Germany: A New Translation of the "Agricola" and
the "Germania."* Trans. H. Mattingly. Harmondsworth, Middlesex:
Penguin, 1948.

Taussig, Michael. *Mimesis and Alterity: A Particular History of the Senses.*
New York and London: Routledge, 1993.

Thomson, James. *The Seasons.* Ed. James Sambrook. Oxford/New York:
Clarendon Press/Oxford University Press, 1981 [1730].

Thwaites, Reuben Gold, ed. *Jesuit Relations and Allied Documents; Travels
and Explorations of the Jesuit Missionaries in North America (1610–1791).*
Cleveland: Burrows, 1897 (CIHM 07534–07607).

Tippett, Maria, and Douglas Cole. *From Desolation to Splendour: Changing Perceptions of the British Columbia Landscape.* Vancouver and Toronto: Clarke, Irwin, 1977.

Todorov, Tzvetan. *The Conquest of America: The Question of the Other.* Trans. Richard Howard. New York: Harper and Row, 1984.

Traill, Catharine Parr. *The Backwoods of Canada.* Toronto: McClelland and Stewart, 1989 [1836].

Trumbach, Randolph. "The Birth of the Queen: Sodomy and the Emergence of Gender Equality in Modern Culture, 1660–1750." In *Hidden from History: Reclaiming the Gay and Lesbian Past.* Eds. Martin Bauml Duberman, Martha Vicinius, and George Chauncey Jr. Markham, ON: Penguin-New American Library, 1989.

– "Sodomitical Assaults, Gender Role, and Sexual Development in Eighteenth-Century London." In *The Pursuit of Sodomy: Male Homosexuality in Renaissance and Enlightenment Europe.* Eds. Kent Gerard and Gert Hekma. New York: Haworth, 1988; *Journal of Homosexuality* 16, 1–2 (1988): 407–29.

Vancouver, George. *A Voyage of Discovery to the North Pacific Ocean, and Round the World; in which the coast of north-west America has been carefully examined and accurately surveyed. Undertaken by his Majesty's Command, principally with a view to ascertain the existence of any navigable communication between the North Pacific and North Atlantic Oceans; and performed in the years 1790, 1791 1972, 1793, 1794, and 1795, in the Discovery sloop of war, and armed tender Chatham, under the command of Captain George Vancouver.* 3 vols. Ed. John Vancouver. London, 1798.

– *A Voyage of Discovery.* Ed. W. Kaye Lamb. London: Hakluyt Society, 1984.

Vaughan, William. *Romantic Art.* New York and Toronto: Oxford University Press, 1978.

Veit, Walter, ed. *Captain James Cook: Image and Impact: South Sea Discoveries and the World of Letters.* Melbourne: Hawthorne, 1972.

Verner, Coolie. *Cook and the Cartography of the North Pacific.* An exhibition of maps for the Conference on Captain James Cook and His Times, April 1778. Burnaby, BC: The Library, Simon Fraser University, 1978.

Visser, Margaret. *Much Depends on Dinner: The Extraordinary History and Mythology, Allure and Obsession, Perils and Taboos, of an Ordinary Meal.* Toronto: McClelland and Stewart, 1986.

von Erffa, Helmut, and Allen Staley. *The Paintings of Benjamin West.* New Haven, CT and London: Yale University Press, 1986.

Wales, William. "Journal of William Wales." Beaglehole II, 776–869.

Warkentin, Germaine. *Canadian Exploration Literature: An Anthology, 1660–1860*. Toronto: Oxford University Press, 1993.

Watt, James. "Nutrition in Adverse Environments 1: Forgotten Lessons of Maritime Nutrition." *Human Nutrition: Applied Nutrition* (1982): 35–45. University of British Columbia Special Collections SPAM 6134.

Weedon, Chris. *Feminist Practice and Poststructuralist Theory*. Oxford and New York: Basil Blackwell, 1987.

Williams, Glyndwr. *The British Search for the Northwest Passage in the Eighteenth Century*. Imperial Studies no. 24. London: Longmans (for the Royal Commonwealth Society), 1962.

– *The Expansion of Europe in the Eighteenth Century: Overseas Rivalry, Discovery and Exploitation*. London: Blandford, 1966.

– "James Cook." In *Dictionary of Canadian Biography*. Vol. 4, 162–7. Toronto: University of Toronto Press, 1979.

– "Myth and Reality: James Cook and the Theoretical Geography of North America." In Fisher and Johnston, *Captain James Cook and His Times*. 58–79.

– "Myth and Reality: The Theoretical Geography of Northwest America from Cook to Vancouver." In Fisher, *From Maps to Metaphors*. 35–50.

Williams, Patrick, and Laura Chrisman, eds. *Colonial Discourse and Post-Colonial Theory: A Reader*. Toronto: Harvestor Wheatsheaf, 1994.

Wilson, Kathleen. "The Good, the Bad, and the Impotent: Imperialism and the Politics of Identity in Eighteenth-Century England." Paper delivered at the American Society for Eighteenth-Century Studies, Seattle, 27 March 1992.

– *The Sense of the People: Politics, Culture, and Imperialism in England, 1745–1785*. Cambridge and New York: Cambridge University Press, 1995.

Withey, Lynne. *Grand Tours and Cook's Tours: A History of Leisure Travel, 1750 to 1915*. New York: William Morrow, 1997.

– *Voyages of Discovery: Captain Cook and the Exploration of the Pacific*. New York: William Morrow, 1987.

Wittig, Monique. *The Straight Mind and Other Essays*. Boston: Beacon, 1992.

Wolfe, Eric R. *Europe and the People Without History*. Berkeley, Los Angeles, and London: University of California Press, 1982.

Woodcock, George. *British Columbia: A History of the Province*. Vancouver: Douglas and McIntrye, 1990.

Wright, J.V. *A History of the Native People of Canada*. Vol. 1 (10,000 – 1,000 BC) and 2 (1,000 BC – 500 AD) Mercury Series: Archaeological Survey of Canada, Paper 152. Hull, QC: Canadian Museum of Civilization, 1999 [1995].

Zimmerman, Heinrich. *Reise um die Welt, mit Captain Cook*. Ed. Peter C. Zimmerman. Rpt. Amsterdam: New Israel and New York: Da Capo, 1971 [1781].

Zogbaum, Heidi. "Cannibalism in the New World: A Case Study in Stigmatization." *Meanjin* 53, 4 (1994): 734–42.

Index

MCGILL-QUEEN'S NATIVE AND NORTHERN SERIES
BRUCE G. TRIGGER, EDITOR